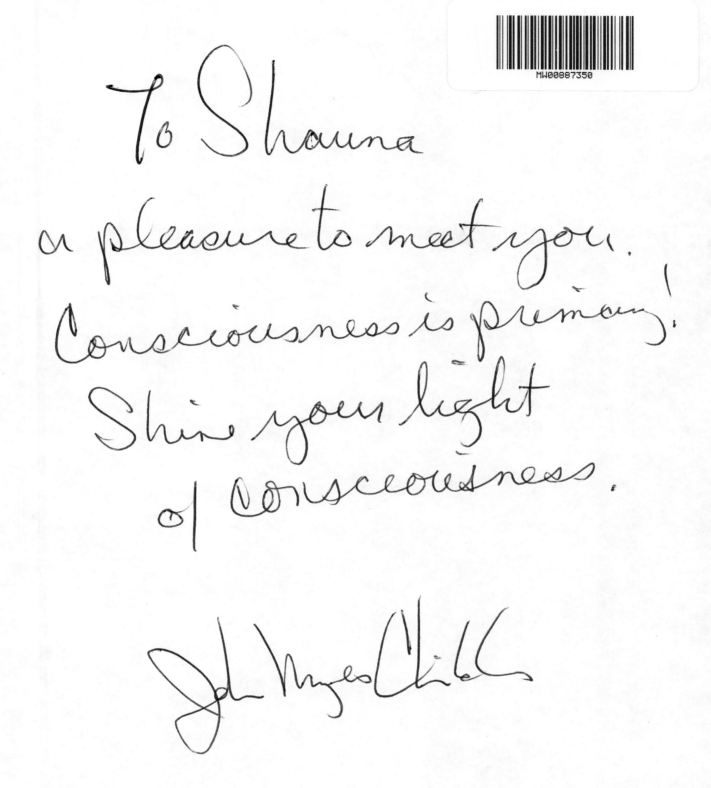

To Shauna

a pleasure to meet you.
Consciousness is primary!
Shine your light
of Conscieousness.

John Hagelin Chopra

A Yoga Pill For Every Ill:
Therapeutic Hatha Yoga:

Conscious Healing

Through Conscious Breathing And Posture

Written and Illustrated

By

John Myers Childers

BALBOA.
PRESS
A DIVISION OF HAY HOUSE

TherapeuticHathaYoga.com

Front Cover – Inner Teacher-Healer-Guide
and Metaphysical Mind Drawing by Cody Childers

Back Cover - Dancing Shiva by Glenn Childers
Invisible Presence by Tristan Childers

Photo by Morgan Smith

A Special Thanks to all of my Students over the many years whose practice,
dedication and support helped make this book possible.

Balboa Press books may be ordered through booksellers or by contacting:

Balboa Press
A Division of Hay House
1663 Liberty Drive
Bloomington, IN 47403
www.balboapress.com
1 (877) 407-4847

Because of the dynamic nature of the Internet, any web addresses or links contained in this book may have changed since publication and may no longer be valid. The views expressed in this work are solely those of the author and do not necessarily reflect the views of the publisher, and the publisher hereby disclaims any responsibility for them.

The author of this book does not dispense medical advice or prescribe the use of any technique as a form of treatment for physical, emotional, or medical problems without the advice of a physician, either directly or indirectly. The intent of the author is only to offer information of a general nature to help you in your quest for emotional and spiritual well-being. In the event you use any of the information in this book for yourself, which is your constitutional right, the author and the publisher assume no responsibility for your actions.

Any people depicted in stock imagery provided by Thinkstock are models,
and such images are being used for illustrative purposes only.
Certain stock imagery © Thinkstock.

ISBN: 978-1-5043-6819-3 (sc)
ISBN: 978-1-5043-6820-9 (e)

Library of Congress Control Number: 2016917442

Print information available on the last page.

Balboa Press rev. date: 11/01/2016

Preface

To read and practice this book you need to have an open mind. Therapeutic Hatha Yoga (THY) is a holistic approach to our being and healing. It includes our feelings thoughts, beliefs, relationships, diet, lifestyle and environment as well as our bodies. It is an approach to life, which lets go of notions and paradigms of separation between body and mind, between physiology and psychology, between matter and spirit.

You are a divine human being. You are a spark of cosmic consciousness. You are a co-creator of life on earth. THY Ultimate Formula for Health and Well-Being explains how to integrate body, mind, breath and spirit to connect to your Inner Teacher-Healer-Guide. Therapeutic Hatha Yoga is a holistic conscious approach to being and breathing healthier so the body's natural ability to heal is realized. This book is to be consciously practiced, not passively read.

This is a guidebook and textbook for teaching yourself and others self-observation, self-empowerment, self-healing and self-realization. This is a manual for conscious healing through conscious breathing. Therapeutic Hatha Yoga is designed to help people to consciously witness physical, emotional and mental edges and limitations, transform and transcend them. As you expand your sense of self, you will experience more sensations not less. Tune into your Inner Teacher-Healer-Guide, dance in the union of opposites and consciously participate in healing yourself, others and the world.

If you want to quickly jump in, go to the section Heal THYself and fill out THY Questionnaire. Search the Sample Practices for one that speaks to you. However, it would be far m beneficial to read the sections before and practice the Conscious Breathing Practices in the THY Ultimate Formula for Health and Well-Being first.

Mission Statement:

Teach People Conscious Healing Through Conscious Breathing And Posture.

Caution!

I am a metaphysician, not a physician. I am recommending that you neither stop nor start any medical treatment. I am a hatha yoga teacher-therapist-consultant. This is a book about practicing Therapeutic Hatha Yoga and consciously participating in your health and well-being. It is not intended as a substitute for the advice and treatment of physicians or other qualified health professionals. Therapeutic Hatha Yoga practices are for expanding consciousness and enhancing the body's natural ability and desire to heal.

A Summary Outline

Of The Contents

$$R_X \sim\sim\sim\sim\text{ Daily}$$

A Detailed Outline
Of The Contents
Introduction

Therapeutic Hatha Yoga – THY

THY Ultimate Formula For Health And Well-Being

Body

Spirit

Therapeutic Hatha Yoga

Therapeutic Hatha Yoga Postures

THY Postures

A Yoga Pill For Every Ill

R$_x$ ∿∿∿∿∿ Daily

Heal THYself

Sample Practices – THY Practices

11

Empower Your Inhalations

Namaste

To my three sons Cody, Glenn and Tristan,

The Family of Humanity and

The Infinite Web of Life.

Introduction

John's Story

This Is My Story Of My Metaphysical Mystical Yoga. It Is *MMM* Yoga. It Is Tasty Yoga. It is Therapeutic Hatha Yoga.

Early Days

I have always been into having a healthy body. For my thirteenth birthday I asked for a set of free weights and a bench press. Through junior and senior high school I practiced the high bar in gymnastics. I rode my bike everywhere in college at a time when there were very few weekend cyclists. After college I lived in Venice, a beach town near Los Angeles, where I swam in the ocean year round--swimming in the ocean was like going to talk to God.

As a child I attended the Unitarian Church with my parents, who raised me as a humanist. This philosophy taught me from an early age the value of human beings, critical thinking, and empirical evidence over blind faith and the acceptance of established doctrines. So not surprisingly, in my teens I wavered between being an atheist and an agnostic, as I became interested in issues of social justice and the war in Vietnam. Wanting to be a doctor, I got into UC Berkeley where I spent two years fulfilling the challenging prerequisites for medical school before changing course and heading to the National University in Mexico City to study history. I returned to Berkeley and finished a degree in Latin American history in 1979.

Finding Meditation and Yoga

Feeling that I had learned little about creativity and the arts, I continued my education at Santa Monica City College, the American Film Institute, and UCLA by studying piano, acting, film-making, and writing, while working as a waiter to support

15

myself. In the early 1980s I read *Journey to Ixtlan* by Carlos Castaneda and *Zen Mind, Beginner's Mind* by Shunryu Suzuki, which got me into metaphysics, shamanism, and meditation. I went to a zazen meditation at the Zen Center of Los Angeles, bought a meditation cushion and started meditating on my own. Later I joined a non-denominational, Christian-based meditation group led by Patrick and Trisha Harbula, who also published the magazine, *Meditation*, which hosted a series of meditations at the Whole Life Expo. I really enjoyed a yoga and meditation workshop taught by Louise Diana and I started taking classes at her home/studio. At my first yoga class, Louise told me that my mid-back was frozen, and it was true: I knew I was very stiff, tight, and rounded in the shoulders and upper back. I had lifted a lot of weights in my youth and I was locked up physically, emotionally, and even intellectually. I felt that I would never be able to touch my fingers behind my back in the Cow Face pose, no matter how much I practiced, but I knew that I needed to "un-knot" my back as well as my life!

Learning to Teach

I was inspired to apply for and was hired for a job as a public school teacher at Washington Preparatory High School in Los Angeles, where I taught beginning Spanish and English as a second language. This inner-city school was rife with gang violence and drive-by shootings. My room was vandalized twice and the bungalow next to mine was burned down. The redeeming feature of this experience was the impressive, talented, and caring staff at the school. Remember that film Denzel Washington starred in about a charismatic and life-changing high-school principal named George McKenna? He was my principal, and I'll never forget the time he said: "Are you having trouble with your students? Do they know you love them?" I was teaching to classes comprised wholly of African-American students, and I thought I was free of prejudice. My parents had sent me to integrated summer camps from the age of ten, and I grew up in an integrated neighborhood just north of Inglewood, where we experienced "white flight" in the 1960s and '70s. My younger brother was the only non-black kid in his class. Nevertheless, being free of prejudice is not the same as genuinely loving children of a different race. Teaching at Washington under the direction of George McKenna truly opened my heart.

Therapeutic Hatha Yoga

Another time he said, "Does a doctor complain that his patient is ill? Do not complain that your students are ill-prepared." I learned to acknowledge that there are different ways of learning, and changed my approach by engaging the body, mind, and cultural background of each student. I enjoyed great success in teaching language acquisition to my students through rhymes, poems, songs, and sayings complete with drawings, rhythm, gestures, and movement.

A Path Worth Walking

During this time, I found my way to the Center for Yoga in Los Angeles, taking beginning classes from Baba Hal. After the sobering realization that I could not even begin to undertake many of the

poses, including straightening my arms in Upward-Facing Bow, I resolved to stick with it. In 1987, I went to the Bodhi Tree bookstore and bought a used copy of *Light on Yoga* by B.K.S. Iyengar, dedicated to his guru, Krishnamacharya of Mysore, India. My immediate reaction to the picture of Krishnamacharya at the front of the book was one of irritation at this "guru" wearing beads and robes and a Western-style wristwatch at the same time. I look back on that moment and believe that I received a type of *shakti-pata*, a form of direct transmission from Krishnamacharya's photograph that has compelled me from that time to follow the path of yoga.

Iyengar described the supreme seeker as someone of great virility and enthusiasm, courageous, learned in scriptures, studious, sane of mind, not melancholy, keeping young, regular in diet, with his senses under control, free from fear, clean, skillful, generous, helpful to all, firm, intelligent, independent, forgiving, of good character, of gentle speech and reverent to his guru. This person could achieve enlightenment in three years. I thought that this was a path worth walking! I took more Iyengar classes and concluded that it would take three years to do the postures correctly. I realized that I would have to stop sitting on furniture all the time if I ever really wanted to become a yogi. I was beginning to be able to sit in full lotus for the time it took to chant three *aums*. With this new understanding, I literally threw away my bed, started sleeping flat on the floor in an effort to straighten my back, and shaved my head. My students at the high school freaked out, but I was determined to stay on my newly found path.

Finding a New Home

It was a quiet time for yoga in the 1980s at the Center for Yoga in Los Angeles: classes were small with few people seriously practicing. We passed around a copy of Joel Kramer's 1980 Yoga Journal article *Yoga And Self-Transformation* like it was a scared text. His concept of lines of energy in the body grabbed my imagination. The Ashtanga master Tim Miller gave a lecture and I felt that I had met a true American yogi. I took Brian Kest's class on Thursday nights and he told me I should come to the newly opened YogaWorks in Santa Monica, but that was a forty-five minute drive and I lived close to the Center for Yoga with a monthly pass. Nevertheless I got YogaWorks' newsletter and I was deeply moved and inspired by the articles of Eric Schiffmann and Rod Stryker. After having shaved my head, a lot of Buddhist energy had come my way. A friend of mine suggested I check out nearby Kanzeonji Buddhist Temple and Siva Ashram Yoga Center just north of Little Tokyo in L.A. I went and found four practitioners there, two doing Full Cobra pose with their toes on their shaved heads :-)! They could also do headstand for ten minutes and sit in full lotus for half an hour! I started taking classes with them.

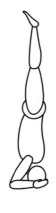

From my perspective the modern world and modern thought were upside down.

A few months later I moved into the temple/community center, and here I found a home. I did not return to my teaching job at Washington High in the fall, but instead gave away all of my belongings and sold my car. I lived like a monk, practicing yoga and meditation. My teachers, the Reverend Ryugen Watanabe, Zenryu, and Shinryu all had impeccable posture, balance and flexibility. The teachings were mostly about Zen with little discussion about yoga, although we referred to Swami Satchitananda's *Integral Yoga* for descriptions of poses as needed.

I began to yearn for more detailed hatha yoga technique in my practice, so after living at the temple for nine months, I went to the parent organization of the Center for Yoga, the White Lotus Foundation in Santa Barbara. Wanting more than the traditional teacher training offered there by Ganga White and Tracey Rich, I arrived with two duffle bags, a check for $1,000, and a proposal to create my own work/study teacher-training programs. Ganga accepted, and I lived in a tent on the White Lotus property for a couple of months and then took the teacher-training program for the Ashtanga-like "Flow Series," which was surprising to me after having attended less rigorous classes at the Center For Yoga in Los Angeles. However, Ganga's unique approach to yoga and his lectures on it were inspiring, and in many ways his teachings gave me the confidence to pursue a life as a yogi, and ultimately, to write this book.

Teaching Yoga

After obtaining certifications in both Zazen Meditation and Hatha Yoga, some friends invited me down to Orange County to teach. So in August 1990, I began my yoga-teaching career at a metaphysical bookstore in Costa Mesa, called Visions and Dreams. I immediately found that most individuals who were interested in yoga at that time were not prepared to do the rigorous Flow Series. Feeling an obligation to best serve the interests of my students, I created a more accommodating introduction to the program by incorporating beginning postures, and the movement and breath repetitions of the newly emerging viniyoga practices from Krishnamacharya's son, Desikachar. "Full Spectrum Yoga" is the name I chose for the eclectic style of yoga I began teaching in 1990. I wanted a name that reflected both the visible and invisible elements of our being, the rainbow color of the chakras, and the stillness and movement innate in the hatha yoga tradition.

Conscious Healing Through Conscious Breathing And Posture

In 1991, I became a father. I rented an old house, took my small group of students, and created a yoga studio out of the Childers' family living room. To make ends meet, I began teaching Spanish at the Waldorf School of Orange County and as a substitute for the Santa Ana Unified School District. My son Cody was born in October, his brother Glenn two years later and Tristan two and a half years after that. All three were be born at home, under the care of a midwife. All three also attended the Waldorf School Of Orange County.

In September of 1992, I was one of the five original teachers to launch Yogaworks of Orange County, which became Yoga Place in 1995. From 1992 until 1999 I taught three-to-twelve classes a week, as well as taking workshops from a wide variety of renowned yoga teachers including Gary Kraftsow, Indra Devi, Eric Schiffmann, Rodney Yee, Rod Stryker, Tim Miller, Rodger Cole, Anna Forrest, Karin O'Bannon, and others. During this same period, I also taught 8 yoga classes a week to patrons of the Sports Club/Irvine.

I was a very interactive teacher, walking around the room while I taught. While continuing to lead the whole class, I would adjust and direct attention to various elements of individual postures. I became better and better at noticing people's injuries, imbalances and abnormalities in posture, breath and movements. I often taught large classes and sometimes there would be a line of people to speak to me after class. They wanted to know what posture would be good for their specific issue like knee pain, stiff hips, frozen shoulder, carpal tunnel syndrome, plantar faciitis or low back pain. With no examination beyond what I observed during class, my students thought I could prescribe a practice for them right on the spot. I feel I have given a lot of good advice on how to practice yoga postures for specific needs. It has been very gratifying to have students come up to me and tell me how "key postures and practices" have helped them over the years.

However, it started to feel like I was doing my students a disservice by just giving snap suggestions at the end of class. Not all snap suggestions worked and some students needed more customization of key postures. I told my employers that I would like to have a space to have private clients for extended consultations. Hatha yoga's popularity was beginning to blossom in 1994. There was a full page story on how yoga was going mainstream in the OC Register featuring pictures of me teaching a class with a woman recovering from breast cancer. Yogaworks and Sports Club Irvine offered me a room to have regular private clients in addition to dozens of classes.

In 1995 I acquired my first serious long term yoga therapy individual student-clients, a man with torn plantar facia and broken shoulder, and a teenage girl with scoliosis. I had a holistic approach to the body, mind and breath though I had never focused on the same issue week after week and month after month. I was very present and they were very disciplined. I was a beginner. I would often stand there pondering with my body-mind what the next step in the healing process was. One time the man said to me, 'take your time.' as I had yet to find the yoga pill for his plantar faciitis. They both did home practices that I wrote out for them, and with conscious effort both healed. Both did additional lifestyle changes to help heal them. The girl with a scoliosis curve of 31 degrees of deviation went to 18, 12 to 8 degrees in less than one year. In two years it went to 0 degrees in less that two years. I gained a lot of confidence in my ability to help people heal consciously integrating body, mind and breath. I gained more individual students, and their unique set of issues. I joined the International Association of Yoga Therapists in 1996.

In addition, I had long-term corporate lunch and after-work classes with clients such as Fluor/Daniel, Chevron, Practice Builders, Varco, and Kingston Technologies. I led yoga therapy workshops at the Medical Ayurveda Rejuvenation Center of Newport Beach, Omadawn of Seal Beach, the Desert Yoga Center in Palm Springs, and the Reno Yoga Center.

On January 1, 2000, I opened my own studio, Full Spectrum Yoga, in Newport Beach, California. A variety of students and colleagues wanted to join me and I created the first two-hundred-hour Yoga Alliance-certified teacher-training program in Orange County. Over eighty students graduated over the following four years and many went on to teach yoga. In my own studio, I was able to offer therapeutic workshops on a wide variety of issues including low back pain, shoulders, bunions, plantar faciitis, sciatica, heart wellness, knees, carpal-tunnel syndrome, hips, lymph edema, and neck and jaw issues. My handouts and experience from these workshops was helped to create a

21

foundation for this book. However, after a series of challenges, I closed the studio in November 2004, and look back on it as an important learning experience.

I moved my practice to the D'Amore Natural Healing Center in Newport Beach, where I currently have a room for individual and small group yoga therapy sessions. These small group yoga therapy sessions, allow me to give personal attention to each individual's specific needs. The process has enabled me to refine my teaching while exploring challenging issues in a safe environment. I attended the International Association Of Yoga Therapist conferences and did a forty-five minute presentation on plantar facia. I have worked with people trying to avoid or recover from having surgeries of the hip, knee, neck, low back, shoulder, thumb and foot, as well as people who have suffer from many types of cancer, cysts, and autoimmune disorders. All in all, I have taught over twenty thousand yoga classes and private yoga therapy sessions over the last twenty-five years.

Looking Back and Looking Forward

Raising a family and teaching yoga full-time over 20 years has had its own challenges and rewards. Many a day, I practiced breathing while doing yard work, cleaning the kitchen, or helping with my sons' homework, instead of taking a class or workshop. Having three young children made family life an important part of my yoga history. I taught numerous Kid's Yoga classes and workshops over the years. Supporting three children made me teach more than I would have if I had only to support myself. I taught seven days a week for five years straight in the late 1990s. My family brought me great joy, however it also isolated me from the yoga community. I attended school plays instead of yoga gatherings or conferences. The result was that I studied and read a lot on my own. On the other hand staying in one place helped me develop a long-term relationship with my students. Many of my students have been with me for five, ten, fifteen, and even twenty years!

Times change. The universe is expanding and life is evolving. It is not always easy to listen to and honor our Inner Teacher-Healer-Guide. In the stillness before we exhale there is a pause in which we can listen to energetic waves of creativity, love and wisdom. This stillness teaches, heals and guides us through life. We have physical, emotional, mental, and spiritual issues that challenge us so our lives can be an upward, spiral path of growth and transformation.

We have the ability to teach, heal, and guide others and ourselves.

The Philosophy
And Practice of Yoga

The word "yoga" means to yoke, join and bind. Yoga carries the meaning of a state of union or communion with the Ultimate Reality, the Supreme Universal Spirit, and Unity Consciousness. Yoga is also a practice to help you become one with that Ultimate Reality. Yoga is basically an ancient conscious spiritual philosophy and practice that includes and goes beyond the five human senses of perception. In modern philosophical terminology, yoga is a metaphysical philosophy because it refers to the studies and practices of what cannot be reached through rational objective studies of everyday material reality. Yoga uses ultimate, universal and infinite concepts to define Reality and our understanding of it. The word Reality, like Self, when capitalized, refers to reality understood beyond the objective five human senses. Yoga seeks to reveal this Ultimate Reality, which is not always easily discovered or experienced in our everyday life. As such, yoga is deeply concerned with explaining the features of Reality that exist beyond the physical world of our immediate five senses. Yoga therefore, uses a logic based on the meaning of life, love and wisdom rather than on a limited material sense of perception. Yoga philosophy and practice are based on direct inner personal experience, not external material reality, and therefore have often been in conflict with classical physical sciences.

Yoga is an attempt to know and understand Reality as opposed to the mere appearance of reality. In classical yoga this meant transcending this physical world and then experiencing the divine Ultimate Reality. Spirit was pitted against matter in a dualist manner in the classical yoga sutras of Patanjali. The physical and the spiritual were separate and to reach the spiritual you needed to transcend the physical body. The body and the material world were obstacles for the yogi ascetics on the path to enlightenment. However, modern schools of integral, hatha, tantric and kundalini yoga have sought a non-dual approach to divine consciousness. Since the divine Ultimate Reality is omnipresent in every aspect of our lives, then the path to enlightenment can be here and now, in our body temple, in our everyday life.

In this book, the term 'yoga' primarily refers to the practice of non-dual Hatha-Yoga, the yoga of physical discipline, to prepare the body to achieve union with the Supreme Universal Consciousness. Yoga is an effort to comprehend our lives and the universe not as composed of a spiritual realm separate from a material realm, but as a whole. Yoga as a metaphysical philosophy examines the true nature of Reality, whether visible or invisible. Yoga's Ultimate Reality is a union of opposites, a play of polarity. Yoga is a non-dual, undivided philosophy that does not separate the body from the mind, the physical from the spiritual or the individual self from the infinite Self. Through posture and breath awareness, hatha yoga offers integration of the physical world of the body with the spiritual world of the soul. Yoga, and specifically hatha yoga, has thrived in America most of all because it brings the body and the mind, the physical and the spiritual, together without religious overtones.

Yoga Is...

The Ultimate Reality that Yoga seeks to know cannot be spoken. There are no words that perfectly describe the wisdom required to understand the Ultimate Reality. There is a being and an "is-ness" to Yoga. Having said that, here are 25 of my favorite popular and traditional definitions of Yoga. Many of these definitions are directly or indirectly taken from the glossary at the end of this book. Remember, as with any ancient tradition, many different forms and branches have evolved over the ages.

1.
Yoga is to be one with the divine.

2.
Yoga is a holistic approach to the well-being of the entire human organism.

3.
Yoga is a practice to end the separation internally between body and mind and externally between you and the web of life.

4.
Yoga is being mindful in the present moment. Yoga is about being in the here and now.

5.
Yoga is the joining of the individual self (jiva) with the infinite self (Brahman).

6.
Yoga is both a dynamic process and a state of being that allows greater Self-realization.

7.
Yoga is the conscious union of the physical with the spiritual.

8.
Yoga is the method by which the restless mind is calmed and the energy directed into constructive channels.

9.
Yoga is the ability to look evenly at life in all of its aspects.

10.
Yoga is a process that involves confronting our limits and transcending them.

11.
Yoga is being completely awake in the present moment to a joyous, unlimited, pure state of being.

12.
Yoga is skillful living.

13.
Yoga is the art of living at the highest possible level attainable by a human being.

14.
Yoga is meditation in action.

15.
Yoga is a process of self-realization, a journey towards awareness, leading us to discover and experience ourselves, not only as individuals, but also as integral parts of the universal life force.

16.
Yoga is the integration of body, breath and mind.

17.
Yoga is a path of loving life not of fearing of death.

18.
Yoga is the perfection of feeling absolute love.

19.
Yoga is deliverance from pain and sorrow.

20.
Yoga is to reach a point we have not reached before.

21.
Yoga is a way of moving into stillness to experience the truth of who we are.

22.
Yoga is the art of opening to and diving into the dynamic creative flow of a life lived consciously.

23.
Yoga is a conscious practice that connects us with the breathing life of all.

24.
Yoga is a path of self-liberation.

25.
All life is yoga.

Therapeutic Hatha Yoga

Therapeutic Hatha Yoga, 'THY', is a system of principles and techniques based on an expanded sense of being and Reality. Therapeutic Hatha Yoga is a credo that you are a powerful co-creator of life, your life, the lives of others, and ultimately of all life on earth. You are a spark of divine cosmic consciousness. You are a conscious human being bearing inalienable gifts of creativity, love and wisdom. You are endowed, invested and empowered to manifest those gifts for life, health and well-being.

Therapeutic Hatha Yoga's Mission Statement:

Teach People Conscious Healing
Through Conscious Breathing And Posture.

Therapeutic Hatha Yoga teaches conscious healing
through the integration of body, mind, breath and spirit.

Therapeutic Hatha Yoga teaches and guides you to consciously participate
in your health and healing regardless of your condition.

Therapeutic Hatha Yoga connects you to your Inner Teacher-Healer-Guide.

'THY' is both an acronym of Therapeutic Hatha Yoga and a reminder that YOU are a divine human being, a conscious healer, a vortex of life energies. In the expression, *Heal THYself* the 'THY' is to reinforce an expanded sense of Self, to heal yourself.

27

- 28 - Therapeutic Hatha Yoga Is Holistic

Therapeutic Hatha Yoga considers the body and all of its parts in relation to our whole being, and the whole of life. The very word health is connected to the Old English word *hal* meaning 'whole'. The development of modern science and technology has intensified the reduction of our concepts of health and well-being to the mere absence of disease. The ancient Greeks Aristotle and Hippocrates, the father of Western medicine, were much more holistic in their approach to the study of medicine than today's modern medical institutions. For ancient Greeks the nature of the parts of the body could not be understood without grasping the nature of the entire organism and life as a whole.

There is one common flow, one common breathing.
All things are in sympathy.

Hippocrates.

The idea of a *holistic* medicine is that all the properties of a human being, including the physical, biological, chemical, social, economic, mental, linguistic, cultural and spiritual are mutually interactive.

Good health is not the mere absence of disease and its symptoms.

Modern medicine is allopathic medicine. The word allopathic is defined as a system of medicine to combat disease. *Allopathic* literally means *against the disease or pathogen*. So often modern medicine treats only the symptoms and not the source of a disease. Once the symptoms are gone the doctor might say, "You are as good as new." The goal seems to be to restore you to a previous state, but with no added growth of awareness or consciousness from the experience to live more skillfully. Our allopathic medicine may "fix" the physical symptom, but unless there is a transformation of our lifestyle, our consciousness, we could unconsciously re-create our condition again, even if we have had surgery or taken medicine for it. This is especially true for chronic conditions such as cancer, coronary heart disease, low back pain, diabetes and autoimmune disorders. Therapeutic Hatha Yoga is not intended to replace or be a substitute for modern allopathic medicine. Therapeutic Hatha Yoga is a multidimensional system of integrating body, mind and breath for radiant health and well-being.

Good health is a state of complete
physical, emotional, mental, social and environmental well-being.

A holistic sense of self is more than a skin encapsulated ego sense of self, a self that views it's self separate from the health and well-being of others and the environment. You do not exist, live or heal isolated from life. To holistically heal is to expand your sense of self to include healing your feelings, thoughts, relationships with others and all of life. Ultimately to Heal THYself includes a conscious healing of our emotional, mental and environmental relationships.

Hatha Yoga

Is a Non-dual Metaphysical Quantum Yoga

Hatha Yoga is one of the major lineages in the yoga tradition along with Raja Yoga, the yoga of meditation, Jnana Yoga, the yoga of wisdom philosophy, Karma Yoga, the yoga of service like Mother Teresa and Bhakti Yoga, the Yoga of love and devotion. Hatha yoga, often called forceful yoga or the yoga of physical discipline, is focused on aligning the breath and spine to prepare the body-mind to awaken to the divine. The word *hatha* is composed of two words, *ha* meaning sun and *tha* meaning moon. Hatha yoga is about uniting the feminine Shakti with the masculine Shiva. Hatha Yoga is a practice that weaves the opposing energies of the sun and the moon, masculine and feminine, together into one continuous flow of breath, *hamsa*. Based on Hatha Yoga the fundamental approach of Therapeutic Hatha Yoga connects your body, mind, breath and spirit. HathaYoga is based on the notion that the body is not just a material food tube, but rather as a temple made of an immortal substance. Hatha yoga and Tantrism hold the non-dual view that the physical phenomenal world (samsara) and the spiritual transcendental Reality (nirvana) are coessential and are one. Thus creating the possibility of *jiva-mukti*, of living a liberated life on earth.

Hatha Yoga is a non-dual practice in that it unites the apparent dualities of the world such as sun and moon, body and the mind, physiology and psychology and physical and spiritual and weaves them together into one whole. Non-dualism is a common thread throughout the history of yoga and in the better-known schools of Hatha, kundalini, Vedanta, bhakti, and tantric yoga. The difference between traditional hatha yoga, and Therapeutic Hatha Yoga is rooted in this non-duality. The practice of hatha yoga was basically a spiritual practice in which the emphasis was not on healing the physical body, but rather on cleansing and preparing the body, and clearing and stilling the mind to experience spiritual realization and liberation. For Therapeutic Hatha Yoga the emphasis is reversed, focusing primarily on the physical and manifesting, integrating and healing the physical form, and secondly, connecting to spiritual oneness.

THY Inner Teacher-Healer-Guide

The emblem of Therapeutic Hatha Yoga is a symbol of your inner power and authority. It is a symbol of your power to consciously teach, heal and guide yourself. It is a symbol of our conscious spiritual being. It symbolizes our non-dual and undivided Self. THY Inner Teacher-Healer-Guide is a metaphysical mystical spiritual symbol of being.

Your Inner Teacher-Healer-Guide image is based on the symbolic representation of Hermes' staff, called the Caduceus. The Caduceus is a common symbol of medicine and the ancient yoga symbolic representation of the seven major *chakras*, wheel-vortexes of psychophysical energy. Our Inner Teacher-Healer-Guide is the essence of the Ultimate Formula For Health And Well-Being. The wings represent the wings of a swan, *hamsa*, the symbol of our spirit and divine essence in the yoga tradition. They also represent the wings of Hermes, a messenger of the Greek gods. Ultimately, the wings symbolize the power of conscious breathing to connect us to our individual spirit and the infinite spirit.

THY Inner Teacher-Healer-Guide

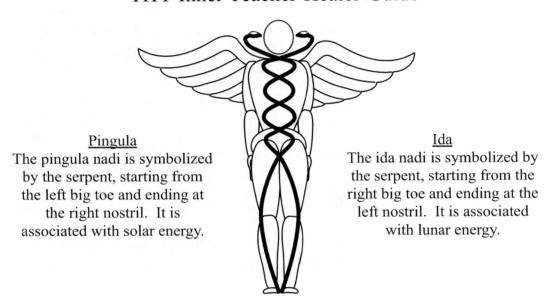

Pingula
The pingula nadi is symbolized by the serpent, starting from the left big toe and ending at the right nostril. It is associated with solar energy.

Ida
The ida nadi is symbolized by the serpent, starting from the right big toe and ending at the left nostril. It is associated with lunar energy.

The two serpents, representing the *ida* and *pingula nadis*, form a double helix coiled around the central channel of the subtle body, called the *Sushumna* nadi. *Nadi*, the ancient Sanskrit word for "duct, tube or pipe" are conduits that carry the life energy known as *prana*, life force. Associated with the spinal column, the *sushumna nadi* symbolizes the path to higher consciousness. Six out of the seven major *chakras* are located where the *ida* and *pingula* intersect. The seventh *chakra* is the crown *chakra* at the top of the head.

The Chakras

Are a Rainbow Path of Manifestation and Liberation.

The chakras, the Sanskrit word for wheels, have many diverse qualities associated with them within the yoga tradition, and have been described differently through the ages. The chakras are spiral vortexes where physiology and psychology are woven together. They are subtle energy centers within a larger dynamic spiral vortex that is you. Along the spinal axis there are 7 major chakras typically described. Note that the first six chakras are located where the Ida and the Pingula meet. All metabolic processes, glands, organs and body parts are associated with these chakra vortexes. Aligning the chakras with posture and breath awareness is essential for good health and well-being.

Each Exhalation Manifests the Chakras.
Each Inhalation Liberates the Chakras.

The Chakras

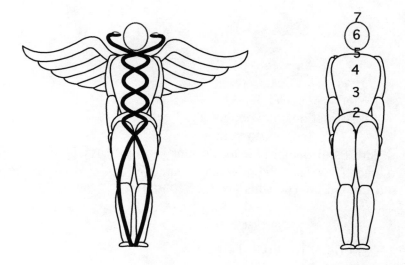

Numbered Positions of the Chakras

Common Chakra Name and Numbered Position
Symbol
Sanskrit Name (pronounced)
Seed Sound
Color
Associated Element
Associated Body Parts
Metaphysical Meditations
Emotional Healing

The Crown Chakra #7

Sahasra (sah-hahs-rah-rah)
Deep Space Transcendental Silence
Radiant Space / The Light of Cosmic Consciousness
Consciousness / Spirit / Perceiver
Pure Being Beyond Thought and The 5 Senses
Top of head, Skin, Cerebral Cortex and Central Nervous System
Experience The Absolute Unity Of Being…
And Release Attachments And Fears.

The Third Eye Chakra #6

Ajna (ah-gyan)
Aum
Violet
Subtle Vibrations of Thought and Feeling
Inner Knowing
Eyes, Forehead, Sides and Back of Head, Pituitary and Pineal Glands
Connect To Your Telepathy and Empathy…
And Let Go Of The Illusions Of Separation.

The Throat Chakra #5

Vishuddha (vee-shood-hah)
Ham
Blue
Ether / Sound
Hearing
Throat, Mouth, Ears, Neck, Shoulders, arms Hands, Upper Back and Thyroid
Listen To Blue Inverted Ether…
And Speak The Truth.

The Heart Chakra #4

Anahata (ah-nah-hat-tah)
Yam
Green
Air
Touch
Heart, Lungs, Shoulders, Arms, Mid Back and Thymus Gland
Touch The Green Hexagon Air…
And Release Your Grief.

The Solar Plexus Chakra #3

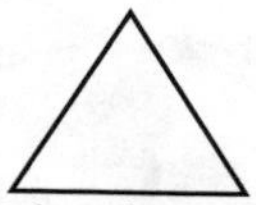

Manipura (mah-nee-poo-rah)
Ram
Yellow
Fire
Sight
Stomach, Liver, Gall Bladder and Digestive System and Pancreas
See The Yellow Triangle Fire…
And Release Your Shame.

The Sacral Chakra #2

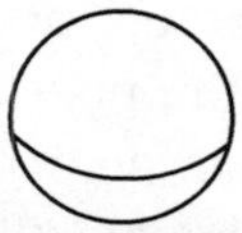

Svadhishthana (svahd-hisht-hah-nah)
Vam
Orange
Water
Bladder, Kidneys, Sacrum, Womb, Prostate and Gonads
Taste The Orange Crescent Water…
And Release Your Guilt.

The Root Chakra #1

Muladhara (moo-lahd-hah-rah)
Lam
Red
Earth
Smell
Hips, Legs, Feet, Rectum Large Intestines and Adrenal Glands
Smell The Red Square Earth…
And Release Your Fear.

Sound Produces Form and Form Is Associated with Color.

AUM / OM

Aum is the seed sound for the Third Eye Chakra, the Ajna Chakra, the sixth chakra. The bottom curve represents the subconscious dream state and has a soft 'a' sound. The upper curve represents the conscious waking state and has a soft 'u' or sound. The curve issuing from the center symbolizes the unconscious deep dreamless sleep and has the sound "m". The crescent and dot represent our divine state of deep space consciousness and have no particular sound save the resonate echo of the first three. The entire symbol stands for past, present, future and beyond time. It represents length, breadth, depth and beyond form. Aum connects us to our father, mother, teachers and our Inner Teacher-Healer-Guide. To a yogi no symbol is more powerful than om / aum. It is a symbol rich with many meanings. It conveys the meaning of the Latin word "omni" as in omniscience, omnipresence and omnipotence: all knowing, all present and almighty.

In the Yoga tradition, vibrant consciousness, sound and frequency are the basis of form and shape, not matter. By amplifying the frequency or consciousness matter will change. Aum is the primordial sound of the creation of the universe. Chant om and raise your vibration and consciousness to change matter and manifest your intentions.

The sound 'A'

The sound 'a' is the first letter of both the English and Sanskrit alphabet. The sound resonates in the body, in the gut, as short 'ah' sound, sounds as a long continuous 'aaaaaaa' sound in the word aum.

The sound 'U'

The sound 'u' resonates in the head, in roof of the mouth as short 'u'. The 'u' sounds and as a long 'uuuuuuu' in the word aum. The 'a' and the 'u' sounds merge together to create a diphthong sound 'au' or 'o' as aum is often spelled 'om'.

The sound 'M'

The sound 'm' resonates in the face, in the lips and nose as a long 'mmm' sound.

The sound of 'Silence'

The crescent and dot symbolize transcendental silence.

Aum is the eternal vibration of deep consciousness.

THY Ultimate Formula
For Health and Well-Being

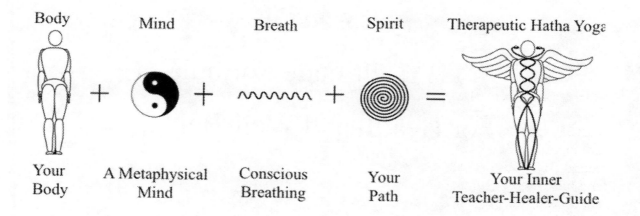

Body	Mind	Breath	Spirit	Therapeutic Hatha Yoga
Your Body	A Metaphysical Mind	Conscious Breathing	Your Path	Your Inner Teacher-Healer-Guide

Your Body
The Ultimate Formula begins with you and your body here and now.
Your body is your temple.

A Metaphysical Mind
The yin and yang is an easily recognizable symbol of a non-dual metaphysical Reality,
where black and white and body and mind are woven together in one unified whole.
Therapeutic Hatha Yoga includes and goes beyond the material world of our five senses.
The Ultimate Formula incorporates your intentions and visualizations.

Conscious Breathing
The smooth sine wave symbolizes conscious rhythmic breathing.
The breath is a bridge between body and mind.
Conscious breathing is a feedback loop for self-healing and awareness.
The key to conscious healing is conscious breathing.

Your Path
Your path is comprised of all of your
physical, emotional, mental, environmental and spiritual relationships.
Your path is symbolized with a spiral.
You are on a path of growth, development and transformation.

Your Inner Healer-Teacher-Guide
The Inner Healer-Teacher-Guide symbolizes a larger sense of Self. It is the ultimate
organization of your body, mind and spirit for creativity, love and wisdom.
You are a powerful being, a conscious creator of life.
You are capable of consciously participating in your health and well-being.

All Therapeutic Hatha Yoga Practices

Are Holistic Practices

Based On

THY Ultimate Formula

For Health and Well-Being.

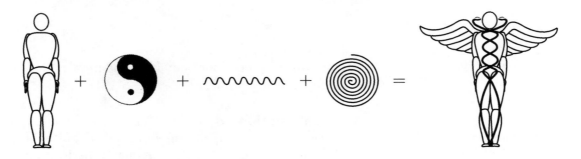

Practice Conscious Healing

Through Conscious Breathing!

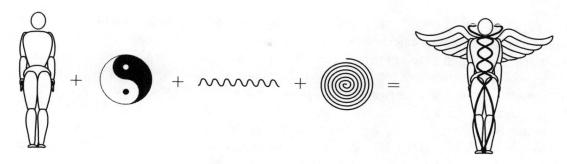

Body

Your Body and 'Te People'

The Ultimate Formula begins with you and your body. Your body is your temple. You are an eternal being in a temporal body. Be conscious of your body. In the yoga tradition, your body is described as a vessel for spiritual growth.

Your body is stylistically represented in this book with these figures I call, 'Te People.' They are neither he nor she people; they are Te People. Te People have no specific gender, age, race or nationality. Te People are terrestrials; they are conscious human beings who live on earth, people just like you and me. These drawings stylistically represent all peoples on earth.

We Are All 'Te People'

Te People are based on my early freehand drawings of yoga postures that I would give out as recommended practices. These early drawings were composed of ovals connected in figure 8s on lined graph paper to form the torso and then the limbs. I used Leonardo Da Vince's proportion ratio in which the head is one eighth of one's height. I tried scanning the drawings into Apple's first personal Mac in 1993, but they were too fuzzy. Then I tried composing Te People in the graphics program Claris Draw. The result is computerized figure drawing shorthand that has enabled me to easily record hundreds of yoga postures I have stylized Te People for us to easily see their structure and alignment with a minimum of distraction. They are designed like this to reduce positive or negative feelings towards the figure. Te People drawings are here to help you understand your body, mind and breath beyond gender, age and nationality.

The head in these drawings is presumed connected, centered and level with the body and the eyes are facing forward. The gaze or the focal point of the eyes is referred to as *dristi*. The most common focal points are the tip of the nose, over the finer tips, out to the horizon, to the ground in front of you and up to the brow point. The eyes are generally open, though also closed for more internal awareness. Our gaze and focus reflect our awareness, feelings and thoughts. Our postures and gaze have an expression and a face to them.

The Face of 'Te People'

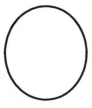

The face of Te People is alert yet calm.
It is a Zen "No-Face," a face reflecting a clear and even mind.
It is a Mona Lisa smiling face.
It is the face you had before you were born.
It is the face of contentment.
It is the face of your Inner Teacher-Healer-Guide.

The Body of 'Te People'

Te People drawings endeavor to honor the bodies sculpted on the ancient temples in India. These ancient yoga bodies had a more tubular shaped body and limbs than the sculpted muscular or ultra thin bodies we so often see in modern yoga books and videos. The bodies of Te People do not include the principles of Ayurveda. This traditional medicine of India describes each individual constitution and body as a unique combination of the three doshas: vata, pita and kapha representing the elements air, fire and water, earth within each of us.

Shiva Nataraja Is the Quintessential Icon of Hatha Yoga

The Dancing Shiva

Shiva Nataraja is the symbol of the "Dance of Shiva". It is both a masculine and feminine image of Shiva, the name of the third god of the Hindu Trinity, who is entrusted with the work of spiritualization as Brahma and Vishnu are with creation and preservation. Nataraja, The Cosmic Dancer, The Lord of the Dance is forever dancing out the rhythms of the universe. In one hand Nataraja is holding a drum ticking out time and in the other hand is holding a ball of fire and burning it up, symbolizing the cycles of creation and destruction. Another hand points to the raised foot, which symbolizes liberation and the other hand is uplifted symbolizing that we need not fear. Nataraja is the master weaver of space and time, of matter and energy. Nataraja is the quintessential symbol of Yoga as spiritual alchemy, of changing the body into spirit. Nataraja is dancing on the back of Mujalaka, the demon of worldly fascinations, or the part of us the stuck in the material world. Nataraja is associated with the transubstantiated body, or the adamantine, divine or rainbow body, a body not made of flesh but of the immortal substance, Light. The body is the dwelling place of the divine and a cauldron for accomplishing spiritual growth. Shiva Nataraja represents health, well-being and enlightenment as whole body/being events.

"Om Namah Shivaya,"
(OM NAH-MAH-SHEE-VAH-YAH)

This mantra has no single translation.
'Om And Salutations To Lord Shiva'
'Om And Salutations To That Which I Am Capable Of Becoming'
'May The Elements Of Creation Abide Perfectly Within Me'

Om Namah Shivaya is the mantra associated with Shiva Nataraja. The sounds of the mantra in and of themselves relate directly to the principles, which govern each of the first six chakras in the yoga tradition in this order: mind, earth, water, fire, air and ether. Notice that this does not refer to the chakras themselves, which have a different set of seed sounds, but rather the elemental principles, which govern those chakras.

Om Namah Shivaya
(OM NAH-MAH-SHEE-VAH-YAH)

om - 6th Chakra,
nah - 1st Chakra,
mah - 2nd Chakra,
shee - 3rd Chakra,
vah - 4th Chakra
yah - 5th Chakra.

The Vitruviun Man The Quintessential 'Western' Body

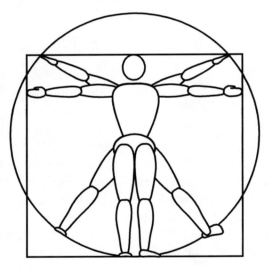

The Vitruvian Man is a world-renowned drawing created by Leonardo da Vinci representing the quintessential human body. The drawing is based on the correlations of ideal human proportions with the geometry described by the ancient Roman architect Vitruvius. It depicts a male figure in two superimposed positions with his arms and legs apart and simultaneously inscribed in a circle, symbolizing our spiritual nature, and square, symbolizing our physical nature. Leonardo da Vinci believed the workings of the human body to be an analogy for the workings of the universe.

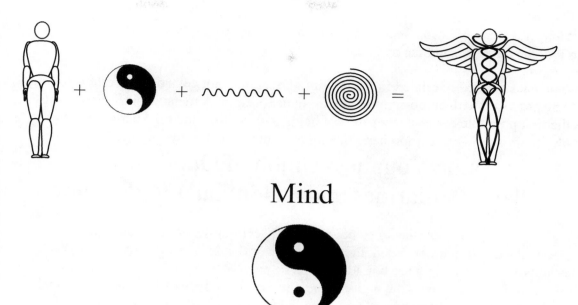

Mind

Mind is the seat of feelings and thought. Mind is what we heed and pay attention to. Mind includes our consciousness, sub-consciousness, unconsciousness and a higher consciousness, a metaphysical consciousness beyond the five senses, a sixth sense of subtle vibrations of feelings and thoughts. Finally, mind includes a supra consciousness, a self-reflective consciousness, a mindfulness, which is conscious of being conscious of itself, our ultimate perceiver or seer or eternal Self.

Most of our daily consciousness is filled with subconscious and unconscious routines and habits. Our day-to-day conscious mind is like an iceberg in that most of our ordinary consciousness is full of sub-conscious behaviors, beliefs and thoughts just like most of an iceberg is submerged below the surface of the water. Yoga quiets the mind so we can see below and beyond the surface of our ordinary consciousness. The yoga mantra *AUM / OM* unites four states of mind, and typically refers to them as—waking, dreaming, dreamless deep sleep and beyond.

You Need an Open Mind to Practice Yoga, A Metaphysical Mind.

An open mind is a metaphysical mind. Metaphysics is defined as the branch of western philosophy that examines the true nature of reality, whether visible or invisible to our mind and senses. The word metaphysics itself derives from the Greek words *meta* meaning beyond or after and *physika* meaning physical. Metaphysics was the term attached to the chapters in Aristotle's works that physically followed the chapters on physics and matter. Aristotle called Metaphysics the first philosophy, the first science, wisdom, the Divine Science and Science of Sciences.
Metaphysics is the study of our existence. For the Ultimate Formula metaphysics is a non-dual, undivided, model of reality that includes the relationship between matter and space, between body and mind, time and causality, and fact and value. Basically,

metaphysics is the philosophical study of being and knowing. Only a metaphysical mind can join the mundane and the mystical.

Metaphysics is directly related to spirituality, though it is not considered a religion. Yoga is to be practiced with an open mind, not as an act of faith. A metaphysical mind focuses on the first principles or ultimate truths of being and Reality, and to experience it as a whole, against trying to comprehend the universe piecemeal or by fragments.

Hatha Yoga Is a Union of Opposites, a Play of Polarities and a Non-Dual Philosophy

The yin and yang symbol illustrates how polar, or seemingly contrary forces, are interconnected and interdependent in the natural world, and how they give rise to each other in turn. Yin and yang are bound together as parts of a mutual non-dual, undivided whole reality. Non-dualism, the undividable unity of the universe, is a common thread throughout the history of yoga and texts like the Upanishads and Vedas. This non-dual holistic philosophy of our being is represented by the yin and yang symbol in.

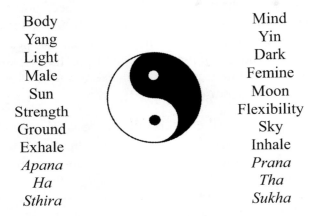

Body	Mind
Yang	Yin
Light	Dark
Male	Femine
Sun	Moon
Strength	Flexibility
Ground	Sky
Exhale	Inhale
Apana	*Prana*
Ha	*Tha*
Sthira	*Sukha*

The Shri Yantra is a Tantric image of unity for meditation and visualization. The Sri Yantra is a classic image of a union of opposites that illustrates that as above, so below.

The Shri Yantra

Modern Science, Classical Physics and

The Age of Enlightenment Separated Body and Mind

To the ancient Greeks, the term 'science' literally meant 'knowledge,' and included all questions about nature, society and humanity. 'Scientific' questions were addressed by natural philosophy, a part of metaphysics as described by Aristotle. Modern 'science' began about 350 years ago, when the Age of Enlightenment or The Age Of Reason replaced Medieval Philosophy. To be 'enlightened' was to be guided by 'reason' instead of the dark superstitions of the medieval era. The cornerstone of the development of The Age of Reason, classical physics and all of modern science was Newtonian physics, the physics of forces of solid matter in empty space.

The central concept in modern science and the scientific method is that all knowledge and truth must be dependent on experimental evidence that is measurable and observable by the five senses. To be 'enlightened' was to let go of knowledge of the heart, psyche, the arts and spirituality in favor of 'science'. The tremendous success of empirical science, rational thought and Newtonian physics in developing the mechanical systems of the Industrial Revolution has in modern times been applied to living systems and human beings with less success.

You Are Beyond Being a Marvelous Machine!

You are not just a collection of parts that constitute a marvelous machine. Describing reality, as being comprised of separate, independent, irreducible and isolated bits of matter has been a cornerstone of modern Western thought. The foundation of Western science was based on the now antiquated notion that reality is made up of solid matter. Matter is a general term for the substance of which all physical objects are made. Matter is described as having mass and occupying space. Historically, matter has been considered inert and space has been considered empty. We have typically thought of reality and our bodies as constructed of solid matter and nothing else. The word atom comes from the Greek *atomos* meaning not able to be cut or divided. Philosophy and science have put forward the idea that reality is built from solid, discrete and unique building blocks called atoms. **This black and white, dualistic model of reality not only separates matter from space, it separates body from mind, and physical from spiritual.**

A sound body is the product of a sound mind.

The foundation of our modern allopathic medical model is based on dualism. It is a model that separates material from spiritual as well as body from mind. This dualistic medical model often presents the body as a machine to be 'fixed', independent of any thoughts, feelings or beliefs. Furthermore, our Western medical model typically reduces our body to a sum of parts and then studying them independently. This has created a world of specialists who rarely include holistic elements of our posture, breath, personality, diet and lifestyle in their treatments. This mechanistic and reductionist thinking has a subtle and not so subtle implication that the body is a machine and we do not need to be consciously involved in our healing. This model presents people and their role in society as divided individuals whose physical form is basically independent from feelings, thoughts and beliefs.

Up until recently modern science has examined all of creation, including your heart, as a precise mechanical clock, as a ticking machine. The scientific method, the foundation of what we call modern science, made empirical and objective experimental activity paramount. Only what could be measurable and observable in a repeatable experiment was considered science. Matter was measurable, and the invisible world of feelings, thoughts and beliefs were not. Matter was primary and ultimately even our consciousness, our soul, has been reduced to being simply a product of our 'gray matter', our brains.

The prevailing belief that everything can be explained 'scientifically', compels us to think that only what can be 'scientifically' tested, can be true, and therefore meaningful to us as humans. Thus, modern medicine has generally omitted the value our feelings, thoughts, relationships and beliefs in our healing. As a result, modern medical science downplays and ignores the placebo effect as an unimportant anomaly when in reality it is amazing that our invisible thoughts, feelings and beliefs can have the same affect on our body's biochemistry as if we had taken a pharmaceutical pill.

Visualizations, intentions, love, prayers, meditation and beliefs in healing lose meaning in the context of empirical science because their efficacy is difficult to objectively test. However, there are now hundreds of holistic mind-body studies, that are mostly ignored by modern medicine, that support a holistic approach to mind-body wellness.

Your Mind Matters to Your Immune System.

In matters of individual holistic healing, the problem of validating claims with empirical scientific methods is challenging. Trying to prove the effectiveness of the healing power of a yoga posture for one specific issue, independent from that person's consciousness, breath, diet, relationships, environment and lifestyle, is impossible. The difficulty arises out of the attempt to rationally and objectively scientifically study something, which, by its very nature is whole, personal and subjective, and cannot easily become an object of scientific study separate from the rest of that person. Self-reflective living systems such as our immune system and ecosystems are too complex to be understood by purely reductionist and materialistic thinking.

Quantum Physics and Ancient Yoga Wisdom

Maya is the yoga word for illusion or the illusionary world, implying a veiled world behind the five senses. *Maya* also means to measure, indicating the divisive power of the Divine to create the physical world. Normal, everyday objects obey the laws of conventional Newtonian physics and can be measured. These rules break down on the sub-atomic level and an entirely new branch of theoretical physics, known as quantum physics has had to be developed to explain what happens on this sub-microscopic level. Einstein was the first to embrace quantum physics but with reservations on the grounds that it made everything unpredictable. In quantum physics, unlike Newtonian physics, at the atomic level, matter has no fixed form and atoms are neither solid nor indivisible. Atoms are 99.999% space, a vacuum quantum space, with wave-particles appearing and disappearing. Electrons are described as having uncertain, non-deterministic "smeared" orbital paths around or even through the nucleus. Quantum physics describes atoms as "no-things," as fields of vibrations. There is some sort of residual energy, vacuum space energy, bit of information or zero point energy at the foundation of all that we think of as solid matter. Matter is fundamentally made up of energy, frequencies and vibrations.

Matter is the illusion of something.

Space is the illusion of nothing.

There is a wholeness, a quantum field, a consciousness and a Divine presence everywhere and in everything. In deepest outer space there are still microwaves. In the deepest vacuum where there is no matter and no light, there are still electromagnetic oscillations. Solid matter and empty space are ultimately an illusion, *maya*. It is an illusion that you are a solid and separate individual disconnected from everything and everyone else.

We have to deal with a wholeness that is completely foreign to classical physics.
Niels Bohr, Quantum Physicist - Nobel Laureate

The Observer Effects The Observed.

Modern science, based on the concept of solid matter separated by empty space, has considered the observation of the matter and the natural world to be objective, passive and receptive. Modern science is based on this notion that reality can be objectively observed. Modern science has believed that you could separate yourself from things, people and life, and passively and secretly observe them without affecting them. Quantum physics, post-modern science, challenges that premise.

Quantum physics states that the observer affects the observed. For example, wherever physicists look for an electron they find one. The act of observation collapses an invisible wave-particle function into an electron. When under observation, electrons seem to be "forced" to behave in one way or the other by just observing them. Light photons behave like waves or particles depending on how you consciously choose to observe them. The act of conscious observation literally effects the outcome of the experiment.

How You Consciously Look At People Effects Them.

The expression, "Sticks and stones can break my bones but words can never hurt me," is now considered false in biochemistry. If you look at someone with love in your eyes it creates one chemical neuropeptide, and if you look at him or her with hate and scorn it creates different one. There are many examples of how the observer effects the observed. Dr. Masaru Emoto experiments show that consciousness, thought and prayer have a profound effect on the crystalline structure of water molecules.

I regard consciousness as fundamental.
I regard matter as derivative from consciousness.
Max Planck, The Originator of Quantum Theory - Nobel Laureate

Quantum Entanglement: We Are One

Niels Bohr went on to develop the theory of quantum entanglement and won the Nobel Physics Prize. Interestingly, he chose the yin and yang symbol for his Nobel coat of arms. Bohr determined that once two particles were in contact, then separated in space, still maintained a sense of being whole. Thus when one photon was forced to change its spin, the other changed at exactly the same instant. The change is so simultaneous that no communication even if it was traveling at the speed of light could inform the other photon. Einstein famously described this as "a spooky action." Researchers have no clear theoretical explanation of a Reality beyond the speed of light, and thus beyond our concepts of three dimensional space and linear time. The yoga tradition defines this deep space beyond time as *kasha*, radiant-space. It is where creativity, love and wisdom come from. All of life is sharing one cosmic mind, one absolute unity of being. We are sparks of one cosmic flame. We are spiral vortexes in an infinite sea of consciousness. Quantum physics, like the ancient yoga, indicates that our consciousness and how we view our selves, others and the world has a meaningful effect.

The Post-Modern-New Millennial Yoga Manifesto

Consciousness Is Primary, Matter Is Secondary.

The state of your conscious effects what you observe.

You are an active ingredient, a conscious co-creator, in the health and well-being of yourself, others and the world. Conscious relationships become primary and any actual physical exchange secondary. You can no longer claim that you are passively observing yourself, others or the world. All life is interconnected. All consciousness is interconnected. We are one.

The term post-modernism originates in the late 20th century as a movement in the arts and architecture. It is a departure from the austere forms, structural utility and the notion of objective reality of the rational tenets of Age of Enlightenment. Post-modernism embraced imagination, intuition and fantasy. The Post-Modern-New Millennial Yoga Manifesto turns the perception of the modern world and thought upside down. It is a revolutionary concept for modern thought that the gray matter of our brain is no longer considered to be the source of consciousness, rather it is consciousness that is the source and foundation of matter. Like the ancient scriptures of the *Upanishads*, where the term Yoga was first used, quantum physics suggests that the material world of the five senses is a veil covering a deeper Reality of subtle vibrations.

Our Five Senses Are Limited and Can Be Deceptive

Our five senses give only a limited view of Reality. Our senses perceive only a small fraction of the electromagnetic spectrum and electrochemical signals that are present.

The walls of your room look and feel solid,
until you receive a cell phone call that passes right through them.

The world looks flat when you drive down the highway,

The Post-Modern-New Millennial Yoga Manifesto is a about a quantum paradigm shift in our perception of reality and ourselves. It is similar to the paradigm shift in consciousness, belief and thought of 500 years ago when Copernicus and Galileo said that the sun does not rotate around the earth. Even though it appears to our five senses that the earth is still and that sun is rotating around it, the earth is really rotating around the sun. Even though it appears to our five senses that matter is solid, the particle accelerators of today have shown atoms not to be solid, but in fact 99.999% empty vacuum space. Atoms seem to be composed of a bit of information in vast quantum field sprinkled with subatomic wave-particles. It seems that a mysterious quantum energy-space-consciousness is the ultimate foundation of atoms and Reality. The *Upanishads*, Vedanta, Integral Yoga of Sri Aurobindo, traditional Hatha-Yoga and Therapeutic Hatha Yoga hold that life is already in matter and consciousness is already in life. Therapeutic Hatha Yoga is about being conscious of a wholly holy other realm of reality.

The Post-Modern-New Millennial Mind

The Post-Modern-New Millennial Mind is a mind that matters. According to ancient yogis and quantum physics we create reality with our consciousness. There is no out there separate from in here. We are co-creators of reality. Your consciousness, thoughts, feelings, beliefs and relationships affect your physical form, and they affect those around you. A Post-Modern-New Millennial Mind is a mind that is sensitive to the invisible world of feelings, thoughts and beliefs of life all around us as well as the visible physical world.

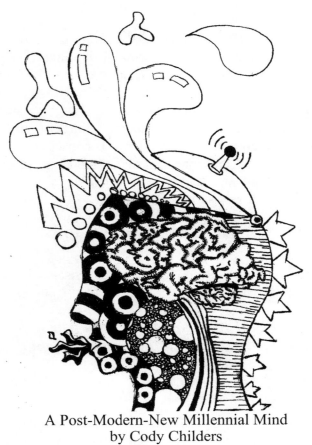

A Post-Modern-New Millennial Mind
by Cody Childers

A metaphysical mind does not separate body from mind, physiology from psychology or masculine from feminine. Your attitude effects you, and to a lesser degree everyone around you. Visualizations and intentions connect your physical form with formless feelings, thoughts, beliefs and spirit. A metaphysical mind can 'sense' and 'tune in to' the invisible waves of creativity, love and wisdom. Be conscious of what you say, feel, think and believe.

The Post-Modern-New Millennial Yoga Manifesto is a Revolution In How We Think and Perceive.

Be Conscious of the Dynamic Relationship Between the Right-Handed Left Brain Way of Thinking, and the Left-Handed Right Brain Way of Thinking, Between Masculine and Feminine, Numbers and Art, Word and Image, and Between the Tree (Me) and the Forest (We).

A post-modern-new millennial mind is a holistic mind-body. In many ways what is described as mind-body is like describing our left and right hemispheres of the brain. It is a mind that integrates the masculine, linear, reductionist and rational left-brain, which controls our right hand, and the feminine holistic, intuitive, image beholding and artistic right brain, which controls our left hand. The Age of Enlightenment or Age of Reason has focused almost totally on the qualities of the left hemisphere of the brain and in doing so, suppressed the qualities of right hemisphere of our brain and the feminine side of life distorting our culture, society, relationship with nature and our ability to heal. It is time to create a more holistic relationship between the left and right hemispheres of our brain, between mind and body, between masculine and feminine.

Let There Be a Dynamic Peace, a Play of Polarities, Between Earth Father and Sky Mother, as well as, Mother Earth and Sky Father In Our Thinking, Behavior, Culture and Healing.

The Most Powerful Drug in the World

The most powerful drug in the world is the placebo. Placebos are pills, injections, surgeries, and other treatments that contain no known active ingredients. Placebos are often called dummies by modern medical institutions. However, placebos work all of the time taken in clinical trials.

You Will See It When You Believe It,

Rather Than You Will Believe It When You See It!

The placebo effect points to the importance of perception, beliefs and the role of our consciousness, thoughts and relationships in our healing. Nevertheless, modern medical and pharmaceutical institutions continually deny, ignore and avoid the natural healing intelligence of the body-mind connection. To the linear materialistic mind the placebo effect is one of the oddest phenomena in medicine since placebos, without "an active ingredient", often work as well as the treatments they are compared with in clinical trials. **Modern medical institutions treat the research on the placebo effect as an inconvenient truth, instead of embracing the power of the wholeness of the body-mind connection.** Nevertheless, there is a now a growing field called 'evidence based' mind-body medicine.

Placebos are scientific proof of the mind's ability to heal the body.

The most powerful pharmacy in the word is your mind.

One explanation for placebo effect is that the caring and hopefulness that the patient feels while being treated translates into an expanded sense of consciousness, which manifests in surges of specific hormones and other biochemical exchanges in the brain and body.

This is all centered in the hypothalamus, which creates neuropeptides based on our emotions, consciousness and beliefs that are released into the blood stream. These then go on to trigger therapeutic immune responses in our cells. One class of hormones implicated so far is the endorphins. They carry messages through the bloodstream to the endocrine and immune systems where they induce the production and release of other biochemicals that contribute to healing.

Even according to traditional medical organizations, including the American Cancer Society, placebos seem to affect and heal people in up to and beyond 1 out of 3 patients. Many put the percentage of healing due to the placebo effect between 40%and 66%. Our invisible field of subtle vibrations of beliefs, feelings and relationships affects our physical structure.

> The efficacy of any pill or practice
> is a co-creation with the individual.
> Be aware. You are your own temple.
> Does it work for you?
> Your sense of things affects them.
> Consciousness matters.

Change your thinking and change your life.

Louise Hay

Let's Toast To Your Good Health!

When we toast to our health, we are directly implying that our thinking, intentions, visualizations and consciousness can play a role in our health and well-being. How we view our health and medicine are greatly effected by the outdated dualistic concepts of matter and space. A strictly materialistic approach to our bodies constricts our being and limits our natural healing abilities. If we view ourselves as just a physical machine, we do not have to be consciously involved in our own healing, and not encouraged to call on our lifestyle, visualizations, prayers, meditations or even our breath to facilitate our healing.

Having Sharing and Caring Relationship Helps Us Rally!

A materialistic dualistic model of reality often creates feelings of separation, loneliness, alienation, and sadness, which suppress our psycho-neuro-immunology. We are meant to feel and have meaningful relationships with others, society and the web of life. One of the most amazing things about the placebo effect is that it makes a difference if we emotionally feel cared about by the people administering the placebo. It seems that the most powerful of the most powerful drugs is the feeling and belief that you are being cared for. Many studies suggest that an encounter with a doctor or other healer is enough treatment to initiate a recovery. How it is shared with us increases the effectiveness of the placebo. Experiencing sharing and caring relationships revives us.

What is the difference between illness and wellness?
The first begins with 'I' and the second with 'we'.

Swami Satchitananda

Share the Gift of Yoga. Find a Yoga Buddy / Partner.
Co-create A Local Healing Circle, Network, Community.

In the yoga tradition, the word community has implied a spiritual community, which was typically isolated from the rest of society. Historically yoga has had an initiatory community structure, and was all male up until about a hundred years ago. A yoga practice presupposed a teacher, historically called the *guru* and a community of devotees, practitioners and students. The word '*guru*' literally means 'teacher' and in the yogic tradition is referred to as the 'remover of darkness,' and or the 'weighty one.' The Kula-Arnava-Tantra speaks of six levels of being a guru. When you share yoga with a friend or family member, you become 'the 'impeller' and are literally taking the first step onto the path of becoming a guru/teacher. Deepen your yoga practice by creating a sharing and caring relationship. Share the gift of yoga. Historically, a yoga community has been based on a system where practitioners invite friends and family to join them.

Six Levels of Being a Guru/Teacher
In the Kula-Arnava-Tantra Tradition

1. The guru, as impeller, stimulates interest in the would-be-practitioner.
2. The guru, as indicator, points out the form of practice for which the initiate is qualified.
3. The guru, as explainer, expounds the practice and its objectives.
4. The guru, as revealer, shows the details of the process.
5. The guru, as teacher, presents the dynamics of the actual practice.
6. The guru, as illuminator, lights up in the lamp of spiritual and physical knowledge the disciple.

A Post-Modern-New Millennial Yoga Community

The 21st century now has a yoga industry with corporations selling everything and anything yoga including mats, clothes, classes and teacher trainings. Yoga enthusiasts are not viewed as students and practitioners of yoga in a corporate market based setting as much as they are viewed as customers and consumers of yoga. Ultimately we must be careful of this commercial yoga industry model, which puts profits before people and the depth of the teaching of yoga. Today people who practice yoga are likely to be 'members' of a corporation or health club, rather than devotees and students of a particular yoga teacher, school or ashram. Thus a modern 'yoga community' is typically referring to a loose knit group of members, students and teachers, who share a bond together as they live and work in separate communities. This bond, regardless of the market place limitations, is a powerful source of strength, inspiration and support for healing for many.

Post-modern yoga communities can and are for forming friendships, coalitions and alliances beyond the market place. With the advent of the festivals, conferences, cell phones, Internet and social media, contemporary yoga communities now exist on local and global levels. Post-modern yoga community devotees now easily link into personal and social networks to foster the health and well-being of their community and the planet.

The words 'devotee' and 'vote' come from the Latin *votum,* 'a vow, wish, promise to a god, solemn pledge or dedication.' A post-modern yoga community combines being devoted to a personal yoga practice, an individual rite if you will, and being devoted to a social practice, the right to vote and participate in the general health and well-being of the local and global communities. Recognizing the holistic benefits of yoga and its inherent compatibility with the principles and values of the United Nations, the General Assembly of the United Nations has proclaimed June 21st International Day of Yoga. Members of post-modern yoga communities devote time to the personal rite of practicing postures, and to the social right of practicing voting in their community. A post-modern yoga devotee fosters a metaphysical mind and a non-dual rite-right practice of yoga, a personal rite and social right of devotion to health and well-being.

All of life is yoga.

Sri Aurobindo

The Medicine Buddha Mantra

*Teyata om bekanze
bekanze maha bekanze
radza samudgate soha.*

It is like this. Medicine Buddha, You are the Supreme Healer.
Please remove mental illness/pain,
physical illness/pain and the great illness/pain,
the illusion of duality, the root cause of our suffering. Now I offer.

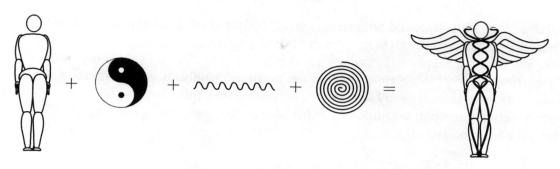

Breath

The Breath Is a Bridge Between
Body and Mind, and Between Physical and Spiritual.

The Latin word for breath, *spiritu*, literally means both breath and spirit. Our breath unites our material physical form with our formless feelings, thoughts and beliefs. The breath is a bridge between our physiology and psychology. Our breath responds to changes in our emotions and thoughts, as well as changes in our levels of physical activity. Our invisible feelings, thoughts, beliefs and spirit ride on the wave of the breath throughout our bodies. Our breath is our friend to help teach, heal and guide us. Being conscious of the breath brings the mind and body closer together. Being conscious of the breath is an ideal way to harness and focus the power of the mind to heal.

   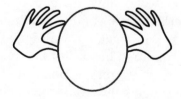

Cup your hands over your ears or place your thumbs over your earflaps.
Listen to the vibrant ocean of consciousness in your breath.
Listen to the power and authority in your breath.
Conscious Breathing Practice 1

How to Breathe?

People constantly tell me they do not know how to breathe. For most people, normal breathing is basically a totally unconscious experience. The books they read in school about their lungs and body did not create a meaningful personal awareness of breathing. A lifetime of external awareness has left many of us ignorant of an inner awareness of the breath, and how it effects and affects us physically, emotionally and spiritually. It is difficult for most of us to accept and claim the power and authority of our own breath. Granted there is no one-way to breathe for everyone all the time. We modify our breathing depending upon the situation. Most of the time, our exhalations are slightly longer than our inhalations.

Breathe Through Your Nose!

The nose knows how to breathe. The nose, with its intricate design, is the best choice for optimal breathing during both rest and exercise. Conscious breathing begins with breathing in through your nose. Breathing through the nose filters, warms and moistens the air and conditions it for the lungs. The olfactory sensors in the nose stimulate the mind creating even greater consciousness and awareness while breathing. Breathing in through the mouth is basically having only four of your senses activated. The sense of smell is connected to our instincts and to our intuitive wisdom. Breathing through the nose is essential for developing self-reflective consciousness. Yoga is to be practiced breathing through the nose.

Conscious Healing Begins with

Being Conscious of Breathing Through Your Nose!

Inhaling through the mouth stresses the lungs and contributes to respiratory conditions such as asthma. Unfortunately, many people are totally unaware of their breath and habitually suck or sip the air in through their mouths. People do this unconsciously between sentences while talking, walking and even eating. Inhaling through the mouth not only fails to condition the air for the lungs, it tends to create a sympathetic nervous response, an emergency stress response in the body, a fight-or-flight response. Breathing through the nose triggers the parasympathetic nervous response, a rest and relax response, which calms and soothes the body and mind. Observe the breath in yourself and in others. How often are people around you breathing through their mouths or their noses?

Invite the breath in to your body-temple.

Draw the breath in through your nose.

Feel the Breath on the Inside of the Nostrils
And Soften Your Forehead as You Inhale.
Conscious Breathing Practice 2

The Yin and Yang of Breathing

Basically, we have an in-breath and an out-breath, an expansion and a contraction. Together they equal one breath. The image of the yin and yang helps us visualize the breath as one whole breath that oscillates smoothly and rhythmically between inhalation and exhalation, expansion and contraction and between nourishing the body and cleansing the body.

Visualize the field of white as the out-breath.

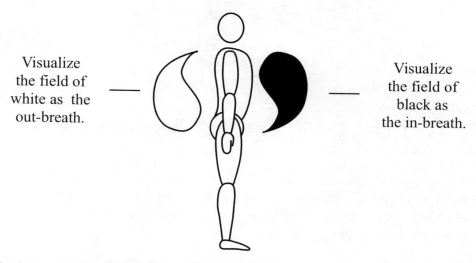

Visualize the field of black as the in-breath.

Anatomically the chest diaphragm separates the chest cavity from the abdominal cavity. The organs of respiration of chest cavity, the lungs and the heart, are separated from the organs of digestion of the abdominal cavity, the stomach, liver and intestines by the chest diaphragm. As we expand on inhalation, we create space in the alveoli and the atmospheric pressure, literally the weight of six miles of air above us, alone can fill us. Inspiration Does Not Suck. We can invite the breath into our body temple by simply expanding our self. As we inhale the ribs expand out and back as the front of the body lengthens and the chest diaphragm descends pressing on the abdominal cavity. As we exhale the body contracts, the ribs are drawn down and in as the chest diaphragm presses up on the chest cavity.

The Rhyme and Reason in Your Breath: the Yin and Yang of Breathing.

For the most part we are unconscious of any rhyme or reason in our breath. Sometimes we inhale longer than exhaling, and sometimes the reverse. Our breathing is changing constantly as we vary our activities, thoughts and emotions.

Equal Ratio Breathing – *Sama-vritti*
Practice Inhaling for the Count of Four
And Exhaling for the Count of Four.
Repeat for 7 Breaths
Conscious Breathing Practice 3

Sama means same, even, smooth, equal and or flat. *Vrittii* means whirling consciousness or fluctuations of thought. Being conscious of an even smooth, rhythmic breath is one of the first steps in yoga.

Let our in-breaths and our out-breaths be woven together
In a rhythmic circular manner like the yin and yang symbol,
Like wings in flight, like an oil derrick smoothly moving
Up, around and down as you breathe.

The Chest Cavity and the Abdominal Cavity

Therapeutic Hatha Yoga focuses on expanding the chest cavity first, and then drawing the breath down into the abdominal cavity. THY exhalations focus on contracting the abdominal cavity and condensing the belly first, and then on contracting the chest cavity expelling the breath up and out of the body.

Draw the breath down and into the body from the chest cavity on inhalation and expel the breath up and out of the body from the abdominal cavity.

The field of white represents the exhalation contracting the body from the abdominal cavity to the chest cavity expelling the breath up and out of the body.

The field of black represents the inhalation expanding the body from the chest cavity to the abdominal cavity drawing the breath down and into the body.

The Heart and the Anchor of the Breath

The addition of an image of a heart to the yin, and an anchor to the yang of breathing adds psychological and emotional components to the expansion and contraction of the breath. Inhaling to the heart is a perfect image of a holistic integration of our physical, emotional and spiritual sides. The image of an anchor symbolizes a psychological and emotional feeling of stability and security to the yang contraction of the breath.

The Image of a Heart and an Anchor
Combined with the Symbol of the Yin and Yang
Further Helps Us To Visualize Conscious Rhythmic Breathing.

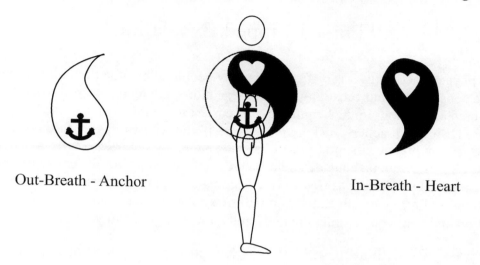

Out-Breath - Anchor   In-Breath - Heart

The Heart of the Breath

Place your hands over your chest. Inhale and expand your heart cavity.
Conscious Breathing Practice 4

The Anchor of the Breath

Place your hands over your abdomen.
Exhale and consciously contract your abdominal cavity.
Conscious Breathing Practice 5

Exhalations Count Too!

During casual breathing most people make moderate efforts to inhale and basically relax to exhale. In other words, people are slightly conscious of their inhalations and basically unconscious of their exhalations. Conscious breathing includes conscious exhaling, not just conscious inhaling. We live in a consumer-driven society. We are focused on consumption and acquisition. All too often people take a huge inhalation and then collapse while exhaling. The easiest way to become more conscious is to be become more conscious of your exhalations is to simply count them as you breathe. When practicing Therapeutic Hatha Yoga count your breaths on the exhalation.

Be More Conscious of Exhalations.
Count Out Seven Exhalations to Yourself.
Conscious Breathing Practice 6

Pursed-Lipped Exhalation

During physical activities it is difficult for many people to breathe through their nose. To be more conscious of our breathing during these moments, focus on an active and empowered exhalation. In the beginning, it is easiest to do this with a pursed-lipped exhalation. Simply practice pursing your lips, as if you where blowing through a straw, which is a great practice in and of itself. Maintain a smooth exhalation as if you were bending, yet not extinguishing, a candle flame. You can empower the exhalation with a 'foggy breath', by exhaling as if you were fogging up a pair of eyeglasses. Pursed-lipped exhalations and foggy breath exhalation will make you more conscious of your exhalation and help you contract the body and gain strength from your core.

Exhale with a Pursed Lips for Seven Conscious Exhalations.
Exhale with a Foggy Breath for Seven Conscious Exhalations.
Conscious Breathing Practice 7

The Pause in the Breath

Pause

The field of white represents the exhalation expelling the breath up and out of the body into a perfect moment of stillness.

The field of black represents the inhalation drawing the breath down and into the body into a perfect moment of stillness.

Pause

In addition to an inhalation and an exhalation there is a pause, a moment of stillness, a space after each. In the yoga tradition, the inhalation is known as *puraka*, the exhalation as *rechaka* and the pause as *kumbhaka*. The pause after the inhalation is known as *antara kumbahaka* and the pause after the exhalation is known as *bahya kumbhaka*. Imagine the pause in the breath like that of a pendulum swinging back and forth into and out of a pause and a moment of stillness.

All too often we tense and lightly hold our breath at the end of the inhalation and then lightly collapse the heart and chest cavity as we exhale breaking the rhythmic flow of our breath. Be conscious of the pause in the breath. We breathe smoother and more rhythmically when we are conscious of a pause and a moment of stillness in our breath.

*Let there be a smooth rhythmic moment of stillness, of
Spaciousness between inhalations and exhalations.*

Be Conscious of the Pause-Stillness-Space
In the Breath for Seven Breaths.
Conscious Breathing Practice 8

The Wisdom of Paradoxes

The paradoxical contradiction in the yin and yang symbol is that black and white are mutually exclusive opposing forces, yet they contain an element of each other. The field of white is not all white and has a small circle of black in it, while the field of black has a small circle of white in it. The essence of one is paradoxically found in the other.

A paradox is a counterintuitive statement

That illustrates an apparent contradiction

That actually expresses a deeper truth.

Dynamic Tension in the Breath

In order to sustain a stable smooth vibrant rhythmic breath the two opposing forces of the breath need to be balanced. The exhalation, centered in the abdominal cavity, represented by the field of white is balanced by an element of the inhalation, a small circle of black, which you could visualize as balancing the exhalation by holding the heart lifted. The inhalation, centered in the heart cavity, represented by the field of black, contains an element of the exhalation, a small circle of white, which you could visualize as balancing the inhalation by holding the navel in.

Great art is the result of

Dynamic tension between light and dark.

Great breathing is the result of

Dynamic tension between exhaling and inhaling.

The Deeper Truth

The deeper truth is that the apparent contradiction
Of adding dynamic tension to the breath
Actually smoothes evens and balances the breath.

Hold the essence of the lifted heart
while you exhale to the navel.

Hold the essence of the navel in
while you inhale to the heart.

Practice dynamic tension
Between the heart cavity and the abdominal cavity,
Place the thumb and forefinger of one hand just below the collarbones, and
The thumb on the navel and the forefinger on the pubic bone
of the other hand.

Dynamic Tension in the Exhalation
Keep the heart lifted as you exhale for seven breaths.
Conscious Breathing Practice 9

Dynamic Tension in the Inhalation
Keep the navel in as you inhale for seven breaths.
Conscious Breathing Practice 10

Three Diaphragms Involved with Breathing

There are a number of anatomical structures that act as diaphragms, membranes or partitions within the body, including the iris and the eardrum. Consider that there are three diaphragms involved with the physical act of breathing. The first is the throat or vocal diaphragm at the larynx. The second is the chest diaphragm, thoracic diaphragm, or simply the diaphragm. This chest diaphragm is a sheet of internal muscle that extends across the bottom of the rib cage separating the heart and lungs from the organs of digestion. It separates the heart cavity from the abdominal cavity. The chest diaphragm is responsible for vast majority of musculature used for breathing and is the diaphragm most associated with breathing. The third diaphragm is the pelvic floor or the pelvic diaphragm. It is composed of a webbing of muscle fibers connecting the tailbone and the pubic bone. Remember to keep the heart lifted as you exhale, and the navel in as you inhale.

1. **Throat Diaphragm**
   Heart
   Cavity

2. **Chest Diaphragm**

   Abdominal
   Cavity

3. **Pelvic Diaphragm**

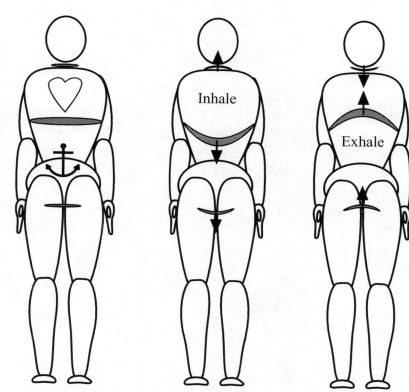

Three Part Diaphragmatic Breathing
Inhale and expand your torso from the top, middle and then bottom,
Focusing on diaphragms 1, 2, and 3.
Exhale and contract your torso from the bottom, middle and then top,
Focusing on diaphragms 3, 2, and 1.
Repeat seven times.
Conscious Breathing Practice 11

Visualize the Body as a Vessel for Consciousness

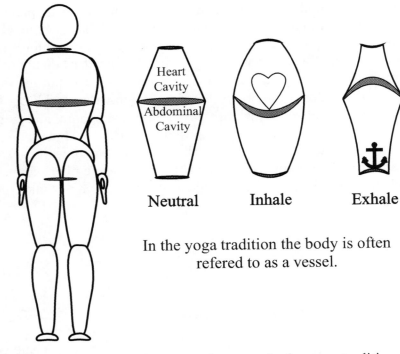

1. **Throat Diaphragm**
   Heart
   Cavity
2. **Chest Diaphragm**

   Abdominal
   Cavity

3. **Pelvic Diaphragm**

Neutral   Inhale   Exhale

In the yoga tradition the body is often refered to as a vessel.

The body is often referred to as a vessel for spirit or consciousness in the yoga tradition. Visualize the three diaphragms as forming a frame for a container, a vessel. Place the thumb and forefinger of one hand just under the collarbones and the thumb of the other hand in your navel and the fingers over the pubic bone.

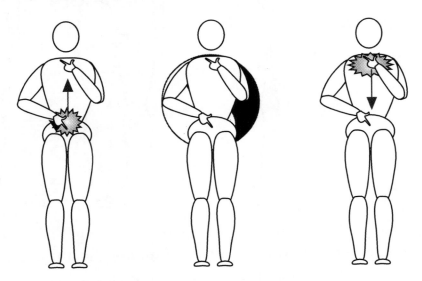

Inhale And Float Your Consciousness, Do Not Bloat It.
Inhale expand your vessel and float your heart, and do not bloat the belly.
Conscious Breathing Practice 12

Prana and *Apana*

In the Yoga tradition, the subtle energy of the in-breath is described as *prana* and the out-breath as *apana*. The word *prana* has slightly different connotations in various yoga texts. *Prana,* in Sanskrit means life and breath. This word *prana* has commonly been defined as 'vital energy' or 'the element that sustains all life in the universe.' *Prana is* also often equated to the Chinese *chi*, Japanese *ki* Polynesian *mana*, Native American *orenda*, African *ashe* and the ancient German *od.* In dozens of modern books, *prana* has been translated as 'life force'.

Apana, meaning not *prana*, expels the life force out of the body through the acts of exhalation and elimination. *Prana* is centered in the heart, encompasses the head and creates a subtle feeing of being lifted and expanded. The apana is centered in the navel, encompasses the pelvis and anus, and creates a subtle feeling of being anchored and grounded. It is a paradox that exhaling the breath up and out of the body creates a subtle feeling of being grounded, and inhaling the breath down and into the body creates a subtle feeling of being lifted. Apana pulls prana, and prana pulls apana.

Inhale *Prana* and Be Consciously Uplifted for Seven Breaths
Conscious Breathing Practice 13
Exhale *Apana* and Be Consciously Grounded for Seven Breaths
Conscious Breathing Practice 14

Exhale = *Apana* = Grounded   Inhale = *Prana* =Uplifted

It is a paradox that
exhaling the breath up and out of the body, the body has the subtle feeling of being grounded and
while inhaling the breath down and into the body, the body has the subtle feeling of being lifted.

Feel the contrast of feeling uplifted, as you inhale the air down and into the body.
Feel the contrast of feeling grounded, as you exhale the air up and out of the body.

The word 'force' is a word used in Newtonian mechanical physics to describe the energy exerted on inert matter to accelerate it through empty space. For the past 350 years, since

Newton and what we now call the Age of Reason or The Age Of Enlightenment, scientists have tried to describe an interconnected reality with discrete and separate 'particles' separated by empty space. By extension they have described society as being comprised of discrete separate individuals. Thus classical Newtonian physics and the Age of Reason have had to add forces to explain how particles, and people, connect together in space and time. This does not explain how discrete matter particles or people create continuous fields of communication that act on other fields. Further quantum physics, particle-wave duality, non-locality, uncertainty and Einstein's general relativity (matter-energy curves space-time) contradict the very concept of discrete and separate inert particles.

You Are a Conscious Living Human Being,

Not a Mechanical Human Doing.

The entire preoccupation of Newtonian physics is to describe reality, and people, as being composed of particle-matter-things. People become human things that do stuff, instead of conscious human beings that are made of Light. Translating *prana* using the language of mechanical physics, we get the expression 'life force', which distorts the conscious and spiritual nature of life and yoga.

The ancient Indian scriptures, the Upanishads, defined prana as life and life as prana. To better reflect the ancient-quantum paradigm, prana might be defined as 'life embracing consciousness' and apana as 'life releasing consciousness'.

Yoga Is Full of Paradoxes!

We inhale more smoothly when we maintain the essence of the exhalation,
The navel slightly in and contracted.
We exhale with more stability when we keep the essence of the inhalation,
The heart slightly expanded and lifted.

It is a paradox that we feel lifted
As we inhale the breath down and into the body.

It is a paradox that we feel grounded
As we exhale the breath up and out of the body.

It is a paradox that in yoga
We connect to our spiritual being through our physical practice.

It is a paradox that our spirits become freer
As we become more physically grounded.

Visualize the Breath as a Wave
Organizing Your Whole Body

Our breath is a fundamental organizing phenomenon of the whole body. All too often we focus all of our attention on discrete muscles to master yoga postures, forgetting the holistic nature of our being. The act of breathing effects us from the top of our head to the soles of our feet. Rhythmic breathing influences the quantity and quality of the flow of blood, lymph and nervous energy throughout the body.

Good Health Is the Natural State of the Body When *Prana* Flows
Easily and Evenly Throughout the Body.

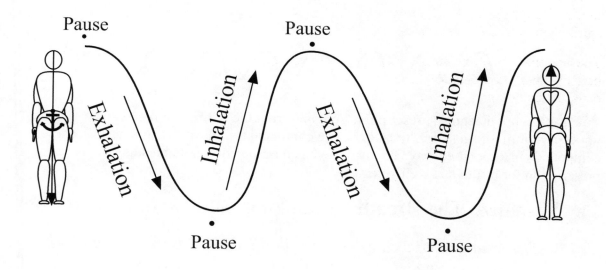

Catch the Wave! Ride It Up and Down through Your Body.
Let the Breath Cleanse and Nourish Yourself From Head to Toe.

Exhale from the top of your head
To the soles of your feet.
Inhale from the soles of the feet
To the top of your head.
Repeat for seven conscious breaths.
Conscious Breathing Practice 15

Conscious Rhythmic Breathing Is
The Single Best Medicine for Every Ill

The single biggest source of prana, life conscious energy, is found in the act of respiration. Therefore, how we breathe has a very profound and immediate effect on our health and well-being. Conscious dynamic rhythmic breathing is thus arguably the single best prescription available for good health. Many studies have shown that conscious rhythmic breathing can lower our heart rate, improve our digestion, reduce stress, release muscle tension and more.

R_x is a symbol meaning "prescription", coming from the Latin verb *recipe*, the imperative form of *recipere*, "to take". It is a command to "take" certain materials and compounds in a specified way. To 'take' seven conscious rhythmic breaths is a prescription for health and well-being.

Visualize The Breath Organizing And Healing You

Visualize your breath as a wave, as a physical process integrating and organizing your tissues, glands, organs, muscles,
Joints and bones from head to toe as you breathe.

Conscious rhythmic breathing
is a feedback mechanism for self-healing.

Nourish and cleanse your body with conscious rhythmic breathing.

Ride your thoughts, prayers, intentions and visualizations for health and well-being on the breath throughout your body.
Conscious Breathing Practice 16

Empower Your Conscious Breath!
Turn Your Yin and Yang into a Count of 6 and 9

Notice that the sine wave used to symbolize breath is slightly uneven. The duration of inhalation to exhalation is polarized in that the inhalation lasts for a duration of 6 counts while the exhalation lasts for a duration of 9 counts with a pause, a moment of stillness between them. Lengthening the exhalation helps engage the lower abdomen and pelvic diaphragm. Yoga utilizes many different breathing ratios. This polarized ratio of 6 to 9 is one of the best ratios to witness our edge, limit and healing. This ratio can be expressed as inhaling for a count of 4 and exhaling for a count of 6. Once you are able to exhale for the count of 9, practice exhaling longer. Try exhaling for the count of 30.

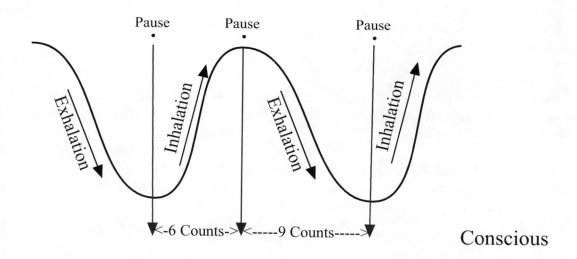

Empower Your Breath
Inhale for the Count of 6. Exhale for the Count Of 9.
Count Out Seven Exhalations
Conscious Breathing Practice 17

Traditional Yoga Breathing Practices

The breathing practices described here are ancient techniques modified over the ages by different yoga schools. There is no such thing as one standardized or universal method to these practices. Even the names can be different.

Ujjayi Breathing

Ujjayi Breathing Is the Ideal Way to Practice Therapeutic Hatha Yoga.

Ujjayi means victory, winning, or conquering breath. During *ujjayi,* as you exhale from the navel, the throat diaphragm and the epiglottis are slightly constricted producing an audibly hollow, deep, soft sound, much like the sound of the ocean. Keep the navel in as you inhale back through a slightly constricted throat diaphragm. By forcing the breath through a constricted epiglottis and larynx, inhalations produce a sibilant `sss' sound, and exhalations produce an aspirate `hhh' sound.

Begin by listening to your breath with your thumbs over your earflaps or cupping your hands over your ears. You can hear the sound of the breath flowing through the throat. Now constrict the throat diaphragm so sound is more audible that you can hear the soft sound without your hands.

In the beginning, it is much easier to create a sound while exhaling. Put one hand in front of your mouth and pretend you are fogging up a pair of eyeglasses. Then see if you could repeat that sound with the mouth closed.

To help create the soft auditable sound on inhalation, bring the chin in and down to constrict the throat diaphragm. Variations of plow and shoulder stand further help to constrict the throat to produce the *ujjayi* sound.

A wall supported shoulder stand is a good way to lightly constrict the throat and begin to listen to the sound of the *ujjayi* breath.

It is easiest to produce a soft *ujjayi* sound on the exhalation. Begin by exhaling for the count of 9 and inhaling for the count of 6.

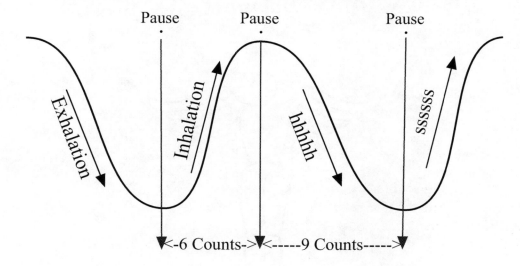

Ujjayi Breathing
Exhale `hhh'.
Inhale `sss'.
Conscious Breathing Practice 18

There is a tendency to over think postures and how they look.
We are often not conscious of how our breath creates
Inner lines of energy and alignment.
Thus many people analyze the postures
Focusing on separate muscle groups
Instead of conscious breathing.

Listen to the sound of the ujjayi breath,
Clear your mind and
Listen to the organizing phenomena of the ujjayi breath.

The sound of the breath helps you focus on the quality, evenness and
smoothness in your body, mind and breath.

Refining and meditating on the tone of the sound of ujjayi breath is a
practice that can last a lifetime.

The Swan Mantra

Hamsa

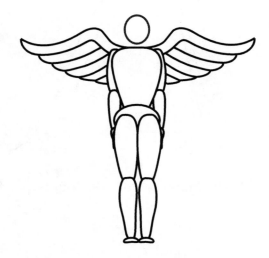

The Wings of the Inner Teacher-Healer-Guide

Symbolize the *Hamsa* Mantra.

The word *hamsa* in Sanskrit is the word for swan or wild goose, and is a symbol of the spirit (*atman*), the divine consciousness. *Mantra* means 'mind tool', 'hymn', 'prayer' or 'call to the divine'. In the hatha yoga tradition, the psyche continually recites the *hamsa* 'swan' mantra. Every exhalation has an internal or aspirant *'ham'* vibration, and every inhalation has an internal or sibilant *'sa'* vibration. Together the out-breath and the in-breath create the word *hamsa*.

The subtle energy currents of a*pana* and *prana* power the *hamsa* circuit. The out-breath carries the subtle descending energy current of apana and the in-breath carries the subtle ascending energy current of prana. Together, they create the *hamsa* circuit, through which the psyche moves up and down the entire body. Meditating, visualizing and tuning into the *hamsa* current creates a foundation for a healing on a psycho-neuro-immunological level. *Hamsa* animates us into being, to teach, heal and guide ourselves, others and the planet.

Exhale – *Ham*
Inhale - *Sa*
Repeat For Seven Breaths
Conscious Breathing Practice 19

70

Every Breath Is a Prayer

The Unspoken Mantra
The *Ajapa* Mantra

According to yoga tradition, every breath creates an unspoken mantra called the *ajapa mantra*. *A* means 'not', *japa* means 'spoken' and *mantra* means 'mind tool', 'hymn', 'prayer' or 'call to the divine'. The sequence *hamsa-hamsa-hamsa*, when repeated can be heard as *so ham-so, ham-so, ham*, which is the Sanskrit pronouncement, *Tat Twam Asi*, which is constantly affirming our true divine essence as we breathe. Every in-breath silently utters the prayer 'Thou art what I am" or 'That am I" and every out- breath silently utters the prayer "I am what thou art" or "I am That", "That" being the divine as expressed in whatever you are sensing and experiencing at the moment be it the birds, the sky or the clothes you are wearing. All of life is a scared expression of the divine.

The word 'universe' is composed of two Latin words, 'uni', meaning one, and 'verse' meaning song or verse. The ajapa mantra is
The one song all of life is singing, chanting and praying.

The *ajapa mantra* is not a beseeching prayer asking for something missing in our lives. Rather, it is an affirmative prayer acknowledging and celebrating the life, creativity, love and spirit that is our life. The *ajapa mantra* is like inhaling 'yes' and exhaling 'thank you'.

The Ajapa Mantra / The Universal Mantra

Exhale - *I am what thou art.*
Inhale - *Thou art what I am.*
Or
Exhale - *I am That.*
Inhale - *That am I.*
Conscious Breathing Practice 20

71

Bhastrika - Bellows Breath

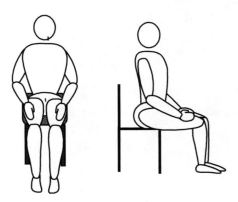

Sit comfortably with a solid foundation. Traditionally, one would sit on the floor, though sitting on the front half of a chair with the spine not resting on the back of the chair is ideal. Rest the hands on the knees

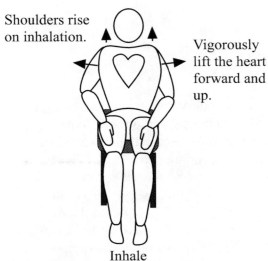

Shoulders rise on inhalation.

Vigorously lift the heart forward and up.

Inhale
Inhale vigorously and lift the chest, thrust the heart forward and raise the shoulders without tensing the neck and face.

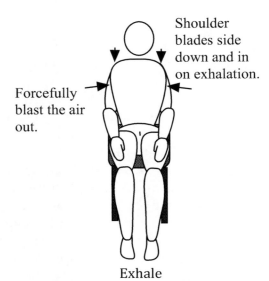

Shoulder blades side down and in on exhalation.

Forcefully blast the air out.

Exhale
A forceful inhalation is followed by an equally powerful and vigorous exhalation pulling the navel in and up.

Practice Bellows Breath with vigorous exhalation and inhalation of equal length.

Listen to your Inner Teacher-Healer-Guide if you have high blood pressure or another major illness keep your rhythm slow and conscious.

During the inhalation the expansion should entirely occur in the heart cavity and not in the abdomen. Inhale deeply as far down as the ribs, but not into the abdomen. Start the

Bellows Breath slowly. Have a tissue handy. Vigorous breathing loosens phlegm and mucus. Consciously build in speed and power. Practice for seven breaths and work your way up to a couple of minutes but no more than five.

For many people, the rib cage and shoulders are stiff and it is challenging to get a vigorous and powerful inhalation and exhalation with the hands on the knees. Pretend your forearms are handles on a small bellows and move them while breathing.

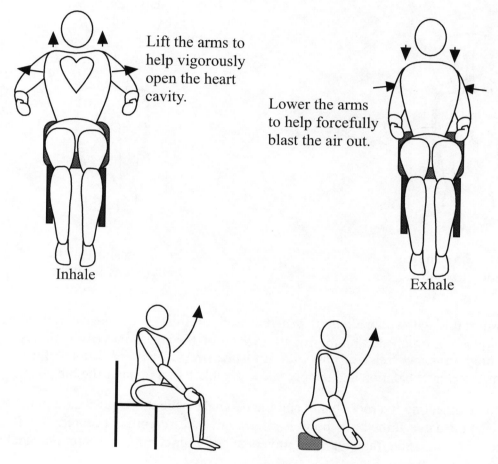

Lift the arms to help vigorously open the heart cavity.

Inhale

Lower the arms to help forcefully blast the air out.

Exhale

Lift the heart forward and up.

Open and close your forearms as you *v*igorously lift the chest, thrust the heart forward and raise the shoulders.

Practice Bellows Breath:
Inhale Vigorously and Exhale Forcibly
For seven breaths, rest and repeat.
Take a moment after to integrate the experience.
Conscious Breathing Practice 21

Kapalabhati - Breath of Fire / Forehead-Shining Breath

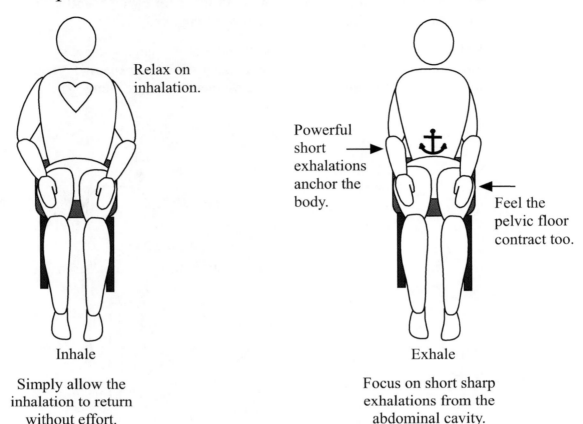

Relax on inhalation.

Powerful short exhalations anchor the body.

Feel the pelvic floor contract too.

Inhale

Exhale

Simply allow the inhalation to return without effort.

Focus on short sharp exhalations from the abdominal cavity.

Sit comfortably with spine aligned. Whereas Bellow Breath the focus is on inhaling to the heart cavity, Forehead Shining Breath focuses on the abdominal cavity during exhalation. Practice Breath of Fire with short, sharp vigorous contractions of the abdomen during exhalation and simply allow the inhalation to enter the lungs.

Focus on connecting the root chakra and the 6th chakra, the third eye chakra at the brow point. The third eye at the brow point is referred to as the command center. Send your intention, visualization, thoughts and prayers out of your command center and anchor them in you.

People with health issues and weak constitutions need to go slowly.
Listen to your Inner Teacher-Healer-Guide.
Practice for a few breaths and take moment and integrate the experience.

Breath Of Fire
Start with 7 short, sharp abdominal exhalations.
Rest and repeat. Again a tissue might be useful.
Conscious Breathing Practice 22

Alternate Nostril Breathing
Conscious Breathing Practice 23

By alternating the flow of air through right and left nostrils, the pingula and ida nadis, the solar and lunar energies of the body and mind are cleansed and balanced preparing you for meditation. Repeat 7 times.

1. While sitting, take the right hand and separate the ring and index fingers like the "Vulcan" gesture of "Live long and prosper".

2. Bend the forefinger and index finger down in a "Vishnu mudra" gesture.

3. Close the left nostril, the ida nadi, with the ring finger. Exhale through the right nostril, the pingula nadi and then inhale through the right nostril.

cover the
left nostril

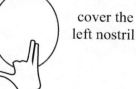

4. Change, open the left nostril and cover the right nostril with the thumb and exhale slowly, and then inhale through the left nostril.

cover the right
nostril

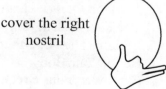

5. Change, open the right nostril cover the left nostril with the ring finger, exhale through the right nostril then inhale through the right nostril.

cover the
left nostril

6. Change, open the left nostril and cover the right nostril with the thumb and exhale slowly, and then inhale through the left nostril.

cover the right
nostril

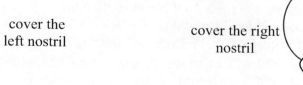

Summary of
Conscious Breathing Practices

1. Be Conscious of The Power And Authority In Your Breath. Listen to it.
2. Feel The Breath On The Insides Of Your Nostrils And Soften Your Forehead
3. Practice Equal Ratio Breathing Inhale - 1, 2, 3, 4. Exhale - 1, 2, 3, 4.
4. Inhale And Expand Your Heart Cavity: Visualize Inhaling To Nostrils Below Your Collarbones
5. Exhale And Contract Your Abdominal Cavity: Visualize Exhaling Out Of Your Navel.
6. Be More Conscious Of Your Exhalations, Count On The Exhalation
7. Empower Your Exhalations: Exhale Through Pursed Lips
8. Be Conscious Of The Pause-Stillness-Space In The Breath
9. Keep The Heart Lifted As You Exhale.
10. Keep The Navel In As You Inhale.
11. Visualizing Three Diaphragms Involved With Breathing Inhale to Diaphragms 1, 2,and 3. Exhale form Diaphragms 3, 2, and 1.
12. Visualize The Body As A Vessel, Inhale And Float The Heart Cavity And Don't Bloat The Belly.
13. Inhale *Prana* And Be Consciously Uplifted.
14. Exhale *Apana* And Be Consciously Grounded.
15. Visualize The Breath As A Wave Organizing Your Whole Body. Exhale From The Top Of The Head To The Soles Of The Feet. Inhale From The Soles Of The Feet To The Top Of The Head.
16. Breathe The Organizing Wave Of Breath Through Your Ill, Wherever It May Be In Your Body.
17. Empower Your Breath Inhale For The Count Of 6. Exhale For the Count Of 9
18. Ujjayi Breathing = Exhale 'hhh' and Inhale 'sss'
19. The Swan Mantra – *Hamsa* Exhale – *Ham.* Inhale - *sa*
20. The Ajapa Mantra – Every Breath Is A Prayer Inhale – I am That. Exhale – That am I.
21. Bhastrika - Bellows Breath Inhale Vigorously. Exhale Forcibly
22. Kapalabhati - Breath Of Fire Practice Short and Sharp Exhalations.
23. Alternate Nostril Breathing - Exhale and Inhale Through one Nostril, and Switch Nostrils, and Exhale and Inhale.
24. Shine The Light - Exhale Sunlight. Inhale Moonlight.
25. The Mind∞Body Infinity Loop - Inhale Body To Mind. Exhale Mind To Body.

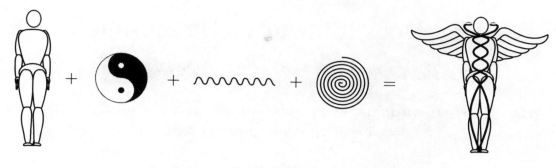

Spirit

Your Path

The Ultimate Formula symbolizes your path of spiritual and physical growth with a spiral. The spiral is one of humanity's oldest symbols of life, growth and renewal. Life spirals. From the heavenly galaxies to the chambered nautilus of the deep, to the bright sunflower, life spirals. Life spirals according to the Golden Ratio *phi,* the infinite or irrational number (1.618…) created from the Fibonacci Series 1,1, 2, 3, 5, 8, 13, 21 … by dividing the later number by the former in an infinite progression. The entire universe, as well as your entire body, has the *phi* ratio embedded in it. The Golden Ratio is an invisible universal source of oneness and wholeness. The spiral connects us to the ancient side of our being and our intuitive understanding of the absolute unity of being.

Yoga Is Not A Religion!

Yoga is primarily a path of elimination not acquisition in the sense that yoga is a practice to help eliminate the stresses and imbalances that obstruct your divine physical and spiritual nature. Yoga is not interested in you adopting a set of religious or holy beliefs. In the yoga tradition, you are already a divine and powerful spiritual being capable of charting and co-creating your destiny, health and well-being.

We are not human beings having a spiritual experience as much as

We are spiritual beings having a human experience.

77

What Does It Mean To Be Spiritual?

To be spiritual is to be one with the Divine.

To be spiritual means to be connected to the source
Of creativity, love and wisdom.

To be spiritual means to be in a state of Yoga, of union.

To be spiritual means to be conscious beyond the five senses including a 6th
sense of empathy and telepathy, and ultimately a 7th sense of pure
consciousness and Infinite Being.

To be spiritual means to be connected to
Our Inner Teacher-Healer-Guide.

To be spiritual is to be conscious
Of the deepest level of one's existence.

To be spiritual means to be altruistic, as we see ourselves
In the lives and faces of others.

To be spiritual means we laugh more and cry more.

Seek real, practical, material life, but see in such a way
That the spirit, which dwells within is not deadened for you.
Seek the spirit, but not with supersensible lust, not out of egoism
But see it so that you can apply it selflessly
In practical life, in the material world.
Apply the ancient words;
Spirit is never without matter, matter is never without spirit,
In such a way that you say to yourselves;
We will do all things in the material world in the light of the spirit,
And so seek the light of the spirit that it may enkindle warmth for our practical deeds.
Rudolf Steiner

Our Spirit and Our Soul Are Two Sides of One Breath.

Atman is the yoga Sanskrit word for Inner Self, Soul, Spirit or pure consciousness. As we exhale our psyche is grounded, manifested and attuned to what I relate to as our soulful atman. As we inhale, our psyche is more lifted, liberated and attuned to what I relate to as

78

our spiritual atman. As we exhale we are more soulful celebrating life here on earth. As we inhale we are more spiritual celebrating our eternal being.

Spirit

Soul

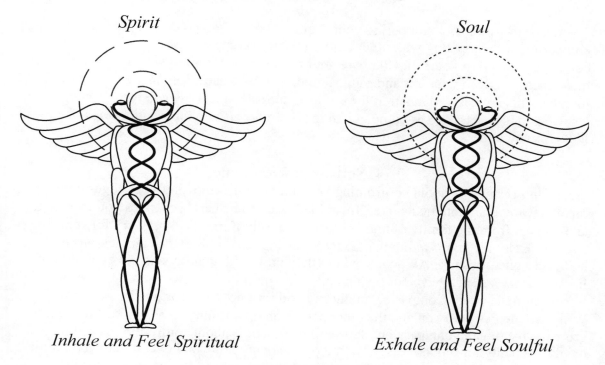

Inhale and Feel Spiritual

Exhale and Feel Soulful

Seven Steps On the Path of Therapeutic Hatha Yoga

1. Gratitude

Gratitude is the attitude with which to begin your yoga practice. Gratitude creates a foundation to step forward on your path. Gratitude reduces anger, fear and sadness. Gratitude opens the possibility of self-observation with no judgment. Bring your palms together in a gesture of reverence and gratitude. Let us be grateful for the gifts of creativity, love and wisdom we were borne with. Let us be grateful that we have the capacity to love and be loved. Let us be grateful for both our many blessings and the lessons we are learning. The purpose of life is not just to consume. It is to grow in wisdom and compassion, and be part of the evolution of life on earth. Be grateful for this life, for this day, for this breath.

2. Self-Observation With No Judgment.

Practice self-observation with no judgment. Simply note what is so with you today. There's no need to judge your observations as bad or good. Your observations are simply what you notice to be so. Non-judgmental self-observation of your breath and posture leads to a sense of self-awareness, which creates the foundation for self-empowerment, and conscious participation in your own health and well-being.

3. Self-Awareness
Practice self-awareness, comparing your Self to no one else. Yoga is neither about comparing nor competing with others. If you want to compare yourself to someone, compare yourself to yourself. Compare your right side to your left side. Be aware of the differences between your left and right shoulders, hips, knees, feet, ankles, wrists and thumbs. This creates a foundation for self awareness. Notice how you were yesterday, last week or 10 years ago as compared to today. Be aware of your relationships, feelings, thoughts and beliefs.

4. Self-Empowerment
Self-empowerment is about confronting your limits and witnessing your edges with breath awareness. Statements like, 'I wouldn't want to be her!" separates you from her, and as such from the family of humanity and the web of life. Feeling sorry for someone else and lucky for you is a trap that undermines the gifts, importance and lessons each and every one of us has. All people add to the family of humanity and the evolution of life on earth. We each have our own path, our own limits, our own gifts to share and lessons to be learned. Comparing another's good fortune or misfortune in relationship to your own, denies both you and the other person an opportunity to be empowered and to grow in wisdom and compassion. Self-empowerment is about confronting your limits and having empathy for others. It is not about power over nature and over other people. It is about our authentic power over our selves and share and care for others and the planet.

5. Self-Reliance
Self-Reliance is an essay written by the 19th century American transcendentalist Ralph Waldo Emerson, which has many metaphysical mystical yoga points of view. Emerson helped introduce Hinduism and yoga to America. Emerson advocated inner spiritual awareness through intuition, all the while avoiding conformity and imitation. *Self-Reliance* is about walking your own path, without feeling the need to conform to the status-quo or how everybody else is. Practice being true to yourself.

There is a time in every man's education when he arrives at the conviction that envy is ignorance; that imitation is suicide; that he must take himself for better, for worse...

Ralph Waldo Emerson from *Self-Reliance*

6. Self-Actualization
Self-actualization is about becoming fully human. Self-actualization is a term used in various schools of psychology to describe the realization of one's full potential.

7. Self-Realization
Self-realization or self-liberation is the ultimate fulfillment of oneself. Self-realization is a popular description of a profound spiritual awakening beyond our individual sense of identity, an infinite eternal sense of Self.

Everything that has Existed, Exists and will Exist,
Exists in Space, in God.

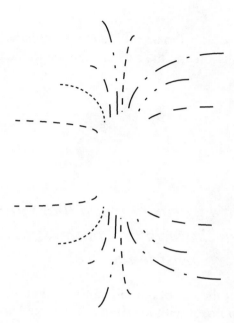

God Is Space...

God, as I imagine God to be, is the quantum-space
of subtle vibrations of spirit, creativity, love and wisdom.
It is the ultimate source of consciousness, life and matter.

John Myers Childers

To Be Conscious of the Space that is You,
Is the Final Frontier.
God Dwells in You, as You.

Matter is not dead and space is not empty.
The Divine Presence is everywhere.

'God is the breath inside the breath.'

The Great Mystic And Yoga Poet Kabir

What does it mean to say, "God is the breath inside the breath?" Certainly God is more than the oxygen in the inhalation and the carbon dioxide in the exhalation.

I interpret Kabir's words to mean that God is in the pause,
In the stillness, in the space,
Inside the breath.

The pause-stillness-space at the top of the inhalation and at the bottom of the exhalation are excellent moments to connect with the divine, God, the Universal Spirit.

Traditional Yoga Names For God

In the diverse tradition of yoga, God has many names. Divine, Brahman, Ishvara, Lord, Creator, Unchanging Reality, Universal Spirit, the Great Self, Absolute Being, Absolute Self, Transcendental Self, and Supreme Being are some of the yoga names associated with God.

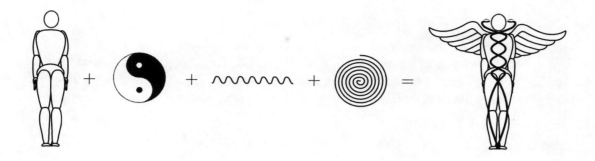

Your Inner Teacher-Healer-Guide

Connecting to your Inner Teacher-Healer-Guide is a metaphysical mystical experience. It is ultimately about connecting to your consciousness. Your Inner Teacher-Healer-Guide is the conscious integration of body, mind and breath, of your hand, heart and head. Connecting to your Inner Teacher-Healer-Guide produces a holistic consciousness and awareness of how and where your physiology meets your psychology. A new language of how your body and mind are connected and influence each other is being created with terms like evidence based mind-body medicine, neuroplasicity, psycho-neuro plasticity and psychoendoneuroimmunology. Connecting to your Inner Teacher-Healer-Guide is about organizing your mind-body to heal. It is about organizing your posture, breath, feelings, thoughts, visualizations and meditations for health and well-being.

To Develop A Personal Practice Is To Connect To Your Inner Teacher-Healer-Guide.

In the yoga tradition, the word for 'teacher' is guru, the remover of darkness. There are many different types of gurus in the yoga tradition. The term *sat guru`* has been used to describe our inner guru, spirit, creativity, love and wisdom. Therapeutic Hatha Yoga views your Inner Teacher-Healer-Guide as your *sat guru,* your ultimate true teacher.

Expand Your Sense of Self!
Teach THYself!
Heal THYself!
Know THYself!

Our Genes Are Not Our Fate!

They Are Only A Predisposition!

Our DNA is commonly thought of as the ultimate determining factor in our health and well-being. What does it mean when we hear someone say, "You have good genes" or "I inherited bunions from my mother" or "It is genetic?" The implication is that our health and illness are primarily related to good genes and bad genes. The deeper implication is that our mind, yoga, diet and lifestyle have very little to do with how we ultimately are. If we are just a genetic print out, then there is no reason to take action to improve our health. In this model it is easy to become a powerless victim of a genetic fate.

Consciousness Changes Our Gene Expression!

Your thoughts, beliefs, visualizations and intentions create bio-chemicals that pass through the walls of the cells of your body and register on your DNA, not totally unlike how cell phone calls pass through the walls of your room and register on your phone. Your cells are 'listening' to every thought you have and to every prayer you utter. Send healing thoughts to every cell in your body on the deep rhythmic waves of your breath.

Even though we each have genetic predispositions to certain conditions, a variety of current epidemiological studies indicate that comprehensive diet and lifestyle modifications actually change gene expression. Through holistic programs, hundreds of genes can either be up-regulated or down-regulated. In simple terms, genes that prevent many chronic diseases were turned on, and genes that are linked to coronary heart disease, breast and prostate cancer, genes that promote inflammation and oxidative stress were turned off with comprehensive conscious lifestyle changes. These findings are empowering, as they help transform our notions about how we can participate in our health and well-being without drugs and surgery. Just because your mother and father and your sister and brother died of heart disease does not mean you have to. It only means you are likely to be genetically predisposed to heart disease. You can influence your health quicker and to a much greater degree than you have thought.

Shine the Light!

In the yoga tradition, our bodies are described as made of flowers, diamonds and Light, not merely flesh. In the yoga tradition, we are conscious spiritual beings creating and animating a material physical form. Ultimately, we are beings of Light.

Exhale - *Sunlight*.
Inhale - *Moonlight*.

Exhale and visualize yourself as a diamond sparkling in the sunlight.
Inhale and visualize yourself as a flower petal glowing in the moonlight.
Conscious Breathing Practice 24

Your Inner Teacher-Healer-Guide:

• Empowers you, regardless of your condition, to be proactive and directly participate in your health, well-being and self healing.

• Facilitates self-awareness and self-reliance regardless of any physical limitations.

• Gives you the courage to let go of your helplessness.

• Teaches you to witness your limitations and illnesses and transform them.

• Gives rise to a sense of self-esteem.

• Gives you the tools to be more aware of the early warning signs of illness or disease.

• Helps you manage your imbalances.

• Teaches you to become more sensitive to your physical and emotional trigger signals.

• Motivates with a love of life, not a fear of death.

• Celebrates life.

THY Postures

THY Postures are Templates for Conscious Healing

Simply performing an *asana*, physical posture, does not constitute practicing yoga; otherwise contortionists would be self-realized yoga masters. To be considered a yoga *asana*, a pose has to incorporate the principles of yoga.

Classical ancient yoga was a dualistic practice that focused on meditation and *pranayama*, breathing techniques, as tools for yoga ascetics and renunciants seeking to control, withdraw and transcend the physical body to experience spiritual union with the divine. The non-dualistic schools of hatha, tantric, kundalini and bhakti yogas sought to embrace and integrate the physical body with divine consciousness in the daily life. The difference between Therapeutic Hatha Yoga and the classical traditional practice of yoga is that Therapeutic Hatha Yoga focuses on healing the body temple, rather than on transcending it. Therapeutic Hatha Yoga seeks health, well-being and higher consciousness through a full spectrum integration of body, mind and breath that unites the energies of sun and moon, earth and sky, inhalation and exhalation, stability and mobility and physical and spiritual.

The Names of Yoga Postures Are Not Universal

There is no 'standard lexicon' of yoga posture. The Sanskrit word *asana* is a singular and plural word like the word scissors, and used to describe physical yoga posture(s). The original meaning of *asana* was a seat, or sitting position for meditation. Meditation was the focus of classical yoga 2,000 years ago and only a few seated postures, or *asana*, were described. The *Goraksha Samhita*, an early hatha yogic text from the 10-11th century, describes 84 classic *asana* as the most excellent postures and makes reference to 8,400,000 yoga postures in total. Another text says that there is a yoga posture, *asana*, for every creature on earth or a posture for every being. It could be easily argued that there are countless yoga postures. In the 15th century, the term *yoga asana* came to include the more diverse postures from the *Hatha Yoga Pradipika*. Nearly all of the postures we see in today's yoga books and magazines were created by influential yoga teachers of the last century. Different branches of hatha yoga have given different Sanskrit names for similar postures or the same Sanskrit name for different postures.

The names of Therapeutic Hatha Yoga postures, and their countless variations, are secondary in importance to the conscious integration of body, mind breath and spirit.

Based upon the books and teachers listed at the rear of this book, I have created and named dozens of postures and variations. I have attempted to give general common names for the postures, and included Sanskrit only when it seemed appropriate. Naming is a bit like labeling. They both help us recognize something yet confine and limit it. We are infinite beings and each posture has infinite subtle potentials to heal. Each posture is a template for your conscious healing through conscious breathing. Therapeutic Hatha Yoga postures, THY postures, are your postures. They are the postures that speak to you. Please feel free to name your own 'Brand X' posture, 'your yoga pill'.

THY Postures
Are Stable and Comfortable

The *Yoga Sutras of Patanjali,* the most important ancient classical yoga text, mentions yoga postures after *yamas,* moral disciplines including not harming, truthfulness, not stealing and moderation, and *niyamas*, self-disciplines including purity, contentment, study and devotion. Ultimately, good posture incorporates the ethical and moral precepts of no killing, which can be interpreted as reverence for life, since it is impossible to live without taking life for nourishment. In classical yoga, our moral and personal disciplines precede our physical discipline. Practicing yoga asana is a path to understanding our breath, mind, concentration and meditation. Patanjali described *asana* as being both *sthira* and *sukha,* stable and comfortable, at the same time.

Yoga Postures Are a Paradox of Being
Alert Without Tension, and Calm Without Dullness.

There is a balance between muscle strength and joint flexibility. Good posture, be it standing, sitting, kneeling inverting or lying, is to be stable and comfortable in order to experience stillness and quiet the mind.

THY Postures Are Actively-Yielding & Yielding-Actively

Yoga postures are actively-yielding, building strength and stability and yielding-actively, reducing tension and stress. All muscles are working in reciprocal pairs while moving forward, backward, sideways and or twisting. Therapeutic Hatha Yoga is a combination of reducing inflammation and cleansing the body, and building and nourishing the body. Just as you can create a smooth rhythmic breath through dynamic tension in the breath, you can create a smooth even posture with dynamic tension in the body.

THY Postures Are
Lifted and Rooted Through the Plumb Line

Therapeutic Hatha Yoga postures are aligned along the structural curvature axis of the spine. Good posture is an alignment of our physical skeletal structure with the core gravitational field of the earth. Place your head squarely on your shoulders. Align your middle ear over the shoulder, hip, knee and ankle. *Keep your head centered and level on the shoulders while your feel lifted and rooted.*

THY Postures Can Be In Cat, Dog & Neutral Tilt Positions

A neutral pelvis in yoga postures is halfway between a 'Cat Tilt' and a 'Dog Tilt'. To maintain a neutral pelvis create dynamic tension in the body and breath by holding the essence of the heart lifted as you exhale and the navel in as you inhale.

Cat Tilt / Exhale

Round the back.

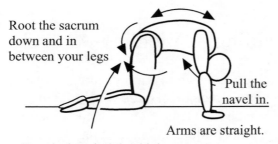

Root the sacrum down and in between your legs

Pull the navel in.

Arms are straight.

Exteriorly spiral the thighs toward the tailbone.

Dog Tilt / Inhale

Arch the back.

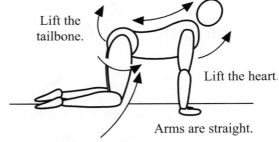

Lift the tailbone.

Lift the heart.

Arms are straight.

Interiorly spiral the thighs toward the pubic bone.

Neutral

Find a balance between dog tilt and cat tilt. Find a neutral pelvis and a plumb line running through your middle ear, shoulder and hip.

THY Postures Are a Network of Dynamic Connections

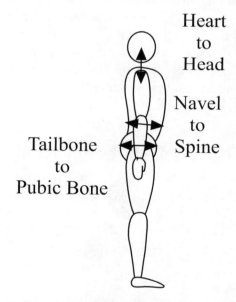

Heart
to
Head

Navel
to
Spine

Tailbone
to
Pubic Bone

We are more than a column of blocks stacked on top of one another. Our skeletal-muscular structure is made strong and elastic through the unison and synergy of tension and compression described as tensegrity. Our skin, muscles, organs and bones are all tied together with an endless web of fascia connective tissue. Yoga postures incorporate a network of lines of energy, *nadis,* kinetic chains and anatomy trains. Maintaining an awareness of these connections will help us stand and move with greater ease in life.

We are also a connection of feelings and thoughts woven into physical form. Our posture is a union of physiology and psychology. Yoga is to be connected to your Self.

The most difficult posture is to keep a smile on your face when things don't go the way you thought they would.

Therapeutic Hatha Yoga postures are not an exterior expression as much as an interior connection and organization of yourself.

The ultimate purpose of THY Postures is to align the chakras, the psycho-physical vortexes of our body, For structural, functional, mental, psychological and spiritual integration.

THY Postures
Include the Back Half of the Body

Just like we tend to focus on our inhalations more than our exhalations, we tend to focus on the front of the body and forget about the back half of the body. This is especially true as we look into mirrors and focus on the front of the body. When you ask someone to stand up straight, they tend to focus on lengthening the front of the body while over arching her or his back and neck. People would benefit from lengthening the back of the body by 'standing down straight' as well as standing up straight.

The Back Half of the Body

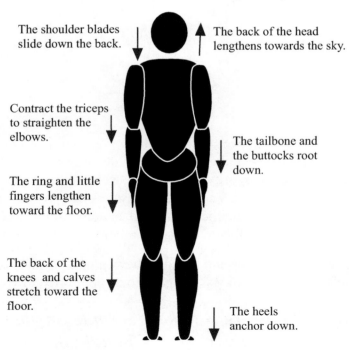

The shoulder blades slide down the back.

The back of the head lengthens towards the sky.

Contract the triceps to straighten the elbows.

The tailbone and the buttocks root down.

The ring and little fingers lengthen toward the floor.

The back of the knees and calves stretch toward the floor.

The heels anchor down.

THY Core

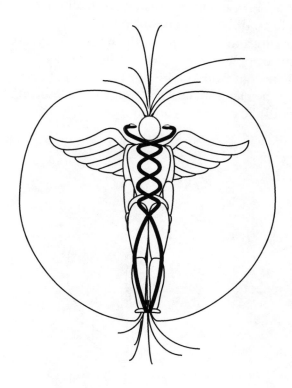

Typically, we think of our core as the muscle groups deep within the abdomen and back that attach to the spine and pelvis. These muscle groups include the oblique, abdominal, lower back, gluteus, psoas and more. From a holistic perspective, our core includes not only the muscle groups attaching to the spine but the spinal column itself and the central nervous system within. Our core includes the cranium and sacrum in addition to the spine and the muscles stabilizing and balancing it.

Our core is also like the electro-magnetic core of the earth. Each has two poles, a north and south and a cranium and sacrum. The heart is the primary source of our electro-magnetic field. The traditional belief that the heart is merely muscle that serves as a pump is incorrect. The heart produces hormones to help regulate our metabolism. Our heart is our single largest source of electro-magnetic energy, even more than our brains. The heart is like a mini-brain that communicates with the brain and body through the nervous system, pulse waves, hormones and electromagnetic fields. Our consciousness combined with the energy generated by our heart creates a dynamic toriodial (donut shaped) vortex field in and around us, which we could refer to as our aura or subtle body.

Your Heart

Is at the Center of Your Core

The word "core" is a late 14th Century English word likely derived from O. Fr. *coeur* meaning "core of fruit, heart of lettuce" and from Latin *cor* "heart". Think of the image of an apple core when thinking about the core of the human body. An apple core goes from the stem through the entire apple to the bottom. When we activate our core, we align a field of energy that radiates out from our being. This field of energy is a subtle vortex field that is sustained by the electromagnic energy of each heartbeat, thought and the subtle conscious energy of the prana and apana in each breath.

At the Center of Your Core, You Are Love

Years before the expressions 'core strength' and 'core workout' became popular, American yogi Eric Schiffmann spoke of connecting to our 'core of goodness'. For Schiffmann connecting to your core is experiencing your spiritual existence as immortal, eternal and true, as God substance, Consciousness and Love. Connecting to our 'core' is connecting to the divine love vibrations inside us.

Our Body of Bliss Is at the Center of Our Core.

The ancient yoga masters of 3,000 years ago visualized the body as composed of 5 *koshas*, bodies, layers or sheaths starting from the periphery of the body and moving towards the core of the self, "the embodied soul.' The five koshas are: *annamaya* kosha—our physical body, *pranamaya* kosha—our breath or vital metabolic functions of the body, *manomaya* kosha—our mental faculties of perception and cognition; *vijanamaya* kosha—our intuitive wisdom and faith, and *anandamaya* kosha—the bliss body. For the ancient yogis, the final destination through the practice of yoga was the *anandamaya* kosha, the body of bliss.

The Center of Our Core Is Still

Like the Eye of a Hurricane

Our spinal core, with its outlying sympathetic trunks and branches, creates a structure capable of generating a double-helix vortex field. Vortexes are the archetypal form for all self-organized structures like red blood cells, trees, hurricanes and galaxies. The *ida* and *pingula nadis* form a double helix of subtle energy that runs up and down, left and right and all around the spinal core of our vortex field. Connecting to our core is connecting to the vortex field emanating from electromagnetic energy of our heartbeat, brain and spinal core and the subtle psyche energy field of the *hamsa* current in the breath.

The quantum physicists know that at center of an atom there is no 'thing', rather there is some sort of bit of information, a 'no-thing', a field of possibilities, an emptiness that generates form, a consciousness. Our true nature, the source of consciousness is non-material.

At the center of our core,
And the ground of all matter,
There is a stillness, a spacious consciousness,
A quantum vacuum, a field of infinite possibilities,
A consciousness that generates all form
And is the source of absolute unity being.

The Kundalini (Pure Consciousness)

Is at the Center of Our Core

The ultimate core in certain tantric yoga traditions is the *sushumna nadi,* the central subtle channel of energy and consciousness in the body. The seven major chakras, vortexes of psycho-physical energies, are located along this central channel. The heart chakra is halfway up the central channel and is the key to connecting to our core. Activating our core in the tantric yoga tradition means opening and aligning the chakras so the kundalini, Pure Consciousness in the *sushumna nadi,* can fill us.

The Mind∞Body Infinity Loop

The Mind∞Body Infinity Loop is a body-breath-mind circuit created on a subtle energy level as we breathe in and out. It is the completed path of the two-way subtle energy currents of *prana* and *apana*. Simply put, exhale your mind to your body and inhale your body to your mind. The Mind∞Body Infinity Loop empowers the *hamsa mantra*. *Hamsa* is the union of Shiva and Shakti, sun and moon and *prana* and *apana*.

The subtle energy current, *prana,* lifts and liberates us as we inhale and primarily runs up the front of the body. However, the *prana* current primarily runs up the back of the head. The subtle energy current, *apana,* anchors and grounds us as we exhale, and primarily runs down the backside of the body. However, the subtle energy current apana primarily runs down the forehead upon exhalation. The crossing point between front and back is at the atlas vertebra, at the top of the spinal column, at the throat chakra and the ether element in the yoga tradition. The Mind∞Body Infinity Loop creates a junction between the mind and the body in the 'ether'. The Mind∞Body Infinity Loop with the electromagnetic field of the heart, power and sustain your living vortex field. The Mind∞Body Infinity Loop helps create an etheric subtle space to resonate with the source of creativity, love and wisdom. The Mind∞Body Infinity Loop honors the Post-Modern-New Millennial Yoga Manifesto, which states that consciousness is primary and matter is secondary.

Patanjali's Sutra 2:47 describes mastery of performing postures as, to loosen effort and meditate on the infinite, (ananta).

Practice the Mind∞Body Infinity Loop Loosen Effort and Be Aligned with and Absorbed In the Infinite.

THY Postures Focus on Consciously Breathing through The Mind∞Body Infinity Loop to Holistically Align the Body's Various Muscles, Organs and Tissues.

Center and Level Your Head With Your Body

Exhale *Apana*.

Exhale Mind to Body.

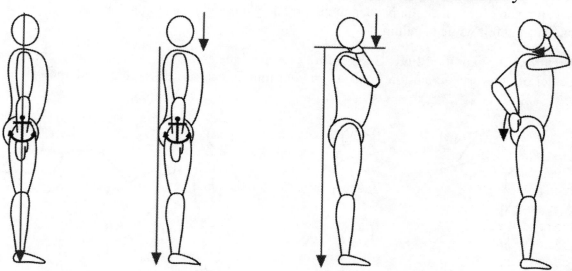

Center and level the head with the body and enhance the mind's ability to help heal the body. Put the back of your hand under chin and center and level your head. Exhale and feel the apana flowing down the forehead and the back of the body. Place the back of one hand on your forehead and the other on your sacrum connecting the forehead to the body. Exhale and feel apana grounding and cleansing you.

Inhale *Prana*.

Inhale Body to Mind.

Inhale and feel prana rising up through the body-mind. Feel it rise up the front of the body and the back of the head. Make a shelf with the back of your hand under your chin and level your head as you inhale. Place one hand on the chest and one on the back of the head and feel the prana rising, nourishing and connected through both areas.

THY Plumb Line Alignment Kneeling

Kneeling is a good way to observe your alignment and to experience the breath through the spine and hips since the pose is undisturbed by any tightness in the legs and hamstrings felt while standing.

Breathing through the Mind∞Body Infinity Loop aligns and empowers your core at the center of our vortex quantum field. Align your middle ear, shoulders, hips and knee.

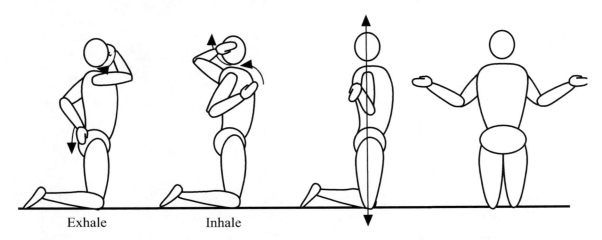

Exhale   Inhale

Place the back of one hand on your forehead and the back of the other hand on the sacrum and exhale down the forehead and down the back of the body. Place the palm of one hand on the back of the head and the other over the heart, and inhale up the front of the body and the back of the head. Visualize the Infinity Loop while kneeling.

Kneel, bend the elbows and release your arms out to the side with the palms up. Lean back a bit and feel the middle ear aligning over the shoulder, hip and knee as you come back to vertical.

When The Head Is Centered And Level With The Body

We Are In Harmony

Notice if the upper back is rounded, or the lower back is too tight or the hip flexors are too tight. Exhale and anchor the pelvis while contracting the belly and create a solid plumb line to center head with the body.

The Yin and Yang, and the Yang and Yin of
The Mind∞Body Infinity Loop

Exhale   Inhale

Patanjali Sutra 2.48 describes that by meditation and absorption in the infinite, one is undisturbed by the dualities of the world.

The Mind∞Body Infinity Loop

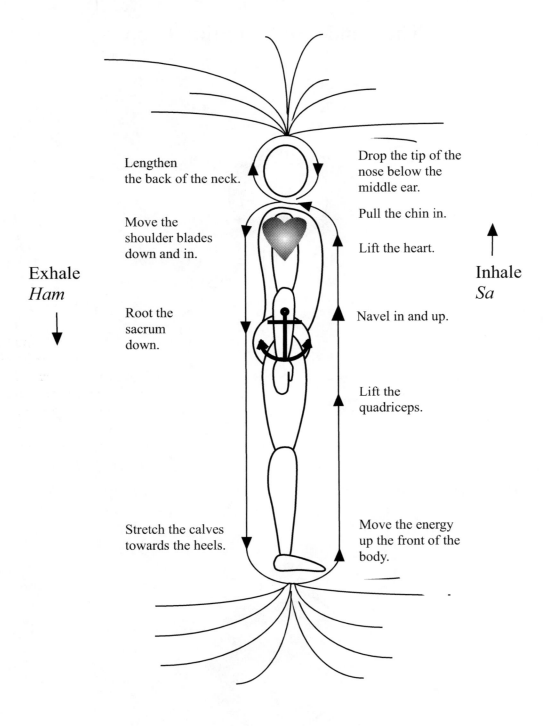

Lengthen
the back of the neck.

Drop the tip of the
nose below the
middle ear.

Pull the chin in.

Move the
shoulder blades
down and in.

Lift the heart.

Exhale
Ham

Inhale
Sa

Root the
sacrum
down.

Navel in and up.

Lift the
quadriceps.

Stretch the calves
towards the heels.

Move the energy
up the front of the
body.

Practice the Mind∞Body Infinity Loop For Seven Breaths
Conscious Breathing Practice 25

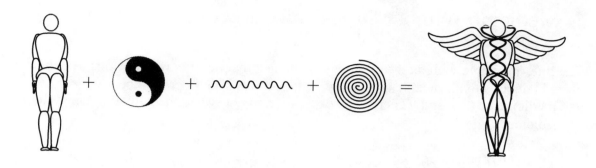

A Yoga Pill For Every Ill

Therapeutic Hatha Yoga is Like A Yoga Pill For Every Ill

It seems like modern medicine has a pill for every ill. After teaching over 25,000 hours of individual yoga sessions, classes and workshops, I believe, there is *'a yoga pill for every ill'*, a specific proactive prescriptive Therapeutic Hatha Yoga practice(s) which can be formulated and focused on virtually any issue or illness, regardless of physical or mental condition. This is not to say that Therapeutic Hatha Yoga can cure every ill, rather that with the Ultimate Formula For Health And Well-Being, a prescriptive yoga practice can be formulated to empower anyone to become a conscious active ingredient in their health and well-being.

People often take pills without any conscious participation. The difference between taking any pill and taking a yoga pill is that consciousness is critical for a yoga pill. Therapeutic Hatha Yoga's Ultimate Formula For Health and Well-Being is a method to integrate body, mind and breath to heal. Yoga pills are comprised of conscious breathing techniques and a key posture or postures that enhances your body-mind's holistic ability and desire to heal. A yoga pill can have instantaneous results, though deep healing requires a change of lifestyle, habits and consciousness.

A Minimum Daily Dose Of Therapeutic Hatha Yoga Is

Seven Conscious Breaths Daily.

Therapeutic Hatha Yoga Is

Medicine Without Drugs and Surgery Without Knives.

The line, 'medicine without drugs', refers to the fact that our diet is our primary medicine chest in regards to our health and healing. Hippocrates said, "Let food be thy medicine and medicine be thy food.' There is an expression in *ayurveda*, the native Indian system of medicine,

"If your diet is good, there is no need of medicine.

If your diet is poor, medicine is of no use."

The phrase, "surgery without knives", refers to a less tangible image of health and transformation. "Surgery without knives" relates to the fact that matter is not separate from consciousness, and that our breath and our intentions, visualizations and thoughts shape, heal and transform our flesh and tissues.

I like to compare how running water is similar to conscious breathing in regards to understanding a "surgery without knives". At first glance, running water appears to have no effect on rock. However, over time, water flowing over a rocky stream bed smoothes and shapes the rocks. Every breath we take flows through our body shaping it like running water shapes rock. This sort of water and rock analogy is especially appropriate for our skeletal structure. It takes years for running water to cut into rock, as it would take years to really change the shape of your bones.

It Might Take 40 Seconds, Days, Weeks or Years To Feel The Full Effects.

Hitching our intentions and visualizations, to our conscious breath and directing them into our softer muscles, organs and glandular tissues could have a more immediate effect. Visualize your tight muscles as a hillside, and your conscious breathing as a giant storm. Let your breathing cut through muscle tightness releasing nerve flow like the storm cuts through the hillside releasing a mudslide. Visualize your organs and glands as soft sand on the beach. Each wave cuts into the shore shaping and transforming it. Each conscious breath can be focused on cutting, shaping and transforming your organs and glands. Consciously directing your breath to specific tissues of our bodies can be visualized as a 'surgery without knives.'

A Yoga Pill is a Daily / 'Dailish' Dose

A yoga pill is best taken everyday, though do not succumb to fear, guilt or shame, if you miss a day or two. Life happens. As with any long-term practice, it is helpful to think of a 'daily' practice as 'devilish' in the sense that your intention is to practice daily. Your practice can be as simple as taking seven conscious breaths daily, and from there you can expand your practice.

What Is the Difference between Medicine and Poison?

The classic question asked of medical students studying to be physicians is, "What is the difference between medicine and poison?" The answer is not black or white. There is no difference between medicine and poison. What makes something poisonous or medicinal is the amount of the substance taken and the context in which it is given. Simply put, too much of anything is not good for you. It is the dosage, which determines whether a substance is going to be toxic or therapeutic. Yoga is a wisdom philosophy of life.

Your breath is a feedback mechanism for determining if you are doing too much or too little. If you are holding your breath, cringing and making a face stop, you are doing too much. If you hanging out in the posture and have forgotten to breathe, you are doing to little. There is a maximum and a minimum edge for every pose. Therapeutic Hatha Yoga involves getting as deeply into a pose as you can, to witness your edge without smashing into it or shying away from it. Conscious breathing keeps your yoga dosage therapeutic. Remember, the breath is primary and the posture is secondary. If you cannot breathe into it, back out of it.

Will I Hurt Myself Practicing Yoga?

One of the most common concerns people have about yoga is whether they will hurt themselves while practicing yoga. To which one of my students once replied, "You will hurt yourself more in life if you do not practice yoga." Whether a yoga posture is harmful can be viewed as a question of dosage. If the posture is one where you immediately wince in pain or hold your breath as if bracing for impact, it is a good indication that it is not the correct posture for you. However, if you can enter and maintain a posture with a smooth, even, rhythmic breath, you have a good chance of releasing tension, and building strength and awareness. The breath naturally organizes the body and mind for optimal health. Your smooth rhythmic breathing is a feedback system to help you to determine when a posture is therapeutic or toxic for you.

Your Breath Is A Feedback Mechanism,

If You Can't Breathe Into The Pose, Back Out Of It.

It is not the external form of a yoga posture, as much as it is the internal organization, integration and consciousness of body, mind and breath that creates a field for healing.

The First Rule of Therapeutic Hatha Yoga Is, Do No Harm.

Abhaya Mudra / The "Fear Not" Gesture

The *abhaya mudra* is made with the open palm of the right hand held at chest level or slightly higher. *Abbaya* is translated from the Sanskrit as fearlessness. There is also a sense of protection, peace and inner security in this mudra.

Yoga Is Not Torture!

Yoga Is Sensational!

The yoga room is not a torture chamber. A yoga teacher does not torture people. It is misleading, confusing and wrong to equate yoga and torture. Yoga is not about you torturing yourself. Holding your breath and wincing in pain will not make you flexible, strong or truthful. Yoga is about consciously witnessing and breathing into our sensations, edges and limits for transformation and healing. Yoga is about practicing postures that cleanse, nourish and lead to greater awareness of our body-mind. Yoga is about breathing consciously. Water boarding torture is a physical posture that you literally cannot breathe into.

The popular slogan, "No pain, no gain" carries with it a subtle and not-so-subtle notion that pain, suffering and even torture are needed to get ahead. It is a myth that we need pain to learn or heal. Pain does get our attention. It has a message for personal growth and well-being through greater reflective consciousness, creativity, love and wisdom.

Conscious Healing through Conscious Breathing,

Is Not the same as, "No Pain, No Gain."

Our world all too often focuses on punishment. People say things like "I have a "bad foot" meaning that it hurts. However, this implies that the foot is misbehaving and needs to be disciplined or punished. It's as if people believe that the body-mind needs to be made painful in order to heal and "be good". This is rooted in the notion that what emotionally motivates us is the fear and pain of death, rather than love and joy of life, to heal and grow.

Modern medicine often focuses on attacking the disease, rather than enhancing the body-mind's natural healing abilities. This dichotomy creates a language and culture of war, punishment and persecution to solve its problems. We have a war on drugs, a war on cancer and a war between the sexes. We 'fight fat' and 'combat stress.' Therapeutic Hatha Yoga is grounded in a language and culture of educating and healing.

Which Posture Variation Is Best for Me?

The posture variation that is best for you is the one you can consciously breathe into the best. If it is too difficult, you cannot breathe into it. If it is too easy, you feel no need to consciously breathe into it. Postures and their variations are templates for circulating blood, energy and awareness in body, mind and breath.

As you heal, as your issues change,
you will need different prescription for good health.
Be your own metaphysician. Your Inner Teacher-Healer-Guide
Can help lead you to which posture is best for you.

How Do I Know I Am Doing It Right?

Stop doing yoga. Start **being** the integration of body, mind, breath and spirit. The pause at the top of the inhalation, and the bottom of the exhalation are excellent places to feel and listen within for intuitive guidance to know if we are doing the posture correctly. If we focus on deep rhythmic conscious breathing, our mind will clear and quiet down, and we will be able to listen and look within. The breath is a wave that organizes your entire body-mind. Be conscious of your breath.

THY Postures Are Templates For Conscious Breathing

To Holistically Align The Body's Various

Muscle Groups, Organs, Glands And Tissues.

Once you have a key posture or a practice to unlock your issues, the question arises "How long do I stay in the posture?" Generally seven conscious breaths are enough to dance with and connect to your issue or condition. If you can reduce the practice down to a key

103

posture, I suggest you take your 'yoga pill' a couple times a day. For deeper healing, you will have to consciously breathe into a posture for two to five minutes or even much longer. Listen for a deep healing in the stillness-pause-space between the exhalation and the inhalation. Look for a sign or a cue to release out of the posture. Conscious rhythmic breathing quiets the doubting mind and focuses the body so we can listen to our Inner Teacher-Healer-Guide. Therapeutic Hatha Yoga is sensational. The breath and body sensations are a feedback system to help us practice yoga consciously, safely and effectively.

Dosage is best measured in conscious breaths not time.

When practicing a challenging posture, practice counting out a few short sweet exhalations, not just holding your breath for a few short seconds. The act of counting keeps the mind focused on the breath and the posture even if only for a few breaths. In intense postures that you can only hold for seconds, the tendency is to hold your breath. For postures you can hold for minutes, practice rhythmic conscious breathing, focus on healing imagery and intentions. When bedridden, simply practice breathing in *nourishing prana,* and exhaling *cleansing apana.* Look for guidance from your Inner Teacher-Healer-Guide in the pause-stillness-space to cue you when to continue or release a pose.

The Moment After a Practice Integrate, Assimilate and Acclimate To a Higher State of Consciousness.

The moment after deeply witnessing your edge, you will need a moment before you can easily respond or move. You might feel vulnerable and defenseless as you acclimate to an expanded sense of self. Do not let these feelings dissuade you from practicing whole-heartedly. Yoga is sensational.

Taking a deep exhalation and a deep pause will require a moment to integrate and assimilate the effects of the posture. It is a bit like a deep-sea diver needing to come up to the surface slowly. Both need to have a decompression moment. Yogis need a moment to decompress and integrate an expanded sense of physical, emotional, mental and spiritual consciousness.

If you act like nothing happened after practicing, probably nothing happened. However, if you feel like you need a moment to integrate, reflect and assimilate the experience, maybe something happened.

It is also common for people to feel a bit exasperated and exhausted after practicing a yoga pose or sequence. As a result, people tend to collapse the heart cavity on the first exhalation immediately after a yoga posture or practice.

Remember to Keep Your Heart Lifted During Your First Exhalation After Coming to Standing or After Exiting Any Yoga Posture.

Practice Restful Awareness

Connect To Your Inner Teacher-Healer-Guide

Settle your body, mind and breath. Most of our consciousness is subconscious like most of an iceberg is underwater. Quiet your body. Quiet your breath. Quiet your mind. Let your fluctuating thought waves on the surface of your mind settle. In the stillness does anything come to mind that has been submerged or suppressed? Can you connect to any feelings or thoughts that are feeding you or eating you?

Stand at Ease

Stand at ease with your hands on your hips, or at your sides, for a moment after taking your yoga pill. Keep your heart lifted. Stand present beyond pride or pity. Stay present! Integrate, witness and be conscious of your breathing. Stay focused, vibrant and uplifted as you take your first exhalation. Acclimate to a higher state. Seek to grow in the wisdom by being present as you heal.

The Evidence Of The Effectiveness Of

Therapeutic Hatha Yoga

Example: Plantar Faciitis

Many research studies have provided empirical data that show the effectiveness of yoga therapy in reducing pain and stiffness, and improving the functioning of much of the body. I have not been able to set up double-blind experiments to provide 'empirical evidence' that Therapeutic Hatha Yoga 'works'. In other words, there is no empirical evidence of the effectiveness of Therapeutic Hatha Yoga. However, I think of my yoga therapy student-clients as funding their own individual yoga research project to heal themselves. All I can say is that my drawings and writings have been able to reduce pain and improve their health and well-being. I would like to thank all of my student-clients over the past 25 years for their support and conscious participation in the development and refining of Therapeutic Hatha Yoga.

Example: Plantar Faciitis

Therapeutic Hatha Yoga has had tremendous success improving the pain and symptoms of plantar faciitis. I would like to thank Dave Gustin, Carla Hughes, Kurt Linn, Phyllis Steele and Jerry King who hired me privately to specifically create yoga therapy for their feet. They, and so many others, have helped to expand my practice of Therapeutic Hatha Yoga.

Therapeutic Hatha Yoga takes the traditional physical therapy exercises for the foot and extends them out to include breath and overall posture. This includes physical, emotional, mental and spiritual ways of being as expressed in our daily habits and patterns of living. If we do not become aware of our unconscious patterns and beliefs, we are likely to recreate the painfully unbalanced condition again, even if we have orthotics, physical therapy and medicine for it. Therapeutic Hatha Yoga is about improving the health of the whole person, while traditional allopathic medicine is about treating a specific injury or disease. We can try to "fix" the symptoms, but unless there is a transformation at a deep level of our physical patterns and emotional conditioning, the environment is ripe for the condition to reappear. Therapeutic Hatha Yoga is first and foremost about creating conscious healing and seeking to change the unconscious patterns that helped create the condition in the first place. Therapeutic Hatha Yoga provides for the possibility of conscious healing, personal growth and even spiritual evolution.

Healing can be both a conscious and subconscious activity. It is especially helpful to consciously witness our healing with chronic conditions such as plantar faciitis. In our culture, we often want to disassociate ourselves from the painful parts of our being. In this manner we are not consciously involved in our own healing process. Without a conscious healing we tend to be disempowered victims hoping that the drugs, the heel cushion, boot or surgery will make it all better. I am convinced that we need to witness our pain, injury or disease to heal quickly. We need to breathe into our pain and ideally transform it into information through breath awareness, thereby discovering what our pain, cramping and soreness are trying to tell us. In the final analysis, cramping is a sign of weak muscles. Through yoga we can lengthen and strengthen weak, injured or diseased parts of our body through breathing and moving consciously into postures. This is what I refer to as the full spectrum integration of body, breath and mind.

There is no need to force any postures on our body by holding our breath and wincing as we practice. The body will not readily accept what it cannot breathe into. Pain is like static on our body's radio dial. We need to tune it in, not ignore it. Furthermore, we are often judging simple sensations as hurtful and bad. There is a message in the pain. There is a message in plantar faciitis and to "fix it", we need first to decipher it. I advocate observation without judgment. This leads to awareness, which hopefully leads to self empowerment, self reliance and self healing. This is Therapeutic Hatha Yoga.

When working with a condition like this one, the dualistic approach of reducing a person to a collection of parts and focusing on the one part that is "broken", does not work as well as integrating that "broken" part with the whole person. This has been particularly true for working with feet.

The plantar fascia is a thin band of fascia (connective tissue) that covers the sole of the foot from the heel to the base of the toes. Plantar faciitis generally refers to a tear or micro-tears in the fascia and the resulting inflammation. It is most often experienced as a dull aching, very sharp or burning pain on the heel or the sole of the foot. Plantar faciitis is the most common cause of heel pain. Its exact cause is not clear. It does, however, seem associated with a number of factors: running, standing for long periods of time, weight gain, and weak foot muscles.

Traditional medical treatment for plantar faciitis include ice, rest, physical therapy, massage, orthotics, ultrasound, a boot to sleep in and cortisone shots. And while these protocols have proven helpful to my clients and students, they generally have offered only periodic or partial relief of their chronic pain and discomfort. Even good traditional physical therapy for plantar faciitis ordinarily only addresses stretching and strengthening the sole of the foot without any broader connection to the rest of the body, let alone one's breath, feelings, thoughts and beliefs.

Typically, the physical therapy my clients have received prior to my yoga program have aimed to strengthen the foot using such exercises as opening and closing the foot like a fist, gripping a marble with the toes, rolling a round object under the foot and grabbing and pulling a weighted towel along the floor. Stretching has commonly consisted of flexing the sole of the foot by pressing the toes up the wall in the corner with the heel on the floor and lengthening the calf and back of the leg while leaning into the wall. These are excellent foot exercises to contract and stretch the muscles in the sole of the foot. However, these exercises have proved insufficient to stop the chronic pain endured by my students.

Therapeutic Hatha Yoga is about improving the health of the whole person, while traditional allopathic medicine is about treating a specific injury or disease. We can try to "fix" the symptoms, but unless there is a transformation at a deep level of our physical patterns, emotional conditioning and or our environment, which in the case of our soles involves our shoes our condition is likely to reappear. Therapeutic Hatha is a program for our whole being organizing our body, breath and mind into a yoga practice tailored to heal and transform us. Therapeutic Hatha Yoga takes the traditional physical therapy exercises for the foot and extends them out to include conscious breathing and overall posture. This includes physical, emotional, mental and spiritual ways of being as expressed in our daily habits and patterns of living. If we do not become aware of our unconscious patterns and beliefs, we are likely to recreate the painfully un-balanced condition again, even if we have orthotics, physical therapy and medicine for it.

I do not consider my students necessarily "cured", but rather they have learned to manage and overcome a predisposition for a specific condition. In other words, I believe they could recreate the painful symptoms of plantar faciiitis if they stopped paying attention to their personal practice. To manage their condition, some practice a few key postures every day, others only when they need to. Some have changed their running routine or changed their shoes. One went on to finished a marathon. Some have lost weight. Whatever solution they selected, all were looking out for the early warning signs of discomfort. All of them have a stronger sense of self-empowerment, self-reliance and self-healing.

Heal THYself

*To Heal THYself Is to Dance the Dance of Shiva,
A Dynamic Cosmic Dance Between Creation and Destruction,
Black and White, Yin and Yang, and Inhaling and Exhaling.*

To Heal THYself Is to Take Up
A Personal Therapeutic Hatha Yoga Practice
And Become A Yoga Practitioner!

Yoga and healing are often described as art forms. What makes great art is the creative tension between light and dark in a painting. To Heal THYself is a dance of creative tension between exhaling and inhaling, being grounded and lifted, and between building and reducing tissue. Therapeutic Hatha Yoga is the creative art of being proactive in your health. It is about taking up a personal yoga practice.

Healing, Like Art, Is Ultimately Subjective To The Individual.

To Heal THYself is about becoming more conscious. It is about becoming, empowered to co-create life and well-being. To Heal THYself is to restore and renew the balance between lunar and solar, yin and yang, reducing and building, and cleansing and nourishing your body-mind. It is about activating the body-mind's inherently self-regulating and self-organizing healing systems.

Therapeutic Hatha Yoga is not focused on fixing or curing your ill, rather it is about facilitating and empowering your body-mind's natural healing abilities, and guiding you to be more conscious about it and to make more conscious choices in your diet, relationships and daily life. To Heal THYself is not about asking someone to 'fix' you. To Heal THYself is about being personally proactive in your health. Remember that the quintessential you is divine and does not need to be 'fixed.' Therapeutic Hatha Yoga is to help you connect to your Inner Teacher-Healer-Guide so you can be more conscious of how to collaborate, cooperate and co-create your health and well-being with qualified health professionals.

To Heal THYself is a paradox.
You must do it yourself, but you cannot do it alone.

A Co-Creator, of Your Life, and All Life on Earth. Heal THYself! You Are a Conscious Being, a Conscious Healer.

"THYself" is an expanded and holistic sense of Self to include a sixth sense and a profound consciousness sense of Life. Your Self is more than a skin-encapsulated ego. You are spark of one divine cosmic flame. You are a vortex field of energy, vibration and consciousness in an ocean of consciousness. We are inseparable from each other and the tribe of all life on earth. We are threads in the infinite web of life. With every thought and breath, we are creating ourselves and to a lesser extent others and the world. Your life is woven into the life all around, in and through you. Your personal yoga practice for health and well-being is ultimately connected to the health and well-being of *all* life around you.

Therapeutic Hatha Yoga Treats the Person Not the Disease.

Fill Out THY Questionnaire

It is more important to know what sort of person has a disease,

Than to know what sort of disease a person has.

Hippocrates

Take a moment. Prescribe to yourself, a moment of self-reflection and take an inventory of what is so with you. Complete the Therapeutic Hatha Yoga Questionnaire, THY Questionnaire. Practice self-observation with no judgment. Be a detective, tune into what makes or does not make, you whole, feel more alive and more conscious. Make a copy of the THY Questionnaire so you can fill it out again at a later date and compare your answers.

THY Questionnaire

Name: _____ Date of birth: _____

This questionnaire is designed to help you get the most out of your Therapeutic Hatha Yoga. People are attracted to yoga for reasons that are clear and not so clear. Our issues and reasons for practicing yoga will change over time. Practicing yoga is walking a spiral path of growth and transformation. Practicing yoga brings you in touch with many aspects of your life. Yoga means union. Yoga involves uniting your physical, emotional, mental, environmental and social facets of your self. Therapeutic Hatha Yoga can help you to heal on physical, emotional, mental and spiritual levels.

Answering these questions will give you a foundation to grow, heal and transform. Yoga is a path with new and different insights at each step of the way. This questionnaire will document where you are right now and give you a reference point as to where you might be headed. This information is to empower you to step onto the path of yoga with greater awareness. Your answers can be long or short.

Define yoga for yourself. Write out a short definition of 'yoga' that works for you. It is important that you have a working definition of yoga if you are to be practicing it.

_____

_____

_____

2. Describe any major physical issues you are dealing with today. Practice self-observation without judgment.

_____

_____

_____

_____

_____

Please indicate with wavy, jagged, smeared, buzzing, tingling, pounding and fine lines on the drawings of any areas of pain, discomfort or disease.

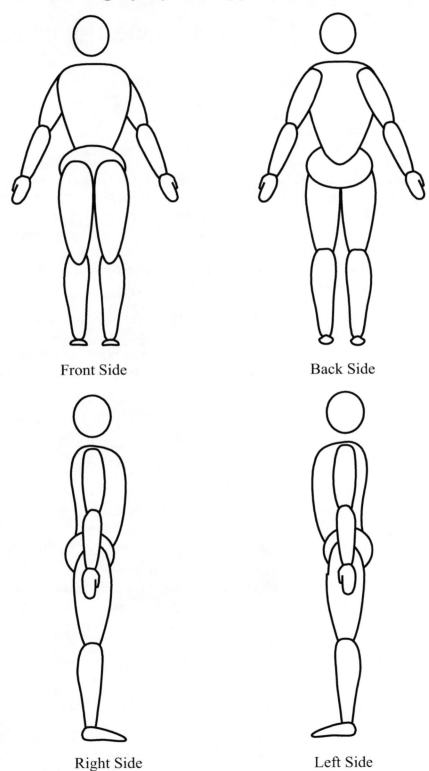

Front Side   Back Side

Right Side   Left Side

3. Please describe any activities that have strongly shaped or physically influenced you. Reflect for a moment on how activities such as gardening, cooking, sports, jobs, hobbies, dance, love, biking, walking, running or golf have shaped you.

_____
_____
_____
_____
_____
_____
_____

4. Please mention any significant feelings, emotions, stresses, issues or relationships in your life. Reflect on how your physiology and psychology are woven together.

_____
_____
_____
_____
_____

5. Please list any thoughts, ideas, books or philosophies that have influenced you.

_____
_____
_____

6. Please mention what you are thankful for.

_____
_____
_____
_____
_____

THY Intentions, Visualizations and Goals

Yoga is a metaphysical practice to develop higher consciousness. It invites us to go beyond the five senses and experience the universe as a play of polarities, a dance, and a sense of self that is greater than the sum of its parts. From this perspective, Therapeutic Hatha Yoga unites our psychology with our physiology and the observer with the observed. Therefore, it is important to remember that our intentions influence our behavior and physical form. Your intentions matter. Intentions and goals help you along the path of self-empowerment, self-awareness and self-realization. They are to help you confront your limits and transcend them. They are part of the art of opening to and diving into the dynamic creative flow of a life lived consciously. Goals and intentions are to help you be happy and healthy.

Intentions are not exactly the same thing as goals. Intentions are oriented towards how conscious you are in the present moment. In this manner, recognize an existing situation or condition, and yet leave the possibility for radical change open. Do not just set your intentions, and then forget about them. Live into your intentions. Be a better person.

Goals help you make your place in the world and be an effective person. Being grounded in intention is what provides integrity and unity in your life. Remembering your intentions provides a sense of meaning in your life that is independent of whether or not you achieve certain goals. Ironically, by being in touch with your deeper values and yearnings you are more effective at creating and reaching your goals.

The *Mandala-Brahmana-Upanishad* makes a distinction between two types of visualizations. The first is the 'deliverer with form', which consists of a manifestation of light from the space between the eyebrows. The 'deliverer with form' is similar to the quantum concept that the observer effects the observed. What vision of health and well-being do you want to deliver, manifest and observe in the world, others and yourself? The second type of visualization is the 'formless deliverer', which is about tuning into, resonating and receiving visions of the transcendental Light of creativity, love and wisdom.

7. Please describe what intentions, visualizations and or goals you would like to focus on for Now, 1 week, 40 days, 3 months, 100 days, a year…

_____

_____

_____

_____

_____ Today's Date:_____

"The doctor of the future will give no medicine, but will interest his patients in the care of the human frame, in diet, and in the cause and prevention of disease."

Thomas A. Edison

The Doctor of the Future

The Patient of the Future

A 'Clinical' Examination To Heal THYself Begins With The Understanding and Awareness That Your Body Wants to Heal

You are connected to the infinite source of creativity, love and wisdom. Walk your path. Follow the Ultimate Formula for Health and Well-Being. Practice gratitude and self-observation with no judgment. Focus on what is so. Be aware! Become empowered and self-reliant enough to take up a personal yoga practice, your yoga pill, with or without a pharmaceutical pill. You are a spark of divine consciousness. You are naturally a

115

powerful creator and healer. Connect to your Inner Teacher-Healer-Guide and prescribe a personal Therapeutic Hatha Yoga practice for yourself or find a yoga teacher to help you prescribe a practice for yourself. If it works for you, take it! Heal THYself!

How is your posture? Where is the issue, limit or ill that you would like to heal? The postures are templates that balance specific areas of the body and bring them into harmony with the whole body. Listen to your Inner Teacher-Healer-Guide and choose a posture that speaks to your ill that balances your posture.

Have an open mind. Reflect and meditate on how you have arrived at the condition you are in. How has the invisible world of your feelings, thoughts, beliefs and relationships help create your condition? Be a detective. Look for clues to why things are the way they are. Are you unconsciously recreating your condition through some behavior, diet or environment? Hold your intention and visualization for health and well-being in your awareness.

Your breath has power and authority to transform and heal you. Your breath cleanses and nourishes you. Your breath is your major source of prana, of life. Conscious rhythmic breathing is the single best medicine for every ill.

Life is about growth, development and transformation. Your ill or condition is part of your growth and spiritual path no matter how strange, ironical or paradoxical that might seem. Expand your consciousness. Be creative. Love. Be wise.

Connect To Your Inner Teacher-Healer-Guide And Choose A Therapeutic Hatha Yoga Practice, A Yoga Pill For Your Ill. It Can Be As Simple As Seven Conscious Breaths A Day. Take A Daily Dose.

$$R_x \sim\!\sim\!\sim\!\sim\!\sim\!\sim \text{ Daily}$$

When Is The Best Time To Take A Daily Dose Of Yoga?

Now is the best time. As for the future, hatha yoga is sun moon yoga. Practicing hatha yoga when the energies of the sun and moon are balanced is considered ideal. The dawn and dusk are thus the traditional times for practicing yoga. In the morning, the mind is clear, though the body is stiff. At dusk, the body is ready, though the mind is less settled. What time-space works for you to take up a personal practice and take a daily dose of conscious healing through conscious breathing?

THY Practices

All The Following Practices Are Based On

THY Ultimate Formula For Health And Well-Being

R~x~ 〰〰〰〰〰 Daily

Your path in life is changing. The issues that are important to us unfold and transform over time. There are evolving stages to both development and healing in our lives.

Your prescription and daily dose of yoga
Will change over time.

Be open to practice a minimum of seven conscious rhythmic breaths a day for NOW,
1 week, 40 days, 3 months, 100 days, a year...

End Warfare

As A Model For Healing

The language of war is regularly applied to the practice of healing. Our modern concept of medical treatment is all too often like an act of declaring war. Disease is equated to a body, which is "under attack" and "besieged by invaders". Doctors "bombard" these invaders with "lethal" doses of medicine.

With this language of war, modern medicine creates a victim consciousness in the patient as the body is seen to be under a "sneak attack." Rarely is the ill body described as mobilizing to repair itself, working to restore balance or in the process of eliminating toxins. The role of modern medicine is not to enhance the body's natural self –healing processes as much as it is to "obliterate the enemy."

The language of war expresses itself in our daily language as we "fight fat" or "combat stress." Warfare has become the model of solving society's problems with expressions like a war on cancer, war on drugs, war on terrorism and a battle between the sexes.

Let go of the desire to use the language of war to help heal yourself, others and the planet. Let go of victim consciousness. You are a co-creator. How have your lifestyle, relationships and environment compromised your health and well-being, and how have they helped it? Meditate on it. Connect to your inner Teacher-Healer-Guide. Practice conscious healing through conscious breathing, and become an active ingredient in your own health and well-being. Expand your consciousness. Stop using the language of war to heal.

Peace and health are not static or inert states of being. Health and peace are dynamic states balancing the energies of life, of inhaling and exhaling, of nourishing and cleansing, of giving and receiving.

Bring A Dynamic Peaceful Balance

To Your Life For Healing And Well-Being.

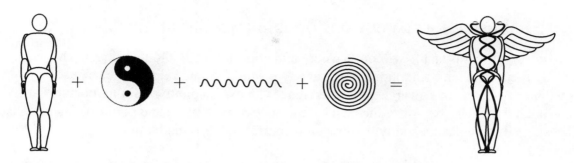

The Mind and Meditation

The Essence of Yoga Is Meditation

Meditation is not what your think.
Meditation quiets the chattering doubting mind and presents you with
clarity, insight and direction.
Meditation expands your consciousness.

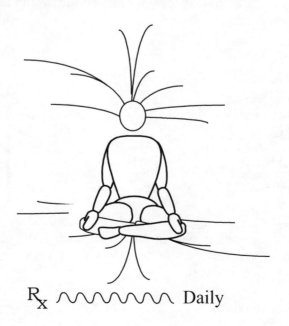

R$_X$ ⁓⁓⁓⁓ Daily

Establish a Firm Yet Comfortable Foundation for Meditation

Create a seat that is stable without tension, and comfortable without dullness. The word *asana* literally means seat, indicating that any posture, asana, is in essence a seat for meditation. Conscious awareness is what makes a pose meditative. Sitting postures are considered ideal as they offer the best balance between stability and comfort. Standing is considered too unstable and lying down too comfortable for meditation.

Level your pelvis by rotating your thighs inward and pulling the flesh away from your sitz bones, the thick, rough surfaced prominences of the hip bone that support weight while sitting. Be sure to have the knees below the hips, otherwise your hips will roll backwards and you will loose your level pelvis. Anchor your sitz bones onto the chair and create a plumb line with the gravitational field of the earth. There are many excellent postures to for meditation.

 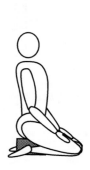 

Begin by creating a seat, which is stable without tension, and comfortable without dullness. Anchor the pelvis onto the seat and lift the back of the head. We sit up straighter when we root down stronger. Connect your legs and feet to the floor. Create a plumb line, through the top of your head, middle of your ear, shoulder and hip.

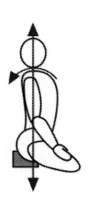  

Plug, root and anchor your sitz bones into the seat through the plumb line the. Get grounded. Lift the heart and roll the shoulders blades slide down the back. The knees are below the hips.

Meditation Is Being Alert Without Tension, And Calm Without Dullness.

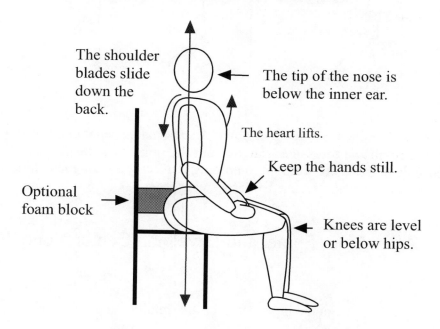

The shoulder blades slide down the back.

The tip of the nose is below the inner ear.

The heart lifts.

Keep the hands still.

Optional foam block

Knees are level or below hips.

Roll your shoulders up, back and down. Lift your heart and gently pull your head back to secure a plumb line through the middle of your ear, shoulder and hip. Drop your chin down so the nose is below the middle ear. We sit up straighter when we root down stronger. If you have trouble sitting up straight, place a foam block, firm cushion or even a rolled up yoga mat between the back of the chair and the sacrum. This is not support for the low back or the upper back. This is support for a solid foundation of the pelvis. The spine is free to move with the undulation of the breath through the body.

Leaning back on the chair will collapse the heart and round the back so the plumb line no longer goes through the hips. Meditation involves a dynamic stillness to align us with the earth and the sky to experience the divine. If you are too relaxed your legs will drift apart, you will begin to slouch and lose your grounded connection.

Still your hands. Palms can be up or down. Hands can be separate or resting on top of one and other. Thumb and forefinger can touch or the fingers can be interlaced together. Find a comfortable position and commit to holding it. Keep your tongue behind your teeth. Let your gaze be soft and focused, or close your eyes.

Align Your Spine, and Level and Center Your Head

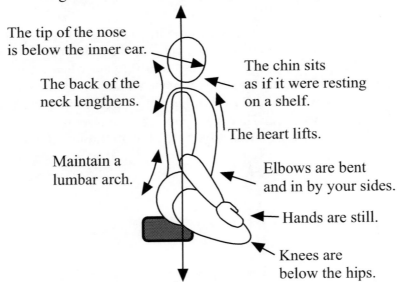

Align the inner ear over the shoulder and hip.

The tip of the nose is below the inner ear.

The back of the neck lengthens.

The chin sits as if it were resting on a shelf.

The heart lifts.

Maintain a lumbar arch.

Elbows are bent and in by your sides.

Hands are still.

Knees are below the hips.

Plug your sitz bones into the cushion and into the earth.

R𝑥 ∿∿∿∿∿∿ Daily

Meditation integrates your body, mind and breath as it connects you to creativity, love and wisdom.

Center and Level Yourself

Meditation quiets whirling, fluctuating thoughts and emotions of our waking consciousness allowing us to witness deeper subconscious and higher conscious aspects of ourselves.

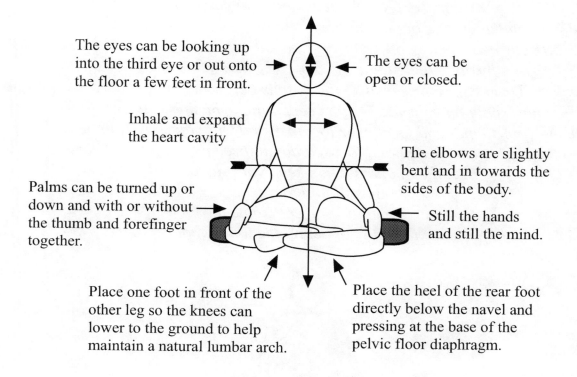

The eyes can be looking up into the third eye or out onto the floor a few feet in front.

The eyes can be open or closed.

Inhale and expand the heart cavity

The elbows are slightly bent and in towards the sides of the body.

Palms can be turned up or down and with or without the thumb and forefinger together.

Still the hands and still the mind.

Place one foot in front of the other leg so the knees can lower to the ground to help maintain a natural lumbar arch.

Place the heel of the rear foot directly below the navel and pressing at the base of the pelvic floor diaphragm.

Raise the pelvis by sitting on a meditation cushion, block or folded blankets so the knees are below the pelvis and the natural curve of the low back can be maintained.

Inhale to the heart. Exhale to the navel.
Quiet your mind and tune in to the divine.

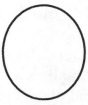

Keep your face soft, mouth closed and your tongue on the roof of the mouth behind your front teeth. Will your hands and arms to be still. Let your brow be soft.

A Brief Guideline to Meditation

Align yourself with the earth.
Establish a firm foundation with your knees below your hips.
Level your pelvis by rotating your thighs inward and pulling the flesh away
from your sitting bones.
Center and level your head with your body.
Roll your shoulders up, back and down.
Lift your heart and gently pull your head back to create a plumb line
through the middle of your ear, shoulder and hip.
Drop your chin down so the nose is below the middle ear.
Keep a half smile on your face as you keep tongue behind your front teeth.
Bring your thumb and forefinger together and will your hands to be still.
Let your gaze be soft and focused about three feet in front of you.
Breathe in and out, yet keep your hands still.
Be still and focused.
Be in the present moment.
Experience the unity of being, the union that is yoga.

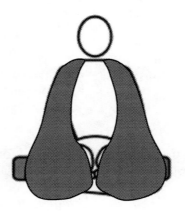

To help still the body, and add a bit of personal ritual to your meditation practice with a specific shawl, piece of fabric or blanket wrapped around you. A candle, picture, crystal, flower or any altar piece will add to your meditative space. An altar is a portal to the Infinite source of creativity, love and wisdom. Your altar, be it as small as a seed in your pocket or as big as the ocean, becomes a metaphysical place to focus on your intentions and visualizations for health and well-being.

Your Thoughts Matter to Your Immune System.
Be Conscious Of Your Intentions and Visualizations.

Meditation Expands Consciousness.

Human thought can be regarded as a result of suspended action, and the pineal gland inhibits the immediate discharging of thoughts into action. This inhibition causes us to look inwards, self reflect and ponder our actions and reactions. Introversion is necessary for self-realization. It displaces attention from the outer world of the five senses to the more subtle sensitivity of the frequencies of an inner world of feeling, thought and imagination. When the external world disappears, the circle of consciousness condenses. In more metaphysical yoga terms, meditation magnetizes spiritual light into the pineal gland. Primary attention is focused upon stilling the body-mind and experiencing our resonating core of consciousness for life, health and well-being.

Classical meditation is described in the last three limbs of Patanjali's Yoga Sutras. The sixth limb, Dharana involves concentration and prolonged focusing of attention on a single mental object. The seventh limb Dhyana is the deepening of concentration toward meditative absorption with the mental object of concentration. Samadhi, the eighth limb of Patanjali's eightfold path, is the union between subject and contemplated object leading to a conscious ecstasy with spontaneous arising thoughts and insight, and finally a subraconscious ecstasy a realm beyond ideas and description, *moksha*, self-liberation, self-realization, *nirvana*.

Meditate On It!

People often say, "Meditate on it" when they perceive someone is in doubt or having trouble making a decision. Meditation centers the body and quiets whirling thoughts so we can be open and see previously hidden creative possibilities and solutions. Here is a 7-breath meditation to help you meditate on any question or issue.

Exhale into the present moment.
Inhale through the nose.

Exhale to the navel.
Inhale to the heart.

Keep the heart lifted as you exhale to the navel.
Keep the navel slightly in as you inhale to the heart.

Exhale from the top of the head to the soles of your feet.
Inhale from the soles of your feet to the top of your head.

Exhale and feel grounded.
Inhale and feel lifted.

Exhale for the count of nine.
Inhale for the count of six.

Exhale and send a question to your Inner Teacher-Healer-Guide.
Inhale and listen for a message, look for an insight and
be open for a creative solution.

Instant Meditation!

The ultimate stillness and clarity of meditation
is in the pause at the bottom of your next exhalation.
Tune into it now.

Exhale into the next pause- stillness-space that connects you to the source of
creativity, love and wisdom.

Manifest and realize creativity, love and wisdom in your life now.

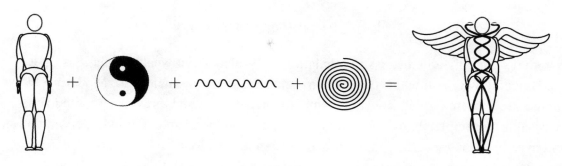

Asthma

Breathe Through Your Nose

Asthma comes from the Greek word for "panting." Panting is by definition is shallow mouth breathing. However, our noses, not our mouths, are designed for breathing. Our noses warm, moisten and filter the air for our lungs. When we breathe through our mouths, we create an alert and stressful response in our lungs, body and mind. Cup your hands over your ears, breathe through your nose and listen to your breath. Slow your rate of respiration and listen to the power and authority of life in your breath.

R_x  Daily

Soften Your Inhalations.

Inspiration Does Not Suck.

As our lungs expand they create a partial vacuum that pulls air into the lower lungs, much like a bellows. You do not have to suck air into your body. Expand and invite the breath in. Feel the breath on the insides of your nostrils, soften your forehead, and soften your inhalation. Relax, you were borne endowed with creativity, love and wisdom. You do not have to suck them in, you need to consciously exhale them out.

R_x  Daily

Consciousness Is Primary

Asthma is not only about stressful inhalations, it is also about weak exhalations. In a fundamental way, asthmatics cannot relax and release their exhalations. Modern society can be stressful mix greed, consumerism and alienation, which prevents people from being able to completely exhale. An incomplete exhalation can result in hyperventilation and over-breathing resulting in too much oxygen in the blood and not enough carbon dioxide. What is the difference between medicine and poison? Dosage! Too much oxygen makes our blood too 'sticky' forcing the lungs into an asthma attack. The Relaxing Crocodile is an ideal posture to relax and yield into your exhalations. With the weight of the body on the abdomen, the exhalation effortlessly becomes deeper and deeper.

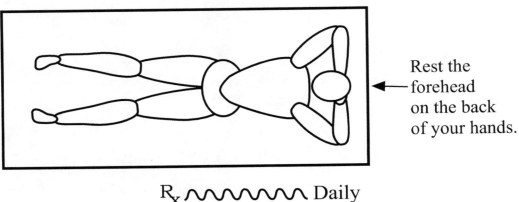

Rest the forehead on the back of your hands.

R_X ∿∿∿∿∿ Daily

Be Conscious Of Your Exhalations. Lengthen Your Exhalations.

 69

Asthmatics do not fully exhale and tend to hyperventilate. Be conscious of exhaling. Stay calm and even in your body, mind and breath. Now empower your exhalations. Inhale for the count of 6 and exhaling for the count of 9 for seven breaths. Practice exhaling for longer and longer to help strengthen your breathing. How long can you exhale? Can you exhale for the count of 30 through pursed lips? Be sure to inhale through your nose.

Practice The Conscious Breathing Practice 1-16
In The Ultimate Formula For Health And Well-Being

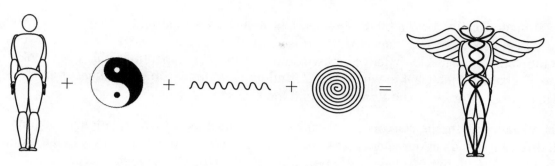

The 6th Sense - Telepathy and Empathy

Be More Compassionate:
Connect to Your Third Eye and Your Third Ear.

We are all familiar with our five senses of smell, taste, sight, touch and hearing. They provide the foundation of empirical science, yet just because you cannot empirically measure something does not mean that it is not real or valuable, such as empathy and telepathy. In the yoga tradition, the five senses are connected to the first 5 chakras, and our 6th sense is about projecting out of our third eye and tuning in with our third ear to the invisible world of feelings, thoughts, creativity, love and wisdom.

The Ultimate Reality, beyond the five senses, is about understanding the play of polarities in a metaphysical dance of life. It is about understanding the difference between fact and value, between knowledge and wisdom. For this, Therapeutic Hatha Yoga looks to the 6th chakra, Ajna Chakra where the *ida* and *pingula nadis* come together for an understanding of our self and Reality beyond the five senses.

In the yoga tradition, the chakras are psycho-physical centers, which are often associated with different glands in our endocrine system. The pituitary and pineal glands in the brain are associated with our 6th chakra. We typically draw the *ida* and *pingula* as coming to either side of the head, though in reality they are more like a double helix coiling around our central channel and meeting inside our heads. Even though we typically only think of the ajna chakra, or third eye, at the brow point between our eyes, there is a backside to our 6th chakra, which Therapeutic Hatha Yoga refers to as our third ear.

The Nasion and Inion,
The Seat of Our Third Eye and Third Ear

Electroencephalography (EEG) is the recording of electrical activity along the scalp. EEG measures voltage fluctuations resulting from ionic current flows within the neurons of the brain. The EEG electrodes are positioned on the International 10-20 System, conventionally defined locations based on the position of the nasion and the inion.

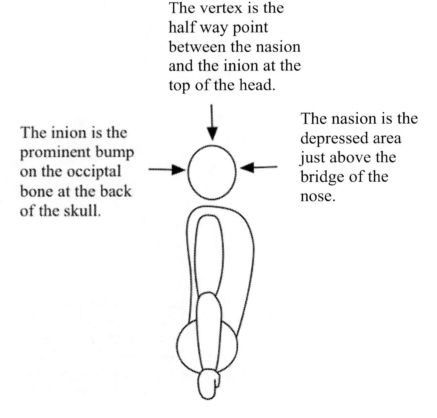

The vertex is the half way point between the nasion and the inion at the top of the head.

The inion is the prominent bump on the occiptal bone at the back of the skull.

The nasion is the depressed area just above the bridge of the nose.

130

Pituitary Gland and the Third Eye

The pituitary gland is the master gland is about the size of a pea. It is located behind the center of our forehead, between our eyes, right behind the nasion. It is the main control center that sends messages to all the other glands. It prompts the proper growth of glands and organs and regulates sexual development. It is referred to as the seat of the mind. It is often described as the seat of your inner eye or your third eye.

Pineal Gland and the Third Ear

This pinecone-shaped gland is located in the middle of the brain behind the pituitary gland. The pineal gland contains pigment, like that found in the eyes, and is connected to the optic center of the brain. It controls the action of light upon our body. The pineal gland is located in the posterior end of the third ventricle of the brain and the pituitary gland is located in the roof of the third ventricle. The pineal gland acts in two ways to inhibit the action of the pituitary gland. The pituitary gland is responsible for activating adolescence and the beginning of sexuality. The pineal gland checks the pituitary gland to prevent premature sexual awakening.

The pineal gland is referred to as our cosmic antenna, divine ear, third ear and the seat of illumination. The pineal gland is known as the seat of illumination, intuition and cosmic consciousness. The pineal gland compares to the pituitary gland as intuition compares to reason. Imagine that the pituitary holds the positive, masculine charge and the pineal holds a negative, feminine charge. It is a mystical marriage when yang and yin, pingula and ida, masculine and feminine energies meet.

Our understanding of how the brain functions, brain wave activity and neuroplasicity is growing and changing with a steady flow of exciting new research. Having said that, the third ventricle connects various parts of the brain and could be called the "seat of the mind." The frontal lobe regulates the emotional side of our nature. The anterior lobe regulates concrete thought and intellectual concepts. It could be that the joining of the essences of the pituitary and pineal glands, our 3rd eye and our 3rd ear, opens our 6th sense of empathy, telepathy and our ability to resonate with the subtle vibrations of creativity, love and wisdom that are all around us.

Tune into your 6th sense, your sense of radiant space, your sense of telepathy and empathy, and resonate with humanity and all life.

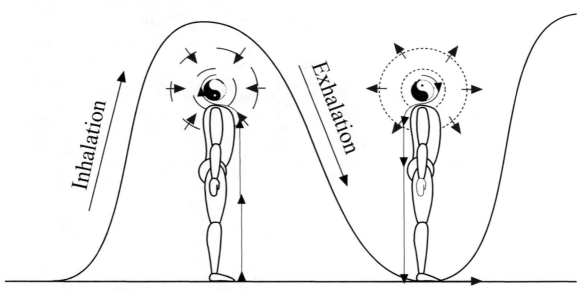

*Inhalations create nerve impulses to the brain
inducing a signal and receiving a telepathic/empathic message.*

*Exhalations create nerve impulses from the brain
radiating a signal and sending a telepathic/empathic message.*

Is Your Antenna Down? Is the Light of Your Inner Teacher-Healer-Guide Turned Off?

The Mind-Body Infinity Loop is disengaged when the alignment and connection between the heart and head, between body and mind, is tweaked. When the head is thrust forward and tilted up so the tip of the nose is above the middle of our ear, the flow of *prana* to the inion, our cosmic antenna, is blocked and obstructed. When the heart is sunken and collapsed, the flow *prana* in the body is reduced. This misalignment compromises the circuit of the Mind-Body Infinity Loop, which lights our Inner Teacher-healer-Guide and powers our ability to tune into the Infinite.

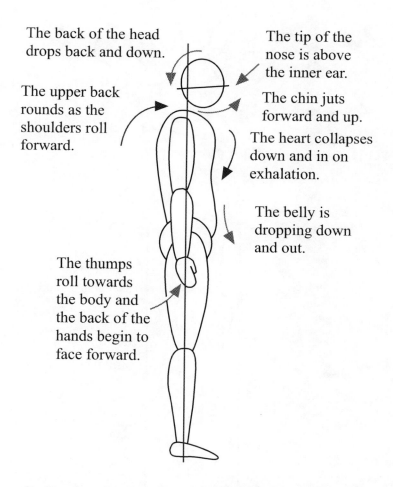

The back of the head drops back and down.

The upper back rounds as the shoulders roll forward.

The tip of the nose is above the inner ear.

The chin juts forward and up.

The heart collapses down and in on exhalation.

The belly is dropping down and out.

The thumps roll towards the body and the back of the hands begin to face forward.

The power to light the Inner Teacher-Healer-Guide is turned off when the muscles and spinal column are pinched and crimped at the back of the neck and head. Poor posture reduces the flow of subtle energy through the Mind∞Body Infinity Loop.

Flip the Switch! Turn on Your Higher Powers. Light Up Your Inner Teacher-Healer-Guide!

The switch to turn on your inner Light is at your inion. The inion is key to complete the circuit for the Mind∞Body Infinity Loop, your connection to the Infinite source of creativity, love and wisdom, and a sense of empathy and telepathy. Place your hand behind your head and feel the occipital ridge on the back of your skull. In the center of the ridge there is a small bump called the inion. It is your toggle switch to connect the circuits for your 6th sense and the Light of your Inner Teacher-Healer-Guide. Place your index finger on your inion and flip the switch for higher consciousness. Flip the switch, by gently sliding the skin on the inion upwards, while lowering the tip of the nose.

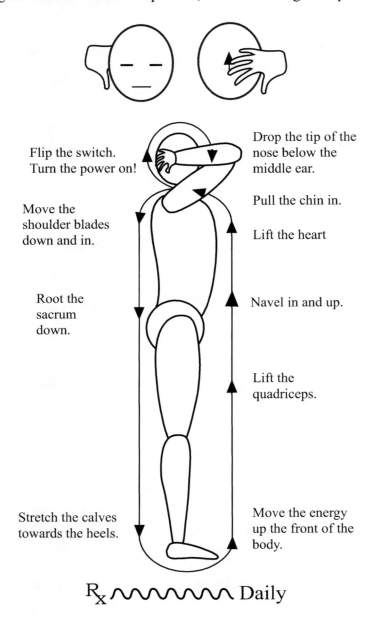

Flip the switch. Turn the power on!

Drop the tip of the nose below the middle ear.

Move the shoulder blades down and in.

Pull the chin in.

Lift the heart

Root the sacrum down.

Navel in and up.

Lift the quadriceps.

Stretch the calves towards the heels.

Move the energy up the front of the body.

R$_x$ ∿∿∿∿∿ Daily

Push The Button To End Thoughts of War!

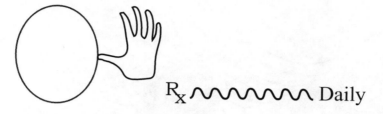

Place your thumb on your third eye- brow point. Gently push to release any tension in your forehead and mind. Align your head with your heart, and push the button, your brow point, to end any thoughts or feelings of war, violence, fear, guilt and shame.

Tune Into Empathy and Telepathy.

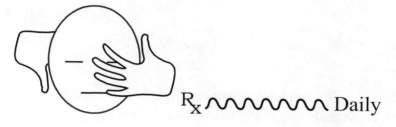

Place an index finger on the inion, your antenna for receiving subtle vibrations on the back of your head, and place the other index finger on your nasion your satellite dish for transmitting subtle vibrations. *Inhale to the inion and receive telepathic / empathic messages. Exhale subtle telepathic and empathic transmissions of creativity, love and life through your third eye.*

Put On Your Cosmic Deep Space Helmet!

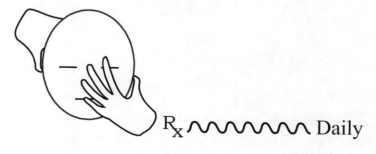

Place your thumbs over your earflaps and then place one index finger on your inion and the other on your nasion. *Listen to the vibrant ocean of consciousness in your breath. Tune into the divine wave-space medium. Inhale the cosmic breeze blowing. Exhale the cosmic river flowing.*

Project and Manifest Your
Intentions and Visualizations Out of Your Third Eye

1. Exhale into the present moment.
Inhale through the nose and soften the forehead.

2. Exhale and contract the abdominal cavity.
Inhale and expand the heart cavity.

3. Hold the heart lifted while you exhale to the navel.
Hold the navel in while you inhale to the heart.

4. Exhale into a moment of stillness.
Inhale into a moment of stillness.

5. Exhale and feel grounded.
Inhale and feel lifted.

6. Exhale from the top of the head to the soles of the feet.
Inhale from the soles of the feet to the top of the head.

7. Exhale, project and manifest your intentions and visualizations
for health and well-being out of your Third Eye.
Inhale and tune into the source of creativity, love and wisdom.

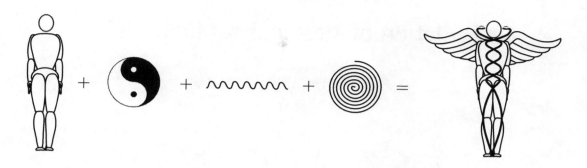

Unleashing Your Super Yoga Healing Powers

The Great Seal - Maha Bandha - The Triple Lock

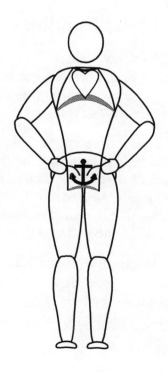

A Bullet Proof Vest and A Magic Bullet

Your Ultimate Core Power

A classic picture of Superman is with his hands on his hips, abdomen in and his chest expanded, looking as if he were practicing the Triple Lock the super pose of Hatha-Yoga. The language of the ancient yogis was no less wondrous than the language to describe superman. Within the yoga tradition, there are many benefits associated with the bandhas. Yoga texts have poetically described the extraordinary power of the bandhas. These powers, *siddhis*, have historically added to the mystery and intrigue of yoga. Their claims are greatly exaggerated in the ancient texts and left out of most modern books. The classic text, the *Hatha Yoga Pradipika*, describes Uddiyana Bandha as "the lion that kills the elephant Death." Jalandhara Bandha as "destroying old age" and by practicing Mula Bandha "even the aged become young." The bandhas are ways to contain, renew and restore our body-mind. Their effects on the body, breath and mind are undeniable and more research is needed to reveal all of their benefits.

The Great Seal - Maha Bandha - The Triple Lock

The three bandhas are described as energy locks, seals or valves that bind back dissipating outward flows of energy, *prana* or life force and also free internal blockages. Bandhas restrain outward flow of *prana* while bringing it back to be redistributed from our core center in order to achieve health and well-being.

The bandhas are learned as a physical movement, yet there are underlying neurophysiologic, mental, and energetic patterns behind the physical, hence the bandhas are affected by awareness and mental alertness as well as muscular-skeletal awareness. Maha Bandha is referred to as the master key. Maha Bandha aligns us with the infinite source of creativity, love and wisdom. Maha Bandha connects us to the core of our being, deep space consciousness. The bandhas are part of any serious Hatha-Yoga practice.

The three bandhas are Jalandara Bandha, the Neck Lock, Uddiyana Bandha, the Flying Abdominal Lock and Mula Bandha, the Root Lock. The practice of engaging all three bandhas simultaneously is referred to as the Master Key, the Great Seal or Maha Mudra. Ultimately, on a mental neurophysiologic level, the bandhas align our spine so that we can tune into the divine.

Jalandara Bandha – Neck Lock

Jalandara Bandha helps reduce neck tension and increase blood flow to and from the head. High blood pressure in the brain can increase tension in the eyes and produce such conditions as migraine headaches and the general sense of "wooliness" of the brain. The venous drainage, from the head and neck area, is clearly indicated to be of great value in correcting tension problems of the face, nasal passages, head and neck areas.

We leak energy, consciousness and life force out through our throats when our heads are not centered and level on the body. when our head and heart are not aligned. In poetic terms, when the jewel of the mind does not rest on the lotus of the heart, our capacity for creativity, love and wisdom is diminished.

Uddiyana Bandha –Flying Abdominal Lock

Uddiyana Bandha has been shown to aid in the strengthening of the chest diaphragm. It stimulates the digestive organs and is recommended for diabetics. Uddiyana Bandha is said to aid in draining a clogged up liver, as well as tone up the pancreas and spleen. Uddiyana Bandha helps eliminate constipation by encouraging the natural peristalsis of the bowel. Uddiyana Bandha connects us to our third chakra enhancing our sense of self-esteem and personal power. Superman is typically drawn and or depicted with the abdomen up and in as if he were practicing Uddiyana Bandha!

We lose energy in our abdomen when our digestive fire is lowered too close to the water element in our body and our navel is not drawn in and up during exhalation. When our fire, our personal power, is disconnected from our heart we lose passion and compassion.

Mula Bandha – Root Lock

Mula Bandha affects the central nervous system producing a stable, calm and grounded sense of being helping to reduce pain and anxiousness. Mula Bandha helps strengthen the hips, low back and the entire pelvic region. The ovaries in the female and the prostate gland in the male receive an increased blood circulation. When our pelvic floor, our pelvic basin, is not water tight, we leak. Increased muscular tone and awareness of the pelvic diaphragm of Mula Bandha is helpful for prolapsed uterus, hemorrhoids, constipation and more. It is part of the Great Seal that unites the physical and the spiritual connecting us to our core of goodness.

Maha Bandha Gives Us a Glimpse of the 7th Chakra

Our 7th sense, our timeless eternal sense of spirit-soul-consciousness, is located in our seventh chakra, at the top of our head. Our spinal cord is surrounded by bone and our brain is locked in a vault of bone known as the cranium. Our bones can resonate with the subtle vibrations of the divine, a timeless perception of the infinite. The expression, 'I feel it in my bones." conveys this seventh sense of Reality. Our sense of the seventh chakra is our sense of timeless radiant space, super consciousness, and deep space consciousness.

In the yoga tradition the body is sometimes referred to as a vessel. The body is our earthen vessel to carry us on our path of awakening consciousness / spiritual growth. *Kumbhaka*, the word associated with the pause between each breath, also means vessel or pot-like container. Visualize the three breathing diaphragms as creating the perimeter for that vessel The pause at the bottom of the exhalation is the ideal place to seal your vessel tight so as not to lose vital prana energy needed to raise consciousness to the seventh chakra. Visualize Your Body As A Vessel, A Container, Of Spiritual Light, Of Deep Space Consciousness.

The Three Diaphragms Used for Breathing

Create a Frame for Visualizing Our Body as a Vessel

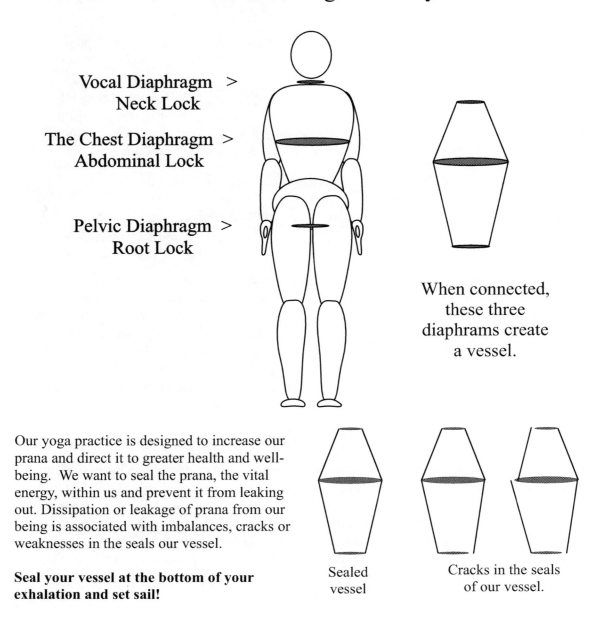

Vocal Diaphragm >
Neck Lock

The Chest Diaphragm >
Abdominal Lock

Pelvic Diaphragm >
Root Lock

When connected, these three diaphrams create a vessel.

Our yoga practice is designed to increase our prana and direct it to greater health and well-being. We want to seal the prana, the vital energy, within us and prevent it from leaking out. Dissipation or leakage of prana from our being is associated with imbalances, cracks or weaknesses in the seals our vessel.

Seal your vessel at the bottom of your exhalation and set sail!

Sealed vessel

Cracks in the seals of our vessel.

Sealing Your Vessel with Maha Bandha

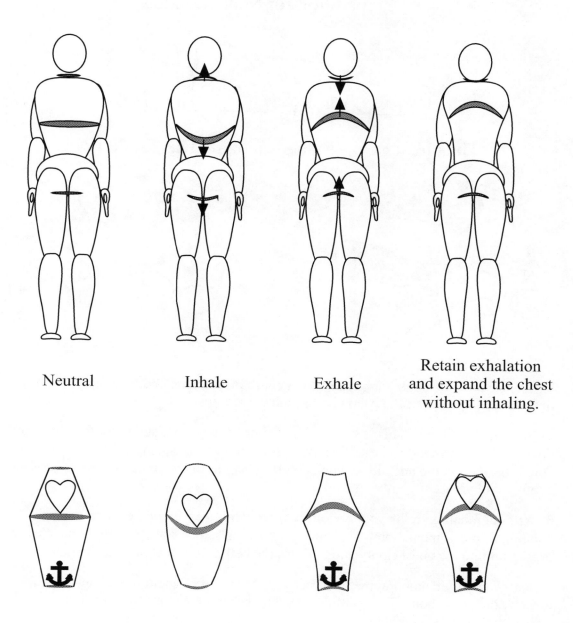

| Neutral | Inhale | Exhale | Retain exhalation and expand the chest without inhaling. |

To facilitate engaging the three bandhas, start on the floor. It is difficult for the abdomen to fly up while standing and working against gravity. Start lying down, ideally with a block under the pelvis so the abdominal cavity is lifted above the chest cavity to assist in its upward flight. Relax the abdominal cavity. Start with your fingertips below your navel and then massage, knead and loosen the viscera along the pubic bone towards the right hip, then work the fingers up to bottom of the rib cage. Massage and knead the abdomen along the base of the rib cage to the sternum and then down the left side to the left hip and then back to the pubic bone.

Massage, Relax and Soften the Abdominal Wall

Preparation for Maha Bandha

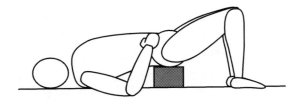

The Great Seal - Maha Bandha - The Triple Lock

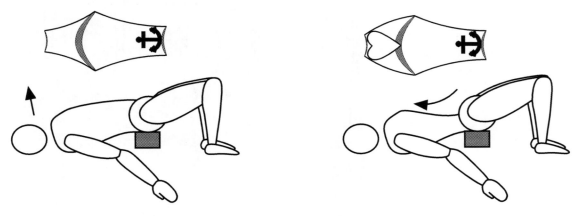

1. Inhale deeply through your nose. Then consciously exhale with an ujjayi breath, through your nose, or exhale slowly through pursed lips.

2. Hold the breath out. This is kumbhaka. Contract the throat and press the chin firmly down and in towards the chest. Seal the throat diaphragm closing the larynx and the epiglottis. This is the neck lock, Jalandara Bandha. In the beginning it might be easier to simply hold your nose with your fingers.

3. Without inhaling, relax your abdominal area while you lift and expand the heart cavity creating a "mock inhalation." The "mock inhalation" sucks the abdominal muscles and organs up into the chest cavity and hollows the belly. This is Uddiyana Bandha.

4. Seal your pelvic diaphragm. Contract your anus and perineum drawing the tailbone towards the pubic bone. This is Mula Bandha, the root lock, and your anchor.

5. Pull the subtle vibrations up through the core of the body from the pelvic floor up through the abdomen and heart to the third eye and all the way to the top of the head. This is Maha Bandha, the Triple Lock or the Great Seal.

6. With the upward flowing prana sealed at the throat with Jalandara Bandha, the downward flowing apana sealed with Mula Bandha and the organs sealed to the spine, with Uddiyana Bandha, the energy moves into the central channel, into our core of goodness, our core of divine spirit.

Many Ways To Practice

A supported posture with the thighs strapped together is a great way to relax and practice the Triple Lock.

Down Dog with the Triple Lock

Down Dog is a great pose to practice the Triple lock as the abdominal cavity is above the heart cavity and the flying abdominal lift does not have to fly up against gravity. Bending the knees and lowering the belly onto the thighs squeezes the abdominal cavity so it is empty and ready to fly up into the heart cavity as the legs straighten out. However, you need not bend the knees to practice the Triple Lock in Down Dog. The Triple Lock will help lengthen down the backs of the legs and out of the hip sockets when practicing Down Dog.

Down Dog or
Adhomukha Shavanasana

Exhale everything out as you sit back towards your heels with the toes curled under.

Hold the breath out. Straighten legs. Mock Inhalation!

Belly Bumps

After you lift the abdomen and hollow out the belly, practice lifting it and then dropping and lifting the abdomen again, and dropping it a few times before you inhale.

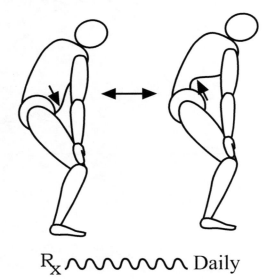

R$_x$ ∿∿∿∿∿ Daily

Bump it up and down slowly yet vigorously.

Traditional Standing Practice of The Triple Lock

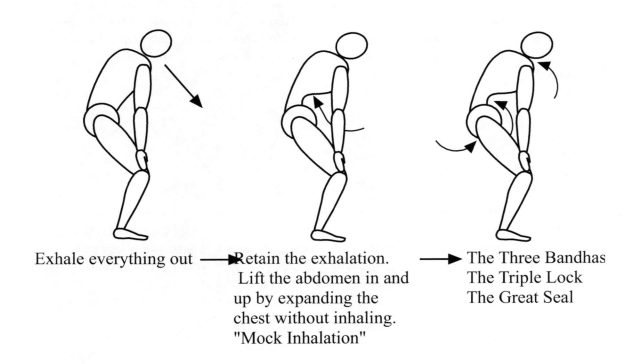

Exhale everything out ⟶ Retain the exhalation. Lift the abdomen in and up by expanding the chest without inhaling. "Mock Inhalation" ⟶ The Three Bandhas
The Triple Lock
The Great Seal

Siddhasana with The Triple Lock / Maha Bandha

Siddha = a seer, sage, prophet or semi-divine being

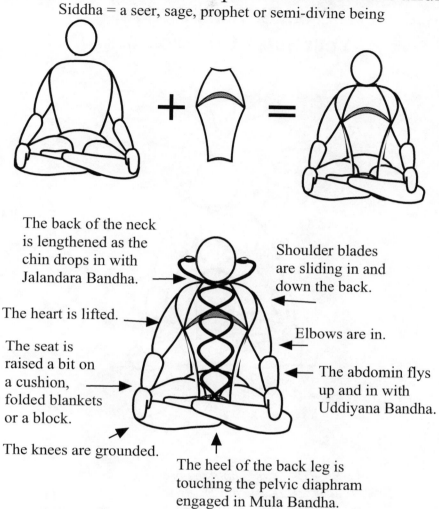

The back of the neck is lengthened as the chin drops in with Jalandara Bandha.

Shoulder blades are sliding in and down the back.

The heart is lifted.

The seat is raised a bit on a cushion, folded blankets or a block.

Elbows are in.

The abdomin flys up and in with Uddiyana Bandha.

The knees are grounded.

The heel of the back leg is touching the pelvic diaphram engaged in Mula Bandha.

Siddhis are supernatural powers to be attained through the practice of yoga. The primary eight siddhis are: *anima*, the power to assume a minute form: *mahiman*, the power to assume an extensive form; *gariman*, the power to become weighty; *laghiman*, the power to become light; *prapti*, the power to reach the proximity of even distant objects; *prakamya*, the power to obtain what is desire; *isita*, the power to shape anything as desired; and *vasitva*, the power to control anything.

In the *Hatha Yoga Pradipika*, one of the few ancient texts that mentions yoga postures in detail, of the 8,400,000 asana, as counted by Shiva, 84 are selected for description. Of those 84, Siddhasana is considered the most comfortable and most excellent. Press firmly one heel on the pelvic floor, just behind the testicles in men and against the vaginal walls in women, and place the other heel in front of the pubic bone. Fix your chin tightly upon your breast. Remain erect with your organs under control, and look fixedly at the spot between the eyebrows. Now apply Maha Bandha and you can unleash your super yogi powers. Awake and become captain of your own vessel.

Awaken Your Higher Consciousness,
Your Seventh Chakra,
Your Super Consciousness!

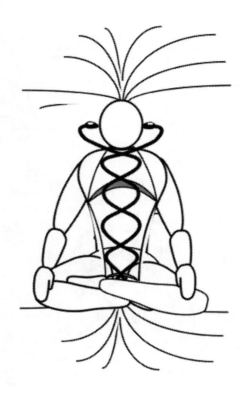

Exhale, and hold the breath out.
Engage the Triple Lock.
Seal your vessel, connect the tip of the tailbone to the brow point, the nasion and clear
the central channel from the 1st chakra to the 3rd Eye.
Align the 3rd Eye with the 3rd Ear.

Inhale the coiled Shakti kundalini, Pure Consciousness,
up through the central channel.
Be moved by the evolutionary transformational creative loving intelligence
Of the kundalini, of pure consciousness, super consciousness, deep space consciousness.
Resonate with the unmanifest energy of the Divine.

As a sealed container The Triple lock creates a vacuum feeling as it expands the container without expanding the space inside. With the Triple Lock connect to the vacuum-void-emptiness, deep space consciousness, a super consciousness at the 7th chakra beyond the space-time continuum. Satori! Samadhi!

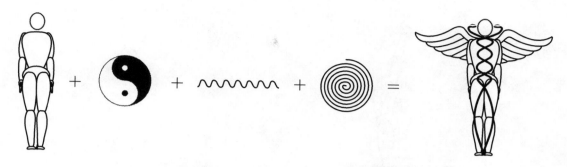

THY Basic Core Practice
For Health and Well-Being

Opening Invocation

The opening invocation reaffirms the concept and principles of yoga in a concise manner, and sets the tone for the class or practice without making people think they have to speak an ancient language to be on a spiritual path or achieve higher consciousness.

Make a comfortable space under your knees and come into a kneeling position.

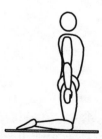

Take your arms overhead. Feel the breath as a wave oscillating through you. As you inhale, feel your arms moving up and back. As you exhale, feel your arms moving forward and down.

Inhale   Exhale

Hold the essence of the exhalation as you inhale, and the essence of the inhalation as you exhale, creating a dynamic stillness, a union of opposites and a wisdom of paradoxes. Move beyond duality and separation into unity, oneness and yoga.

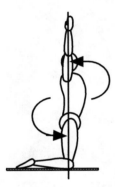

Bend your elbows and lower your arms with the palms facing up. Align the middle ear over the shoulder, over the hip and knee. Welcome yourself in with an open hand, heart and head, a full spectrum conscious integration of body, mind and breath.

Turn your palms forward and sit back to your heels to the best of your ability. Use whatever props are necessary to sit back on your heels, or simple stay on your knees. If you cannot breathe into this posture, or any other posture, back out of it. Practice yoga peacefully. Breathe the body open, flexible and strong. Use breath as a feedback loop so that you may know the difference between what is therapeutic and what is toxic in you practice. Practice yoga safely.

Bring your palms together in a gesture of reverence and gratitude, reverence for all life and gratitude for this life.

With this in our hands, heart and head, set your intentions and visualizations for health and well-being. Exhale into the present moment.

The Opening Invocation with Movement and Breath

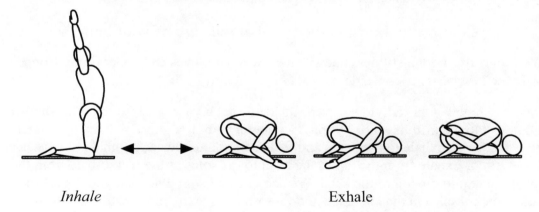

Inhale   Exhale

Inhale your arms aver head.
Exhale and touch the ground.

Inhale to the sky.
Exhale to the earth.

Inhale to the Infinite spirit
Exhale to your individual sprit.

Inhale to the global, to the one ocean we all share.
Exhale to the local, to our local fresh water drinking supply.

Inhale to Earth Mother.
Exhale to Sky Father.

Inhale to seven generations yet to come.
Exhale to this moment, to this time of change and transformation.

Inhale yes, yes, yes. Yes we can take the next step our path.
Exhale thank you, thank you, thank you…

Find a variation of child's pose that works for you.
Take seven slow conscious rhythmic breaths.

Basic Core Practice for Health and Well-Being

Basic Core Practice - Corpse Pose Variation
Shavasana: shava = corpse and asana = pose in Sanskrit

Connect to the embodied soul at the core of your being.

Center yourself. In total stillness and silence, close your eyes and look within. Connect to your Inner Teacher-Healer-Guide.

Exhale and renew your individual spirit. Inhale through your nose, soften your forehead and connect to the infinite spirit. A spirit without a body is a ghost. A body without a spirit is a corpse. Exhale to the navel and feel anchored to the earth. Inhale to your heart and feel lifted. Exhale from the top of the head to the soles of the feet. Inhale from the soles of the feet to the top of the head. We activate and strengthen and then relax and lengthen the muscles in the abdomen and lower back, making our posture stable and comfortable.

Therapeutic Hatha Yoga connects body, mind and breath

To empower the core, lengthen the spine and connect to the divine.

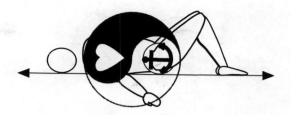

Feel the dynamic stillness of the posture.
Inhale from the soles of the feet to the top of the head.
Exhale from the top of the head to the soles of the feel.

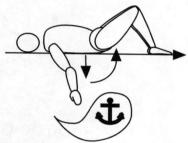

R$_X$ ∿∿∿∿∿ Daily

Inhale to the heart. Draw the breath down to the navel, to the pubic bone. Feel the tailbone on the floor and an arch in the low back. Exhale to the navel, the navel to the spine and the spine to the floor and lightly tuck the tailbone. Exhale and feel anchored to the earth.

If it is difficult for someone to consciously press their lower back onto the floor, they often have back pain and weak core abdominal muscles.

Basic Core Practice - Fish Pose
Matsyasana • matsya = fish

In a certain sense, fish were the first creatures to have a core for they were the first creatures to have a spine and a central nervous system encased in bone,

Experience your spine by gently pressing your head and tailbone on the floor as you exhale. Inhale and float your heart.

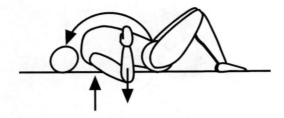

Lift the shoulder blades off the ground by pushing down on the elbows and contracting the muscles behind the heart. Arching the spine, bend the head backwards and place the crown of the head on the floor, creating an arch between the head and the tailbone.

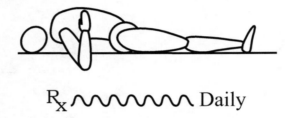

R̶x̶ ∿∿∿∿∿ Daily

Basic Core Practice - Bridge Pose
Setu Bandhasana setu = bridge, bandha = support,

The breath is the bridge between heart and head, body and mind.

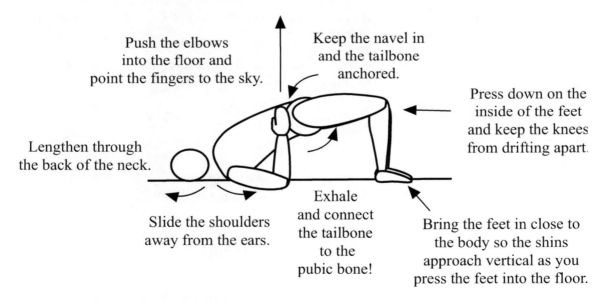

Push the elbows into the floor and point the fingers to the sky.

Keep the navel in and the tailbone anchored.

Press down on the inside of the feet and keep the knees from drifting apart.

Lengthen through the back of the neck.

Slide the shoulders away from the ears.

Exhale and connect the tailbone to the pubic bone!

Bring the feet in close to the body so the shins approach vertical as you press the feet into the floor.

Inhale and expand the heart cavity and lengthen the back of your head.
Exhale and feel the muscles around the hip sockets and buttocks tighten.
Take a deep inhalation, a pause, a deep exhalation and another pause.

R̶x̶ ∿∿∿∿∿ Daily

Basic Core Practice - Leg Extensions Variations
Urdhva Prasarita Padasana
urdhva = raised or elevated, prasarita = extended, pada = foot or leg

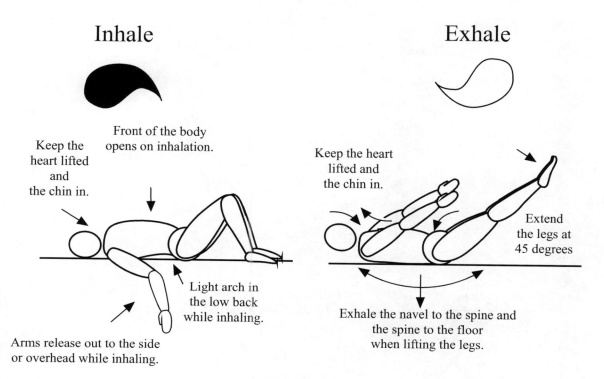

Inhale

Keep the heart lifted and the chin in.

Front of the body opens on inhalation.

Light arch in the low back while inhaling.

Arms release out to the side or overhead while inhaling.

Exhale

Keep the heart lifted and the chin in.

Extend the legs at 45 degrees

Exhale the navel to the spine and the spine to the floor when lifting the legs.

Repeat for seven breaths.

Leg extensions are ideal for integrating movement and breath and building abdominal strength. Bend your knees if your legs and abdominals are not yet strong enough to keep your low back on the floor while you exhale and straighten your legs.

In order to flatten the back, and not stress the low back muscles while lifting the legs many people have to bend both knees at first and then with practice straightening the legs.

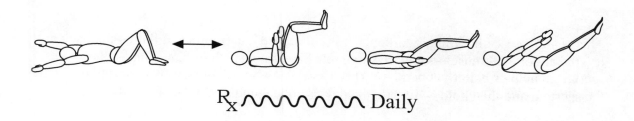

R̲x ᗰᗰᗰᗰᗰ Daily

Practice holding this posture for seven conscious breaths.

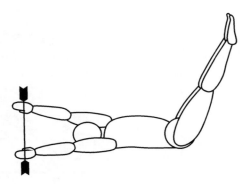

For a more challenging variation, lock the thumbs together or hold a strap to stabilize the arms and shoulders to further help contract the rib cage.

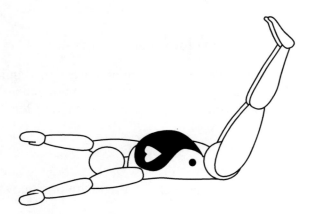

Hold the navel in as you inhale to the heart for seven breaths.

This is an intense abdominal workout. It is so intense that in order to flatten the back and use the abdominal muscles only, most people have to place their hands under their sacrum to help or better yet bend the knees and elbow to establish a firm ground through the sacrum, and then hold it. Exhale the navel to the spine and the spine to the floor.

Basic Core Practice - Reclining Butterfly
Supta Konasana: supta = lying down, kon = angle

Inhale and feel the front of the body open from the collar bones all the way to the pubic bone. Exhale to the navel and lessen the arch in the lower back.

Open the legs as if they were butterfly wings and lightly press the soles of the feet together.

Slide the shoulder blades down the back opening the chest.

Inhale and feel an arch in the low back.

Inhale and feel the pelvic floor expanding and pressing the tailbone into the floor.

Inhale and be soft like a flower petal glowing in the moonlignt. Invite and draw the breath in seven times.

Basic Core Practice - Happy Baby or Dead Bug
Apanasana: apana = out-breath or downward breath

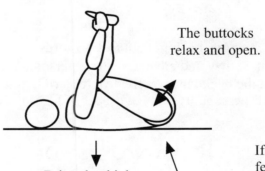

The buttocks relax and open.

Lengthen out through the back of the neck. If the chin juts up and the head tilts back arching the neck, you may place a folded blanket under the head.

Bring the thighs toward the chest.

The low back releases.

If you cannot reach your feet, hold onto the shins.

Lengthen your exhalations and feel the pelvic diaphragm contract. This is an excellent pose to relieve low back tension.

R$_X$  Daily

Basic Core Practice - Cat and Dog Tilts
Balancing Between Being A Cool Cat and Hot Dog
Bidalasana: bidal = cat

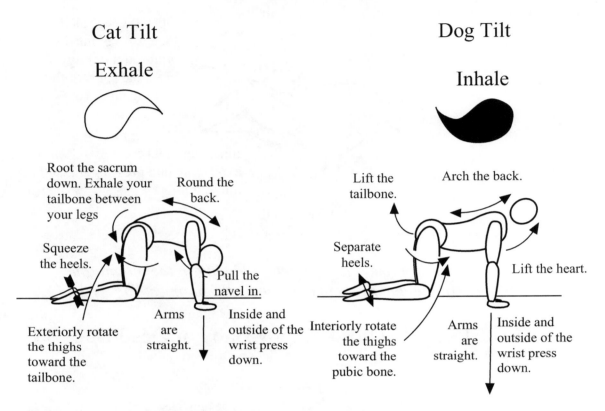

There is always a psychological component to a posture. Too much arch in the low back tends to create an open, showy and adventuresome personality, a 'hot dog' personality. Too much rounding in the back tends to create a reserved, quiet and withdrawn personality, a 'cool cat' personality. Which aspect of life do you need more of to make yourself whole.

R_X  Daily

Find a balance, a neutral pelvis and a plumb line running through your middle ear, shoulder and hip.
Find a balance between being a 'hot dog' and a 'cool cat'.

156

Basic Core Practice - The Relaxing Crocodile

Makarasana: makara = crocodile

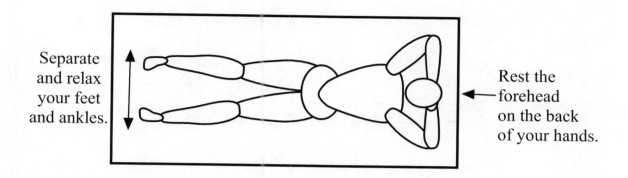

Separate and relax your feet and ankles.

Rest the forehead on the back of your hands.

Let go of any fear or worry.

Lay with your belly flat on the floor. Snuggle your brow point snuggle into the back of your hand and let go of any tension on your brow. Let go of any worry. Let go of any fear. Open your third eye chakra and let creative solutions flow through you.

Inhale to the heart and feel the ribcage pressing into the floor and then draw the inhalation down into the abdomen and feel the belly expand on the floor like a crocodile. As the belly expands onto the floor feel a relax response and a slight arch in the low back. Let the breath flow freely through you.

Inhale and soften your forehead. Exhale and let go of any stress or tension. Repeat until you feel relaxed

Basic Core Practice - The Alert Crocodile

Makarasana: makara = crocodile
Focus on rooting the tailbone down
and anchoring the pelvis to the floor.

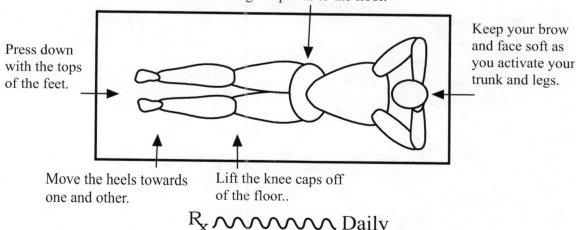

Press down with the tops of the feet.

Keep your brow and face soft as you activate your trunk and legs.

Move the heels towards one and other.

Lift the knee caps off of the floor..

Rx ∿∿∿∿∿ Daily

Basic Core Practice - Locust Postures Variations

Shalabahasana: shalaba = locust or grasshopper

Exhale and press down with the feet, pelvis and arms.

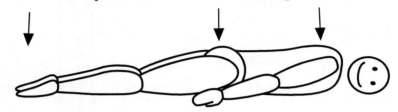

Straighten the arms and slide the shoulder blades down the back.

Lengthen the back of the neck.

Gaze up through the brow.

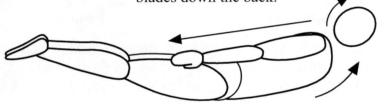

Inhale and lift the heart and the legs.
Hold the pose for 7 smooth rhythmic breaths.
Turn the head to the other side and exhale down.
Practice restful awareness for 7 breaths.
Inhale and lift and hold for 7 breaths again.

To help lift the legs, place a folded blanket under the hips.

To help strengthen the mid-back place a folded blanket under the chest.

R$_X$ 〰〰〰〰 Daily

Basic Core Practice - Cobra Pose Variations

Bhujanasana: bhujanga = snake or serpent

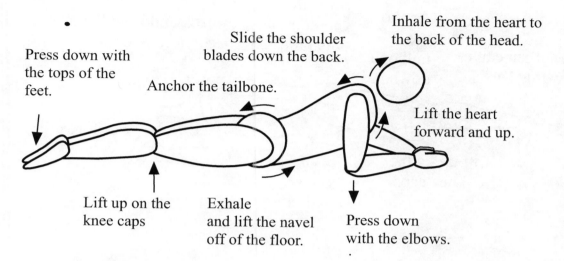

-

Press down with
the tops of the
feet.

Slide the shoulder
blades down the back.

Anchor the tailbone.

Inhale from the heart to
the back of the head.

Lift the heart
forward and up.

Lift up on the
knee caps

Exhale
and lift the navel
off of the floor.

Press down
with the elbows.

Create dynamic tension in the breath, holding the heart lifted as you
exhale and the navel in and anchored as you inhale. Take seven breaths
with dynamic tension and then one deep breath with
a deep pause at the bottom of the exhalation.

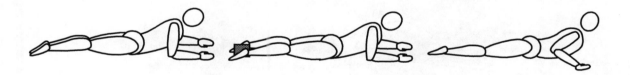

There are many ways to practice. Press a block between your feet.
Hold the arms close to the body and lift your elbows off of the floor.

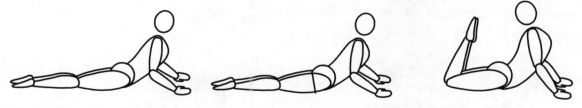

Lift the heart higher, and yet keep the pelvis anchored to the floor. Strap your thighs
together for more awareness and support in the hip sockets. For an intense low back
contraction bend your knees and bring your feet towards your forehead.

R$_x$ ∿∿∿∿∿ Daily

Basic Core Practice - Plank Pose Variations
Chaturanga Dandasana: Chatur = four, anga = limb, Danda = staff

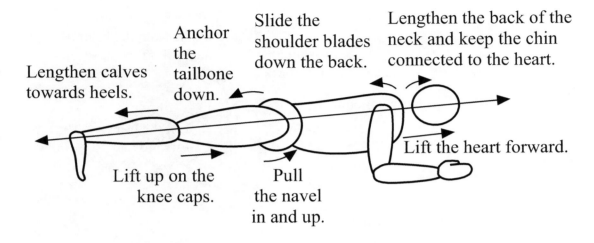

Lengthen calves towards heels.

Anchor the tailbone down.

Slide the shoulder blades down the back.

Lengthen the back of the neck and keep the chin connected to the heart.

Lift up on the knee caps.

Pull the navel in and up.

Lift the heart forward.

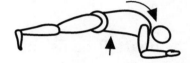

Bringing the navel in too much will round the upper back, slide the shoulders forward and concave the hearty cavity.

Bringing the heart to much forward can pinch the low back and cause the tailbone to lift.

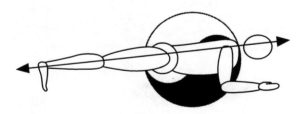

R$_x$ ∿∿∿∿∿ Daily

Plank pose is a balancing act. Stabilize the spine in a neutral position by holding the navel in and the heart lifted, thus avoiding too much arching of the lower back and too much rounding out of the upper back.

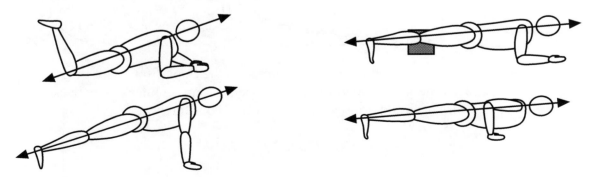

Standing Postures Reflect How We Walk and Walking Is One Of The Best Medicines.
When Standing Facing Forward, Sideways or Twisted, Stand As If You Were About To Step Forward and Walk.

Actively-yield
pushing off from the big toe,
and then root your weight back
onto outer heel.

Yield-actively
onto the outyer edge of the front heel,
and then roll your weight 15 degrees inward
onto the big toe.

In all asymetrical standing postures the hip of the back leg is in a cat tilt, rooting down and forward.

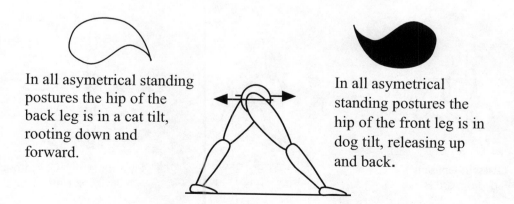

In all asymetrical standing postures the hip of the front leg is in dog tilt, releasing up and back.

All Standing Postures are Grounded and Lifted Through The Mind∞Body Infinity Loop.

Virabhandrasana II
Hero/Heroin II

Parsvakonasan
Extended Angel

Trikonsasana
riangle

Ardha Chandrasana
Half Moon

Virabhandrasana I
Hero/Heroine I

Virabhandrasana III
Hero/Heroine III

Parsvotttanasana
Side Forward Bend

Parivrtta Trikonasana
Twisting Triangle

Parivrtta Ardha Chandrasana
Twisting Half Moon

R$_X$〜〜〜〜〜 Daily

Basic Core Practice - Hero II - Warrior II

Virabhadrasana II *Vira* = hero, heroine, warrior, *bhadra* = auspicious, friend

The head is level with the tip of nose below the middle ear, the chin in and the back of the neck long.

Reach backwards as well as foreward, so that the shoulders are over the hips.

Gaze out to the horizon.

Shoulder blades slide down the back.

Bend the knee so that the shin is 90 degrees and the thigh approaches parallel to the ground.

Turn the rear foot in. Stretch the calf towards the heel.

Lift up on the thigh.

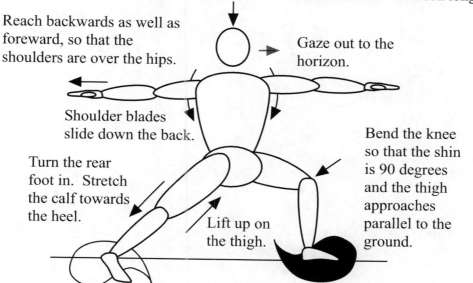

Actively-Yielding Cat Tilt for the rear leg and hip, while pressing down with the big toe to the heel.

Yield-Activily Dog Tilt for the front leg and hip, while yielding into the front heel to the big toe.

Careful not to let the shoulders, neck and chin tense up as you extend out through the arms.

Bending the elbows and turning the palms up will help relax the shoulders down away from the ears.

R~x~ 〰〰〰 Daily

Keep the Heart Lifted and the Tailbone and Sacrum Anchored

In All Standing Postures

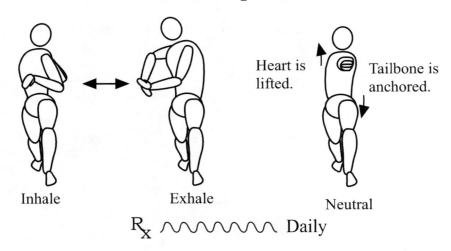

Heart is lifted.

Tailbone is anchored.

Inhale · Exhale · Neutral

R$_x$ ∿∿∿∿ Daily

Basic Core Practice - Plow Pose Variations
Halasana • hala = plow

Palms on the small of the back. Ball of the feet or tops of the feet can be on the floor.

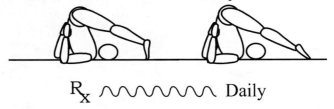

R$_x$ ∿∿∿∿ Daily

Interlace the fingers behind the back.
Rock side to side and get up higher on the shoulders.

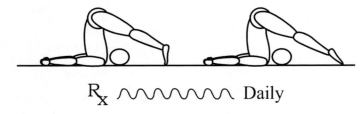

R$_x$ ∿∿∿∿ Daily

For tight shoulders extend the arms down and out.

164

If you are having trouble keeping your legs overhead, use a wall or window ledge for the toes to hold onto. Pressing the heels against the wall is a great stretch.

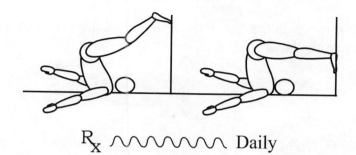

R$_x$ ∿∿∿∿∿∿ Daily

Long delicate, tight or injured necks

might try a couple of folded blankets or yoga mats under the shoulders

to take some pressure off of the neck.

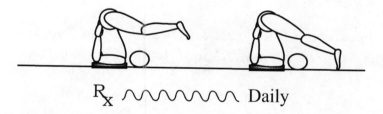

R$_x$ ∿∿∿∿∿ Daily

If There Is No Way To Get Your Legs Up And Over,

Put Your Feet On A Chair Or The Wall.

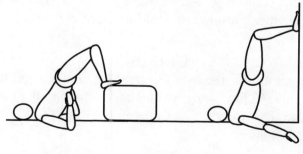

R$_x$ ∿∿∿∿∿ Daily

Roll Slowly Down, One Vertebra At A Time.

Basic Core Practice - Corpse or Restful Awareness Pose
Shavasana: shava = corpse and asana = pose in Sanskrit

The Setup

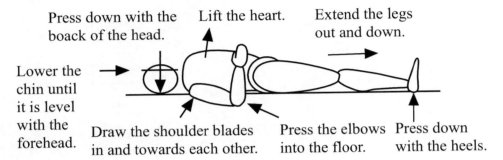

Press down with the boack of the head.

Lift the heart.

Extend the legs out and down.

Lower the chin until it is level with the forehead.

Draw the shoulder blades in and towards each other.

Press the elbows into the floor.

Press down with the heels.

Release, Relax, Renew, Restore, Rejuvenate

Roll the palms open.

Rlease the forarms down and out to the side

Fold the hands across the lower abdomen.

Quiet The Body, Quiet The Breath Quiet The Mind.
Connect To The Embodied Soul At The Core Of Your Being.

R$_x$ ∿∿∿∿∿ Daily

Let the skin on your body relax. Focus on the soles of your feet and notice how relaxed they already are. Let the skin on your chest drape over your shoulders and down to the floor. Let the skin on your palms pool to the center of your hand. Let the skin on your forehead melt away from your brow. Let the light of consciousness shine through you renewing, restoring and rejuvenating you. Hold for several minutes.

Careful!

While standing, it is common for the upper back to be rounded and the head forward. In shavasana, this results in the chin tilting up and back pinching the back of the neck and the head being disconnected from the rest of the body.

Head separated from heart.

Head unlevel.

Neck pinching.

The Solution

Place a small block or a folded blanket under the head so the chin comfortably drops below the forehead.

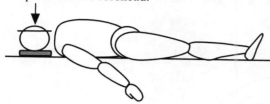

Place a couple of folded blankets under the head.

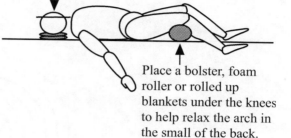

Place a bolster, foam roller or rolled up blankets under the knees to help relax the arch in the small of the back.

R$_X$ 〜〜〜〜〜〜 Daily

More Restful Awareness Variations

Eye cushions are welcome.

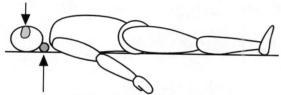

A small foam roller or a tightly rolled up towel at the base of the skull helps release neck tension.

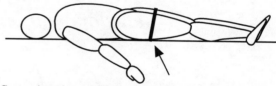

Strapping the thighs together is helpful for people with hip pain. It prevents the legs from turning out too much, which can irritate the hip socket. It also helps the legs fully extend and relax.

Restful Awareness Variations with Yoga Blocks

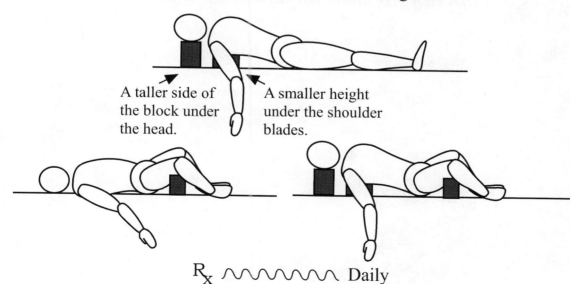

A taller side of the block under the head.

A smaller height under the shoulder blades.

R$_X$ 〜〜〜〜〜〜 Daily

Healing Is A Process

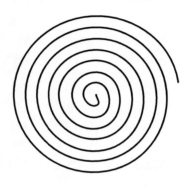

Conscious healing is a path of awareness, growth, development and transformation.

R$_x$ ∿∿∿∿∿∿∿ Daily

Your path in life is changing. The issues that are important to us unfold and transform over time. There are evolving stages to both development and healing in our lives.

Closing Invocation

A closing ritual is important for your health and well-being for several reasons. First of all, it reminds you that yoga is about skillful living and meditation in action. We want to carry our personal practice into our daily lives. Secondly we want to do this safely. A good practice will alter your body and consciousness. I know of a half a dozen times when people have left my class, got in their car and had an automobile accident in the parking lot. One person did this twice! I released that I was being irresponsible to end the class without being sure that everybody was fully awake and present before I said good-bye and *namaste (the Self that is me honors the Self that is you).* So I started having people clap their hands together to be sure everyone was fully present.

Come into a comfortable seated position with the palms facing up or down.

Bring your palms together. Experience the union, the oneness that is yoga.

Exhale your palms together. Inhale for three Aums.

To keep you safe on your path, clap your hand together once.

Rub your palms vigorously together. Create friction, heat and Light.

Place that in front of your eyes and nourish your visions and intentions for health and well-being for yourself, friends and family, and the planet.

Bring your palms together.

Thank you for sharing your energy and presence.

Namaste

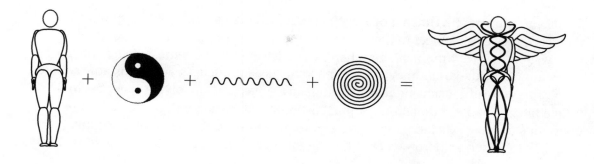

Stress and Anxiety

Take a Deep Breath

The popular expression, take a deep breath has many subtle meanings, though generally it implies that someone, who is mentally-emotionally stressed, take a large inhalation and then exhale and calm themselves. To take a deep breath also implies a prescription to take a different, more profound view of the moment. To take a deep breath is a prescription to be consciously in the present moment, not fearing the future or regretting the past. To take a deep breath connotes that our breath is connected to the bottomless and unfathomable source of being, of deep space consciousness. To take a deep breath is to expand, invite and be open to a different path of action and being.

1. Take a deep inhalation and expand the heart cavity.

2. Hold a brief pause-stillness-space, connect to your Inner Teacher-Healer-Guide and the infinite possibilities of creativity, love and wisdom in every moment.

3. Without collapsing the heart, cleanse and release all stress, anxiety, worry and fear with a deep exhalation.

To take a Therapeutic Hatha Yoga deep breath is to take a conscious deep inhalation to the heart, pause, reconnect to the Divine, to the infinite possibilities of creativity, love and wisdom in every moment, and then exhale letting go of all stress and anxiety. Extending the exhalation increases your awareness and focuses your consciousness to help calm yourself, cleansing and releasing any stress and anxiety. It is easiest to do this with a pursed-lipped exhalation. A pursed-lipped exhalation will make you more conscious of your exhalation and give you more control over the breath. Simply purse your lips together, as if you where blowing through a straw, and blow your stress away.

Shallow Breathing

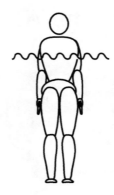

Shallow breathing often like panting and typically done with the mouth unconsciously open, creating a stress response in the body. Shallow breathing utilizes only superficial portions of the ribs and chest diaphragm. Shallow breathing does not fill you to the top, engaging the throat diaphragm or empty you to the bottom, engaging the pelvic diaphragm.

Deep Breathing

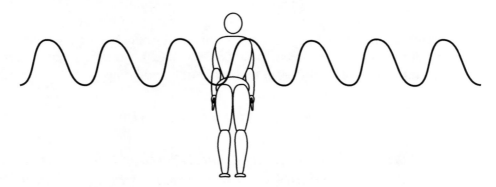

Deep breathing is different from shallow breathing. Deep breathing is more than belly breathing. Deep breathing does not bloat the belly, filling the abdominal cavity beyond the bottom ribs on inhalation, and does not collapse the chest cavity on exhalation. Deep breathing is full diaphragmatic breathing, utilizing all three diaphragms of the throat, chest and pelvis. Deep breathing is inhaling to the top, middle and bottom diaphragms and exhaling from the bottom, middle and top diaphragms. Deep breathing is conscious rhythmic breathing.

The Relaxing Crocodile

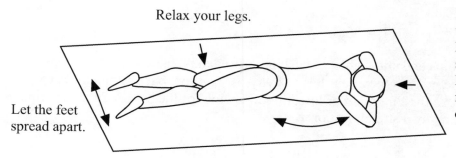

Relax your legs.

Rest the forehead on the back of your hands. Inhale and soften your forehead. Let go of any tension in your brow. Let go of any fear or worry.

Let the feet spread apart.

Practice Slow Deep Conscious Rhythmic Breathing.

We have a somatic nervous system for regulating conscious actions and an autonomic nervous system responsible for regulating the body's unconscious actions. The autonomic nervous system has two divisions, parasympathetic and sympathetic. The parasympathetic nervous system responsible for the body's relaxation response, also referred to as the "rest and digest" response. By contrast, the sympathetic nervous system regulates our "fight or flight" response. A parasympathetic relaxation response can be activated by breathing slowed for about five to seven breaths a minute, instead of the average breathing rates of about 12 to 18 breaths a minute.

The vagus nerve is a parasympathetic nerve, which runs from the stem of the brain to the abdomen and is easily stimulated in Relaxing Crocodile posture. The vagus nerve releases several different chemicals, including acetylcholine, a neurotransmitter that acts as an anti-inflammatory and slows down digestion and the heart rate.

The Yawn Reflex

Yawning or the yawn reflex is a coordinated muscular arousal reflex, mediated by the brain stem. A yawn is a sequence of events that begins with a deep inhalation, a pause-stillness-space and ends with an exhalation concurrent with a strong contraction of the mouth, throat, eyes and face. Yawns have a deep four to eight second pause-stillness-space of integration of body, mind and breath. The yawn reflex is a coordinated movement of thoracic muscles, throat and chest diaphragms, and palate.

Yawning is good for the brain. If you are a little stressed, anxious or 'hot headed' yawning can help. Yawning calms and cools down the brain. Research has shown that yawning works as a natural thermostat, conveying cool air to the roof palate. Yawning is connected with increased levels of neurotransmitters, neuropeptides proteins, and certain hormones in the hypothalamus.

Clear Your Eyes And Open Your Ears To New Possibilities

The yawn reflex stimulates the eyes to tear, a parasympathetic relaxation response in the body. It has been suggested that animals in the wild yawn before they go to sleep at night to open and clear their ears so they can be alert to any sounds while they have their eyes closed.

The Yawning Yoga Pose

Lie down, lift your hips and slide a block, cushion or folded blanket under your hips. Relax the front of the body. Open your heart cavity. If your low back is pinching, try tightening the buttocks for a moment or lowering the height of the block. Take the arms overhead and create a yawn stretch response.

Inhale

The palate rises into the brain cavity and there is a tendency to move the tongue downward and to the rear of the mouth as the jaw opens wide.

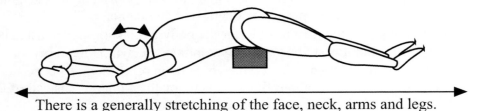

There is a generally stretching of the face, neck, arms and legs.

Hold And Create The Yawn Reflex
R$_x$ ∿∿∿∿∿ Daily

Hold the stretch.

Squeeze out a tear.

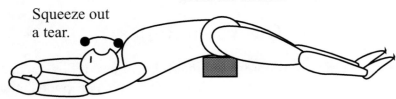

Open your ears.   Experience and intergration and a new awareness.

Feel Calm and Relaxed

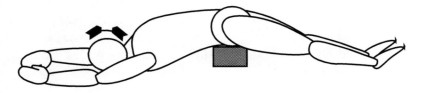

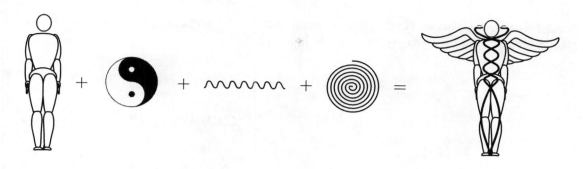

Laughter

You could say that laughter is the best medicine. Laughter creates powerful abdominal contractions, releasing and cleansing psychophysical blockages. We all need a sense of humor; we are human beings. No one is perfectly balanced. The Buddhist might say that we are all stumbling towards enlightenment. The shaman might say that it is deadly serious, but you can't take it too seriously. The world is full of glorious sadness. Life is composed of yin and yang, of humor and seriousness. The ability to laugh is essential to living a whole and happy life.

Witnessing our limits and ills through conscious breathing is often quiet challenging, emotionally and physically. Laughing helps ease our fears and lifts our hopes. Keep your heart and spirit lifted, keep laughing.

Practice Therapeutic Hatha Yoga Laughter Crunches

Laughter requires a contraction. Combining laughter with abdominal contracting postures makes it easier to laugh. Lying on the floor, looking up and not at others in the room, reduces self consciousness. Here are four therapeutic hatha yoga laugher crunches. Each has a different vibration and effect on our being.

Humming Laughter Crunches

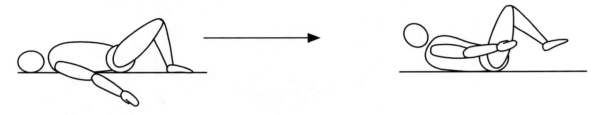

HMM, HMM, HMM, HMM, HMM, HMM, HMM

Rest on your back, breathing rhythmically, with your knees bent and feet on the floor. You can put a blanket behind your head so your chin drops down level or below your forehead. Bring your lips together and begin humming as your exhale and begin to contract the abdominal cavity, bringing your thighs in and lifting the shoulders off the floor as you reach forward. The easiest laugher is the Humming Laugher. It is like chuckling. The vibration is in the mouth. Humming laughter is soft and sweet.

HA, HA, HA Laughter Crunches

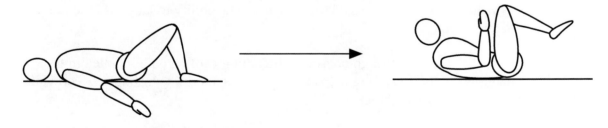

HA, HA, HA, HA, HA, HA, HA

HA, HA, HA Laughter is heartfelt laughter. It is funny land humorous laugh. It is a hearty laugh. HA, HA, HA Laugher is side splitting laughter. Rest. Gather yourself. Open your mouth and start slowly making the sound "Ha." Contract the side ribs, chest, shoulders and arms.

R_x ∿∿∿∿∿ Daily

HO, HO, HO Laughter Crunches

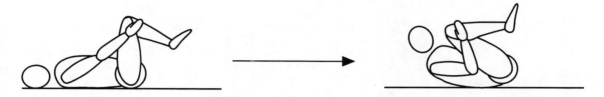

HO, HO, HO, HO, HO, HO, HO

HO, HO, HO Laughter is jolly laughter. It is a happy laugh. It is the merry laughter of Santa Claus, the original Super Shaman of the reindeer herders of Lapland, Siberia and parts near the North Pole. The HO, HO, HO Laughter involves a focused abdominal cavity contraction and is the deepest abdominal laugher crunch. Pull the knees in tight. Squeeze the laughter out by hugging the thighs in tight into your lower belly with your arms.

R~~~~~~ Daily

HE, HE, HE Laughter Crunches

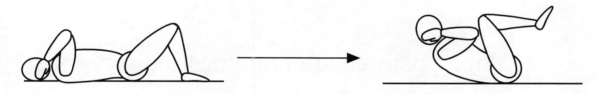

HE, HE, HE, HE, HE, HE, HE, HE

This is a heady laugh, when you think something is funny. HE, HE, HE laughter is centered in the head and the roof of the mouth. Lie down and interlace your finger behind your head. Start to exhale the sound 'he' and contract your abdominal muscles as you lift your head and bring your chin towards your chest as you begin to laugh.

R~~~~~~ Daily

Happiness is not a destination.

Happiness is a path to health and well-being.

Yoga postures are not a destination.

Yoga postures are a path

to health and well-being.

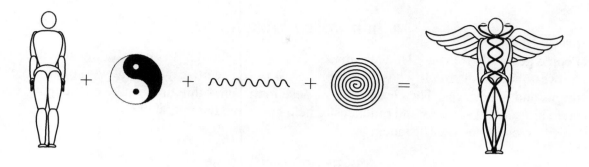

Sitting in a Chair Too Much

Modern culture is a chair-sitting culture. We sit on a dining room chair to eat, an easy chair to watch TV, a bucket seat to drive and a swivel chair to work. We have director's chairs, folding chairs and armchairs. In the bathroom, we have a throne to sit on. The word "chair" comes from Old French *chaiere* meaning 'bishop's throne' and modern French *chaire* 'pulpit or throne' more recently *chaise* from the Latin *chathedra* meaning 'seat'. The word chair has a sense of authority and power, as in a chairperson presiding over a meeting and a big office chair as a symbol of success. Nevertheless, too much sitting in a chair can create imbalances in your back, hips, shoulders and legs.

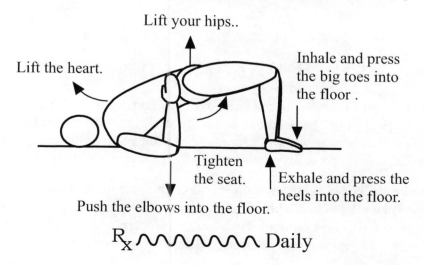

Lift your hips..

Lift the heart.

Inhale and press the big toes into the floor .

Tighten the seat.

Exhale and press the heels into the floor.

Push the elbows into the floor.

R$_x$ ∿∿∿∿∿ Daily

Chair Pose / Utkatasana

People generally translate Utkatasaana as 'chair pose', though it is literally translated as 'powerful pose' or 'mighty pose'. Holding chair pose is certainly a might workout for the thighs and quadriceps. The classical chair pose in the sun salutation can be challenging. Here are some variations and practices to help consciously integrate body, mind and breath in chair pose. Colleagues

Get Off of Your Throne

And Put Those Legs To Work

Find the variation that works best for you.

R_x  Daily

Traditional chair pose is done with the arms over head, knees bent at a 90% angle and the feet facing straight ahead. The head can be facing straight ahead or up at the thumbs. Strapping the thighs together will offer more support for holding the pose longer, keeping the knees and feet facing strait ahead and add to the interior rotation of the hips.

A block between the knees helps strengthen and align inner ligaments, tendons and muscles of the knee joint. The width of the block varies depending on how bow legged or knock-kneed one is. It is best with a foam block. Straightening the arms overhead is difficult for many. The arms can be bent in a variety of positions.

Exhale   Inhale   Exhale

R̽x ∿∿∿∿∿∿ Daily

We typically slump and round the spine into the back of the chair. Adding arm movement in Chair Pose is a powerful practice. It is difficult for many to feel and maintain a natural lumbar, low back, arch while practice Chair Pose. The following sequences can be practiced with a little to a lot of motion. What is most important is to breathe the body open, flexible and strong.

Inhale   Exhale   Inhale   Exhale

Arm Variations in Chair Pose

R̽x ∿∿∿∿∿ Daily

Some Helpful Hints
When Sitting at a Desk all Day or Sitting on an Airplane.

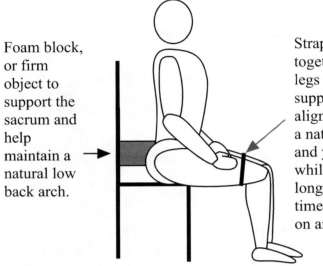

Foam block, or firm object to support the sacrum and help maintain a natural low back arch.

Strap the thighs together so the legs and hips are supported and aligned to create a natural arch and yet can relax while sitting for long periods of time at a desk or on an airplane.

Take A Squat / Malasana
Mala = Indian Rosary or Wreath Pose
Make a wreath with your arms in front of you, over-head, around one leg and behind you.

R_x ∿∿∿∿∿∿ Daily

Malasana with the feet together is difficult. Placing a rolled up yoga mat under your heels will take some stress off of the ankles. Wrapping an arm around one leg is challenging and finally, it is extremely difficult is to wrap both arms around both legs.

182

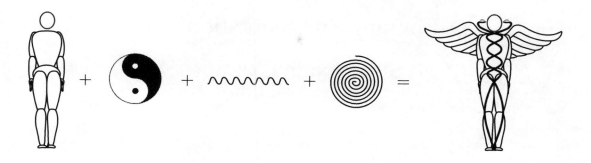

Radiance and Vitality

Sun Salutation Centered Practices

The popularized versions of power yoga, flow yoga and ashtanga yoga are based around variations of the Sun Salutation combined with rigorous standing, seated and strength postures.

Sun Salutations became popular with the teachings of Sri T. Krishnamacharia and Sivananda at the beginning of the twentieth century. Their students, B.K.S. Iyengar, Pattabhi Jois, Swami Vishnudevanada and Swami Satchidananda added to the teachings and taught the Sun Salutation to the world. The Sun Salutation was often taught as a physical activity for youth in India. Sūrya Namaskāra, salute to the sun or Sun Salutation is a phenomenon of modern day yoga that has captured our imagination.

Practice three to ten Sun Salutations of your choice and feel radiant. Add additional postures for enhanced flexibility and strength.

Lunging Sun Salutation:

Surya Namaskara

Inhale

Exhale

Inhale

Hold

Exhale

Inhale

Exhale

Inhale

Exhale

Inhale

Exhale

R$_x$ ∿∿∿∿∿ Daily

The 12 Mantras of the Sun Salutation and
The Fruit that Each Mantra Invokes

Om Mitraya Namaha
Universal Friendship

Om Ravaye Namaha
Radiance

Om Suryaya Namaha
Dispeller of Darkness

Om Bhanave Namaha
Shining Principle

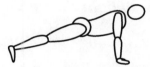

Om Khagaya Namaha
All-Pervading Through The Sky

Om Pooshne Namaha
Mystic Fire
Which Gives Strength

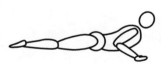

OmHiranyagarbhaya Namaha
Golden Colored One (Healing Gold)

Om Marichaye Namaha
The Pure Light of Dawn,
at the Crack Between the Worlds

Om Adityaya Namaha
Light of the Sage:
An aspect of Vishnu

Om Savitre Namaha
Light of Enlightenment

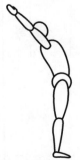

Om Arkaya Namaha
Remover of Afflictions,
Giver of Energy

Om Bhaskaraya Namaha
Brilliant Light of Intelligence

R$_x$ ∿∿∿∿∿∿∿ Daily

Sun Salutation Postures

Salutation Standing / Tadasana / Samashiti

*A Tree Can only Grow as Tall
As It's Roots Are Anchored to the Earth.*

Physical Alignment

Our first challenge to standing up straight is the rounding of our upper backs, which tends to push our heads forward, out of alignment. This is due to a wide variety of things. Physically much of our modern life is spent sitting in chairs. We sit in chairs to eat, work, drive and relax. All of this tends to round our upper backs and thrust our heads forward. Place your index finger on the inion, the shirt button size bump on the back of your head and push the button for higher consciousness with the back of your head.

Flip the switch, the inion, to light the inner light and stand up straight.

Flip the switch so your head is on your shoulders and your heart is lifted.

The Mind∞Body Infinity Loop

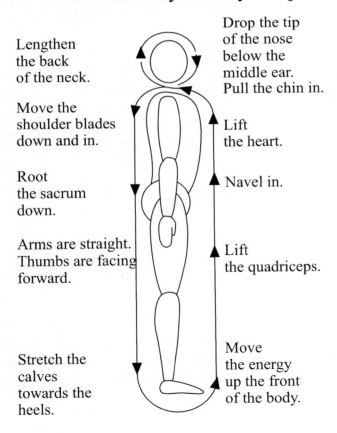

Lengthen
the back
of the neck.

Move the
shoulder blades
down and in.

Root
the sacrum
down.

Arms are straight.
Thumbs are facing
forward.

Stretch the
calves
towards the
heels.

Drop the tip
of the nose
below the
middle ear.
Pull the chin in.

Lift
the heart.

Navel in.

Lift
the quadriceps.

Move
the energy
up the front
of the body.

Achieving physical alignment is ultimately about finding the plumb line that connects you to the deep space consciousness at your core. Starting from your heels it runs up through your ankles, up through the knees, the hip sockets, pelvic floor, spine, shoulder sockets and middle ear. The middle ear is higher than the tip of your nose so the back of the neck is long and not pinched. This plumb line incorporates the natural arches in the spine so that your weight rests fluidly and evenly on the spinal vertebrae.

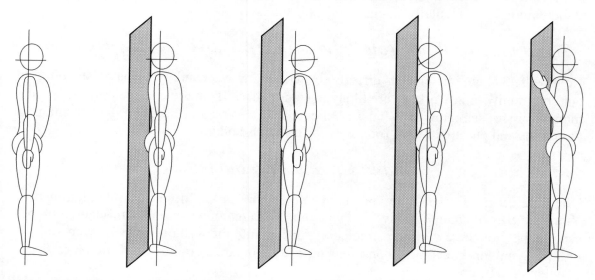

One way to determine if you are standing along the plumb line is to stand against a wall and see if you can touch the all with your heels, buttocks, shoulders and the back of the head. The majority of people have their heads are too far forward and or their upper backs are too rounded to touch the back of the head to the wall without tilting the head back out of a level position pinching the back of the neck. Bending the elbows and bringing the backs of the hands to the wall and keeping the head level is challenging

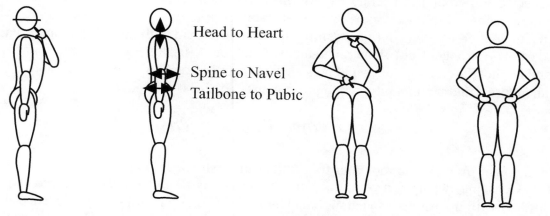

Head to Heart

Spine to Navel
Tailbone to Pubic

Place the thumb on the sternum and the forefinger on the chin is another way to get a sense of whether the chin is level and the heart connected to the head. Place the thumb and forefinger of one hand on the upper chest, and with the other hand place the thumb in the navel and forefinger on the pubic bone to keep the heart lifted as we exhale and the navel in and connected to the spine as you inhale. Standing with the hands on the hips also creates a stable posture that is rooted and lifted.

Therapeutic Hatha Yoga Alignment: THY Alignment

As a holistic practice, Therapeutic Hatha Yoga seeks to unite the physical and the spiritual through the conscious integration of body, mind and breath. It is a holistic approach that joins your physiology and psychology. Our physical form is connected to our formless feelings, thoughts and beliefs. How we stand physically is related to how we stand emotionally, mentally, socially and spiritually.

Stand Up For What You Believe In. You have the Right To Exist.

How we feel about ourselves is directly related to how we stand. If we have 'standing' in our community or at work we are likely to stand taller. If we are confident in life we are more likely to 'stand up' for what we believe in. If we are depressed, our hearts sink into our chests and our upper back rounds even further. Stand up for your life.

Stand Up and Be Counted.

You have the right to speak and be heard. You are a spark of divine cosmic intelligence. You bear gifts of creativity, love and wisdom. You are not a small insignificant grain of sand, rather you are a divine cosmic being, woven into the web of life in an ever-unfolding universe becoming conscious of itself. You are a co-creator of life on earth. Stand up and be counted.

Stand Present Beyond Pride or Pity
For Yourself and Those Around You.

To counter feelings of pity and pride, of anxiety and separation we need to feel protected, connected and grounded. Feeling pity for others disempowers them and ignores their dividing nature. Feeling excessive pride separates us from others. While standing, activate your core, open your heart, straighten your arms and with thumbs facing forward and create a stronger field of energy in and around yourself. This way we can resonate stand by those around us. We stand present for others and ourselves when we stand without pride and without pity. Stand present, grounded and opened minded.

Stand Down To Stand Up!

Stand down! Anchor and root your feet, tailbone and shoulder blades down into the earth. Consciously lengthen your arms and shoulders down so your heart and head can effortlessly lift up. Modern social, political and media culture is full of fear, violence and war. This has a tendency to make us feel vulnerable and unsafe which further leads to the rounding of our upper back in an unconscious or subconscious effort to protect ourselves. Stand rooted to the earth and stabilize in your connection to the web of life and the family of humanity. Stand down and lower your arms and weapons. To 'stand down' is literally and figuratively to stand up for peace, life and harmony.

Salutation Raised hands

Inhale and Spiral Your Arms Overhead

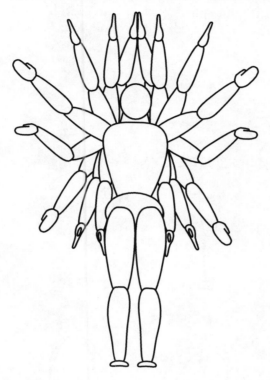

R$_X$ ∿∿∿∿∿∿∿ Daily

Visualize your arms as being the wings of the swan, *hamsa*, your spirit, your Inner Teacher-Healer-Guide, as you exhale *ham*, bring your arms by your side and then inhale *sa* and raise your arms overhead turning the palms forward and then towards one and other. Inhale the arms overhead only as far as you can keep the shoulders relaxed. Bend the elbows if needed. Exhale *ham* and lower your arms again.

Visualize the hamsa current flowing through the Mind∞Body Infinity Loop flowing through you as you raise and lower your arms.

R$_X$ ∿∿∿∿∿∿∿ Daily

Extend lines of energy out of your hands as your exhale your arms down. Inhale and remember to turn the palms forward as you spiral the arms up to the sky.

189

Salutation Forward Fold

Extend Before You Bend: Dive Forward, Out and Down.

Extend out of the hips as if your spine were a beam of light, hinge at the hips, as if they were a flashlight, as you come forward. Then round your back like a wave to reach for the ground.

Bend the knees, if needed to help extend out of the hips and low back.

Salutation Lunge

Raising the arms overhead adds an extra dimension to the inhalation.

Practice the Lunge with Movement and Breath

Exhale   Inhale

Establish a lunge. If you can, hold onto a wrist behind the back and balance, otherwise keep your hands on the floor. Inhale the arms overhead, exhale and lower the chest to the thigh and the chin towards the knee. Inhale the arms out to the side and overhead. Repeat seven times.

Salutation Plank Position

Hold the plank position with a neutral spine.

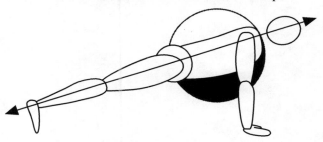

Salutation 8 Point Posture

Lower your knees, chest and chin down to the floor like an inch-worm into the 8 point posture with two feet, two knees, two hands, chest and chin touching the earth—creating the eight points of connection.

Create a small arch in the low back as you keep the hips up as you lower down.

Elbows stay by your sides.

Gaze forward for a bug's eye view of the world.

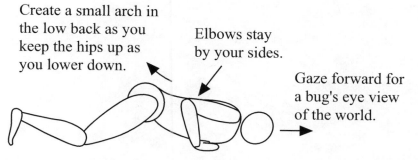

Bend the knees and elbows and lower your knees, chest and chin at the same time.

Salutation Down Dog / Adhomukha Shavanasana

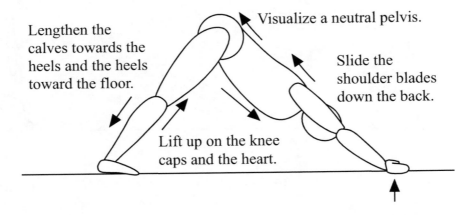

Lengthen the calves towards the heels and the heels toward the floor.

Visualize a neutral pelvis.

Slide the shoulder blades down the back.

Lift up on the knee caps and the heart.

Press down with the inside and outside of the wrist.

Variations and Preparation for Down Dog

R$_x$ ∿∿∿∿∿∿∿ Daily

Salutation Stepping Forward From Down Dog

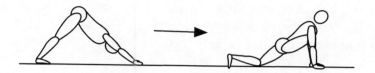

Be sure to exhale everything out first and in the pause, in the stillness, at the bottom of the exhalation step the foot forward. You can step the foot forward twice or thrice too. You can also shift the weight to one arm and lift the other in the pause at the bottom of the exhalation to step forward.

Stepping forward from Down Dog is challenging for many of us.

Try lifting one arm up before you move the rear leg up.

Practice Moving One Leg In And Out

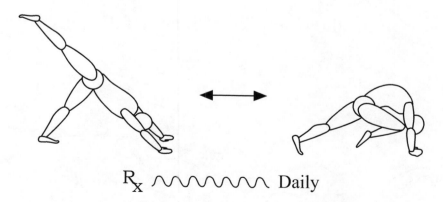

Rx ∿∿∿∿∿∿ Daily

Inhale and lift the leg back and up.

Exhale the knee forward to the touch one arm and then the other.

Salutation Up to Standing

The Spine Is Like A Ray Of Light.

The spine, like light, has wave and particle aspects. The spine is a series of waves, when you focus on the lumbar, thoracic and cervical curves. The spine is a beam of particles (photons), when you focus on a line of individual vertebrae.

You can come up to standing with a flat back, with the spine extending out of the hips like a beam of particles, or you could round up like a wave of light.

Rounding Up Like A Wave

To help extend the arms, hands and fingers out from the core commit to a hand gesture or *mudra*. Holding your thumb and forefinger together will add energy and awareness to your movement.

Extending Up Like A Beam Of Photons

'A' Series Sun Salutation

Exhale   Inhale   Exhale

Inhale   Exhale   Inhale

Exhale-Hold 5 breaths   Inhale

Exhale   Inhale   Exhale

R$_x$ ∿∿∿∿∿ Daily

'B' Series Sun Salutation

Exhale   Inhale   Exhale   Inhale

Exhale   Inhale   Exhale

Inhale   Exhale   Inhale   Exhale

Inhale   Exhale   Inhale   Exhale-Hold 5 breaths

Inhale   Exhale   Inhale   Exhale

R$_X$ ∿∿∿∿ Daily

After 3-10 Sun Salutations
Select A Posture Progression To Practice

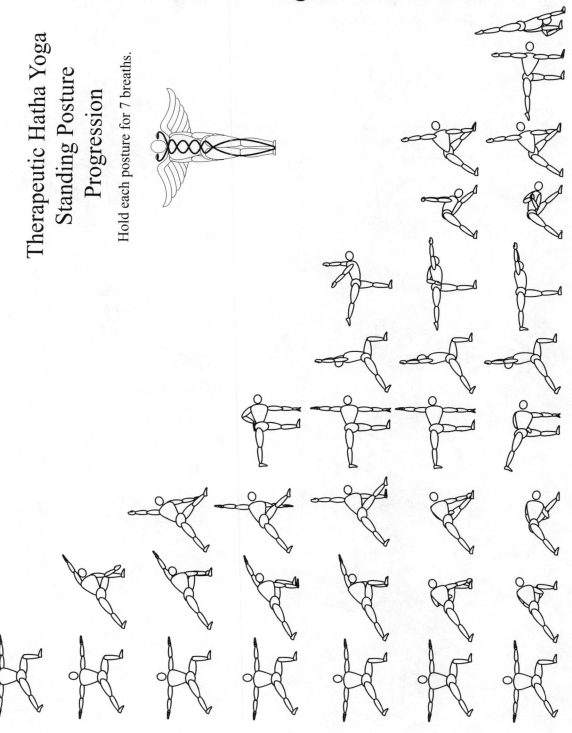

Therapeutic Hatha Yoga
Standing Posture
Progression

Hold each posture for 7 breaths.

Repeat On The Other Side

Twisting Extended Angle Progression
Parivrtta Parsvakonasana
Inhale to the heart. Exhale to the navel. Keep the navel in and inhale to the heart. Keep the heart lifted and exhale to the navel.

R~x~ ∿∿∿∿∿∿∿∿ Daily

Asymmetrical Forward Folds /Parsvotttanasana

Extended Hand to Big Toe / Utthita Hasta Padangustha

Extended Hand to Big Toe is one of the most challenging common standing postures.
Here are some ways to prepare for it.

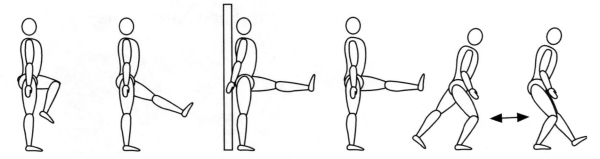

Practice balancing on one foot with one knee bent. Using the wall for balance can be helpful. Moving the extended leg back and forth while standing develops coordination, strength and balance.

Straps, chairs and tables can support you while you extend out of the posture.

Marichyasana I

Standing From Marichyasana I To Extended Hand To Foot.

Balancing on the floor, while holding onto the extended foot and then leaning forward and coming to standing is a challenging thrill.

Back Bending Progression

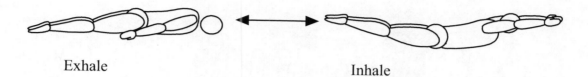

Exhale   Inhale

Salabhasana-Locust

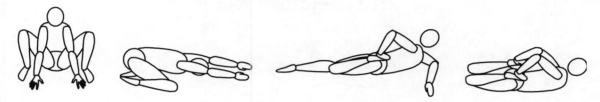

Bhekasana-Frog

Dhanurasana-Bow

Parsva Dhanurasana-Side Bow

Urdhva Dhanurasana-Upward Bow

R$_x$ 〰〰〰〰 Daily

Ustrasana-Camel Pose

Supta Vajrasana-Reclining Thunderbolt Pose

Laghu Vajrasana-Little Beautiful Thunderbolt

Kapotasana-Pigeon

Picha Mayurasama - Peacock Feather & Variations

R$_x$ ∿∿∿∿∿∿ Daily

Visvamitrasana

Vishvamitra was the name of a king long ago who had a crisis of consciousness and renounced his kingdom. He witnessed his own greed, lust, pride and anger and become a sage. At the moment of his enlightenment, he heard the famous Gayatri-mantra, which is sill chanted by Hindus world wide today.

R_x ∿∿∿∿∿∿ Daily

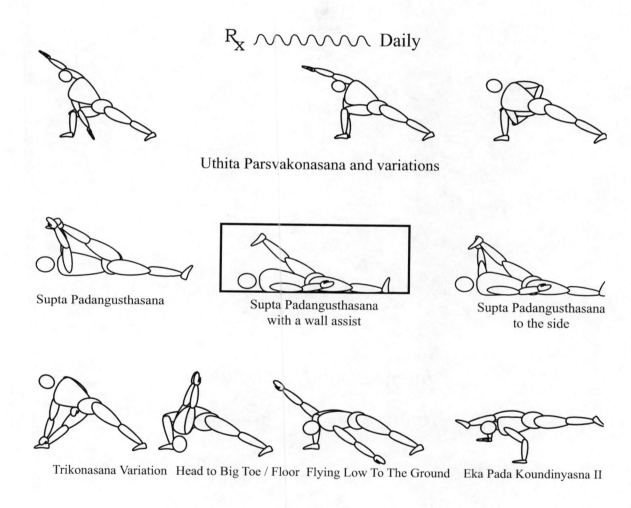

Uthita Parsvakonasana and variations

Supta Padangusthasana

Supta Padangusthasana
with a wall assist

Supta Padangusthasana
to the side

Trikonasana Variation   Head to Big Toe / Floor   Flying Low To The Ground   Eka Pada Koundinyasna II

Visvamitrasana Preparation

Visvamitrasana II

Visvamitrasana

Take A Moment for Closure at the End of Every Practice

Integrate and Acclimate

to a Higher State of Consciousness.

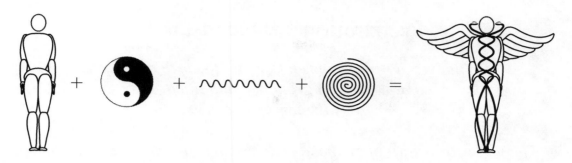

Headstand:

The Queen/King of Healing Postures

The headstand is often described as the king of yoga postures. Certainly the headstand is a fabulous pose conveying a feeling of preeminence. It is one of the easier beginner/intermediate hatha yoga postures and helps develop concentration and focus. In many respects, the headstand is the king or queen of yoga pills for every ill because it literally turns everything upside down, revitalizing the whole system. The headstand can be a bit challenging for people who are not in good physical condition. Nevertheless, many of the benefits of the headstand can be reaped completing only the preparation stages of practicing the headstand and these are accessible to most people.

The headstand is contra-indicated for people with high blood pressure, ear infections, a detached retina or serious neck issues.
If you experience pain or discomfort, stop.

Headstands reverse the flow of gravity affecting all of our tissues and organs. This helps cleanse and nourish of the body at the deepest levels. Iyengar recommends headstand as a therapeutic practice for asthma, backache, loss of memory, bronchopneumonia, chills, cold, cough, colic, colitis, constipation, diabetes, diarrhea, displacement of uterus, dysentery, eyes, flatulence, gout, halitosis, headache, heel spurs, hernia, impotency, insomnia, kidneys, liver, menstrual disorders, piles, tonsillitis, varicose veins, anemia, appendicitis and more.

Preparation for Headstand

What is your physical relationship to earth and sky?
How are you grounded and lifted?
Where is the top of your head?

The vertex or crown of the head is the topmost point of the cranium,
between your inion and nasion.
The vertex is at the center of your vortex field.

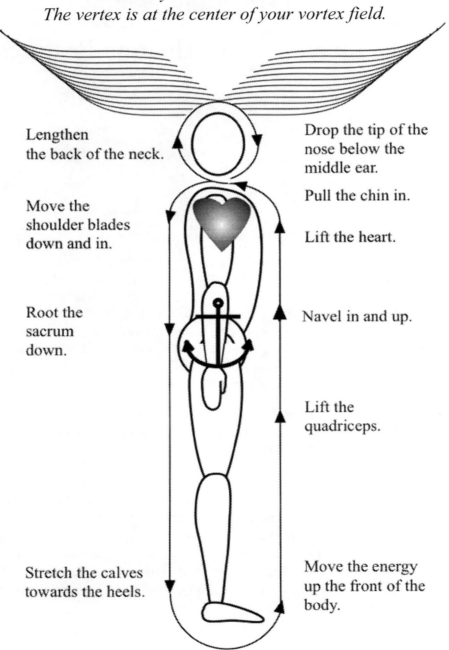

Lengthen
the back of the neck.

Move the
shoulder blades
down and in.

Root the
sacrum
down.

Stretch the calves
towards the heels.

Drop the tip of the
nose below the
middle ear.

Pull the chin in.

Lift the heart.

Navel in and up.

Lift the
quadriceps.

Move the energy
up the front of the
body.

Dynamic Tension in the Pose

All yoga postures reflect an element of dynamic tension, of being stable and comfortable, rooted and lifted, and exhaling and inhaling. People tend to hold their breath while balancing. It is only through dynamic tension and stillness can we sustain our balance. All of the elements of standing up straight are present in headstand, generally, the places where we are out of alignment or lack awareness while standing are multiplied when we invert into headstand. The most common challenge I see is lack of awareness about the relationship between the navel and the spine while inverted.

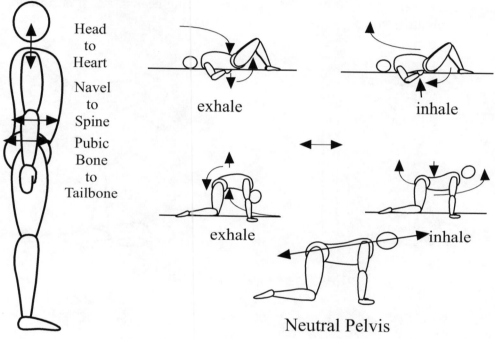

Head
to
Heart

Navel
to
Spine

Pubic
Bone
to
Tailbone

exhale

inhale

exhale

inhale

Neutral Pelvis

Holding dynamic tension between inhalations and exhalations,
with a neutral pelvis, will add stability to the pose.

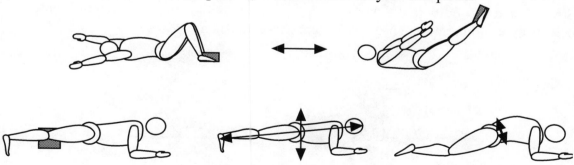

Core strengthening postures help maintain dynamic stillness while inverted.

Extend Out from the Center of Your Core

Conscious extension through the legs is required for balancing in headstand. Often the legs are waving around during headstand. Only by activating the legs and feet can we create the dynamic stillness for staying in headstand. Note: If the weight falls to outsides of your feet while standing, you will typically have challenges keeping your big toes together when upside down.

Practice extending out through the legs and feet.

People forget to extend out of their legs when practicing headstand. It is common to see legs waving about as someone goes up into headstand.

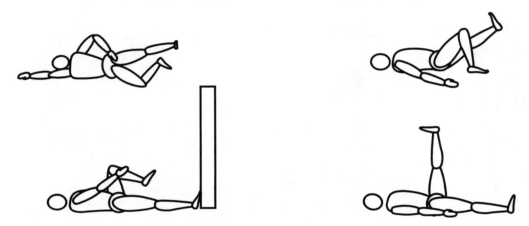

Exhale and straighten the knee.

R$_x$ ∿∿∿∿∿ Daily

Extend Out of the Shoulders

You have to push down with your arms and shoulders to get up into headstand. Your shoulders have the responsibility of holding you up, so you do not strain your neck. Strength and flexibility in the shoulder girdle are required to distribute weight evenly between your forearms and head while practicing headstand.

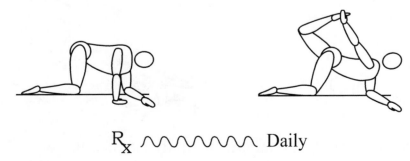

R$_x$ ∿∿∿∿∿ Daily

You Have to Be Able to Shoulder the Load To Wear the Crown.

Forearm Balances

Peacock Feather / Picha Mayurasana

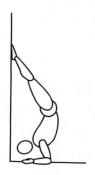 

R$_x$ ∿∿∿∿∿∿ Daily

Focus the power of the exhalation, through pursed lips or ujjayi breathing, to lift you. It is easy to start breathing through your mouth during strenuous moments. Consciously start breathing through your nose again. Be aware of holding your breath. Maintain an even dynamic tension. Many would say that it is safest to be proficient at practicing peacock pose before attempting to practice headstand. Regardless of what percentage of weight your arms and shoulders carry, an awareness of your shoulders is required.

Connect to Your Vertex and the 7th Chakra

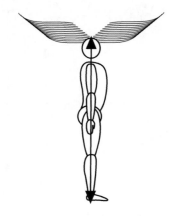

Connect to a 7th sense of Reality, a sense of Absolute Unity of Being.
Connect the individual with the infinite space of
creativity, love and wisdom.

The headstand is an ideal pose to connect to our 7th sense because as the headstand turns how we see the world upside down. Our 7th Chakra flips the notion that matter somehow creates consciousness, to the notion that consciousness somehow creates matter. Our 7th Chakra, our 7th sense, is located at the top of our cranium. Our brain and nervous system are encased in bone, and together they form the organ of perception for our 7th sense. It is a pure perception of the Divine. Feel the resonance of the timeless eternal subtle vibrations of creativity, love and wisdom in your bones during and after practicing headstand.

Feel the resonating subtle vibrations of the 7th Chakra in your bones!

Practice Connecting to Your Cranium

Can you feel where the top of your head is?

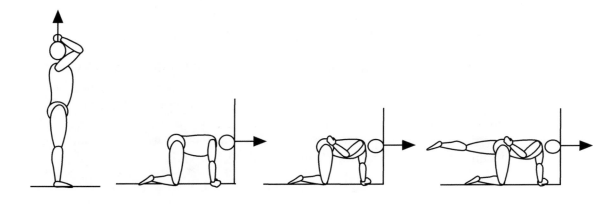

Balancing on the forearms and pressing the top of the head against a wall, while keeping the navel connected to the spine is a great way to create a strong sense of dynamic stillness.

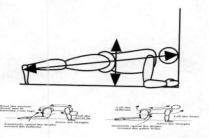

Variations On Rabbit Posture For Connecting To The Top Of The Head

R~~~~~~~~~ Daily

Create a Stable Foundation for Your Headstand

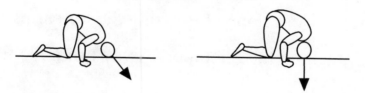

Centering the top of our heads on the floor is essential to both prevent neck stain and to align the spine. Be sure the top of the head, not the forehead, is pointing straight down on the floor.

Elbows one forearm length apart.   Make A Tripod   Place the head about 8 inches from the wall.

  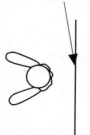

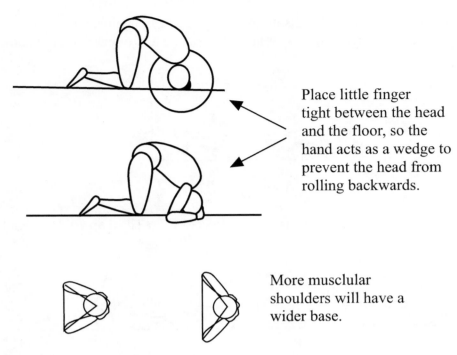

Place little finger tight between the head and the floor, so the hand acts as a wedge to prevent the head from rolling backwards.

More musclular shoulders will have a wider base.

Placing the hands, and especially the little fingers, neatly and tightly around the top of the head to create a cradle for the crown of the head. This will help prevent you from falling backward toward the wall. Arm placement is critical to establish a firm tripod base. The tendency is to have the elbows too wide. When the elbows are too wide you have less ability to balance and to resist falling forward back down to the floor.

Practice Being Conscious of Pressing the Forearms Down and Lengthening the Shoulders Away From the Ears

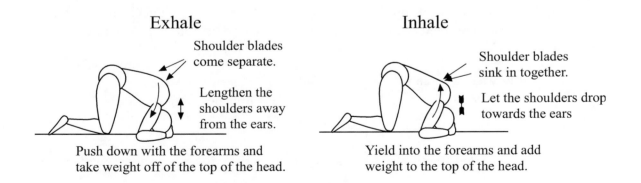

Exhale

Shoulder blades come separate.

Lengthen the shoulders away from the ears.

Push down with the forearms and take weight off of the top of the head.

Inhale

Shoulder blades sink in together.

Let the shoulders drop towards the ears

Yield into the forearms and add weight to the top of the head.

R$_x$ ∿∿∿∿∿ Daily

Be Sure the Forearms Are Pressing Down During the Headstand!

Lift Off

Lifting the feet off the floor is a coordinated movement. Ideally you are lifting off the floor or lightly jumping up with control as opposed to kicking up wildly and hoping to you will make it. With practice, the feet will stay together. Start with your elbows placed a bit too close together because when you put weight on your arms, they will spread out.

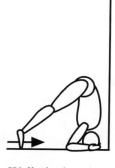

Walk the legs in toward the body as far as possible.

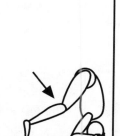

People with tight hamstrings will have to bend the knees.

Lift the feet off of the floor with as little jump up as possible.

Lift your hips and put your feet on the wall to stablize the posture.

Hold it! Balance! Breathe into a Dynamic Stillness.

Exhale and pull the navel in as you lift the feet off of the wall.

Keep your feet together and tap the wall with your toes until you can balance.

Extend the legs keeping the feet together.

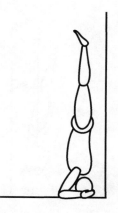

Create dynamic stillness.

The Summit

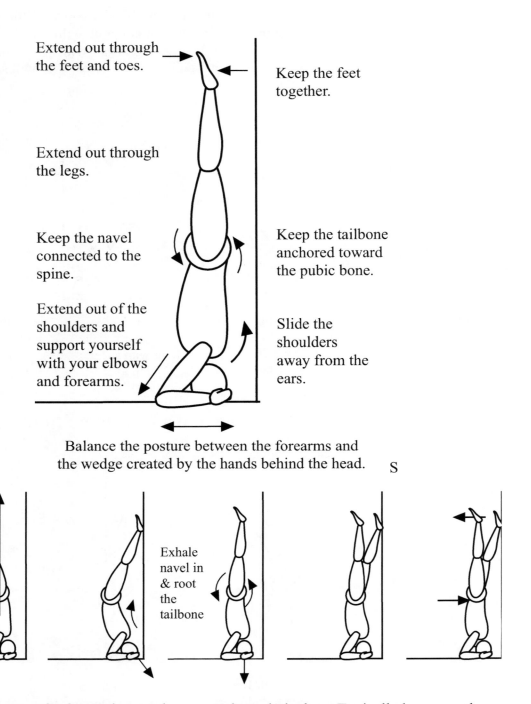

Extend out through the feet and toes.

Keep the feet together.

Extend out through the legs.

Keep the navel connected to the spine.

Keep the tailbone anchored toward the pubic bone.

Extend out of the shoulders and support yourself with your elbows and forearms.

Slide the shoulders away from the ears.

Balance the posture between the forearms and the wedge created by the hands behind the head.

S

Exhale navel in & root the tailbone

If the legs are too far forward, extend more up through the legs. Typically however, the low back and the neck are arched too much and the legs rest on the wall. If that is the case, exhale and pull in the navel and root the tailbone down to lift the legs off of the wall. It might be easier to lift one leg away from the wall first, and then slowly exhale and lift the other leg away from the wall.

The Descent

Lower on exhalation. The longer and slower the exhalation, the smoother and more even the descent will be. With practice you can come in and out of headstand with your knees together and later with your legs straight.

Counter Poses

Even if you feel no tightness or discomfort in your neck, a counter pose is highly recommended after headstand. Balancing on the head involves a lots of tiny muscles, which might still be tight, and you might not feel the stiffness for a while. Any variation of shoulder stand or plow is ideal releasing any residual compression in the neck and shoulders.

Any shoulder stand or plow pose variation is

a good counter pose to headstand.

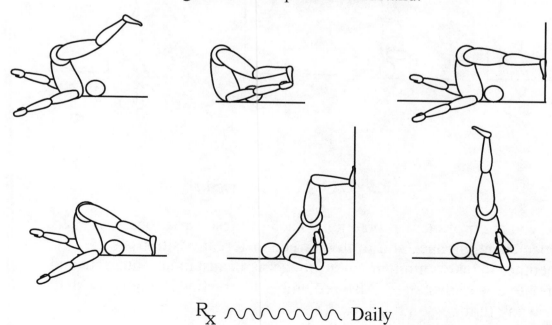

R_x ⌇⌇⌇⌇⌇⌇⌇ Daily

Different Arm and Hand Positions For Headstand

People have been taught headstand from many different sources and methodologies. Here are some of the most common hand and arm positions. The positions are shown from the most common to most difficult.

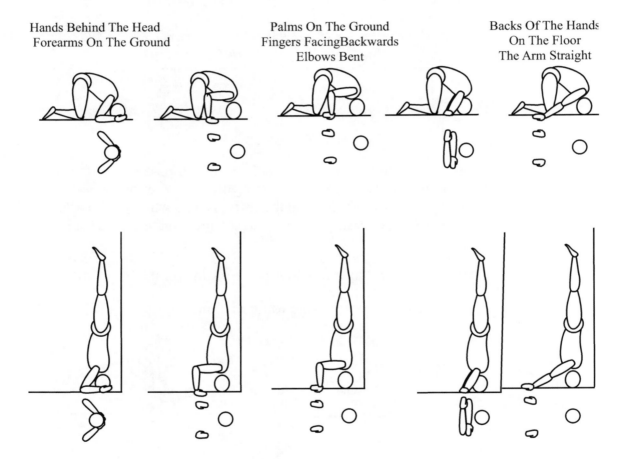

Once you are proficient at practicing each of these variations, practice changing back and forth between different positions. Remember to take a moment after practicing headstand to integrate and acclimate to a higher state. Also remember to practice a counter pose to release any tightness in the neck.

How Do You Wear Your Crown?

Actively-Yielding or Yielding-Actively.

The principle of actively-yielding and yielding-actively are examples of the play of polarities in yoga. Yoga is a wisdom philosophy. Healing THYself is a dance in the gray zone between activating and yielding.

The Vertex Headstand and the Bregma Headstand

The vertex headstand is most popular in recent years. However, if you look at older pictures of hatha yoga you see more bregma headstands. I notice that people tend to start with a vertex headstand for a few breaths, though if people hold a headstand for a minute or longer the posture becomes more willowy and flowing like a bregma headstand.

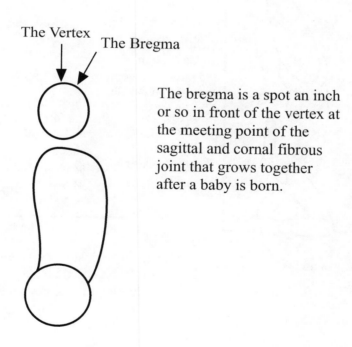

The Vertex

The Bregma

The bregma is a spot an inch or so in front of the vertex at the meeting point of the sagittal and cornal fibrous joint that grows together after a baby is born.

In the bregma headstand, the pelvis will come forward a bit as the lower back arches more than in a crown or vertex headstand. The low back is a little more relaxed in a bregma headstand and in a way a bit more stable. A vertex headstand is a bit tippy as it is a bit more rigid. In the bregma headstand you are still pushing down with the arms though the low back and abdominals can relax.

The Bregma
yielding/actively

The Vertex
actively/yielding

Relax the abomin as you inhale and acitvate the ribs and lower abdomin as you exhale.

Yield in the low back as you inhale and push into the arms as you exhale.

Careful not to yeild too much into the back of the neck.

Keep the feet together.

Extend out through the legs.

Keep the navel connected to the spine.

Push down on the forearms and slide the shoulders away from the ears.

Push with your elbows and forearms and balance with the back muscles.

Balance the posture between the forearms and top of the head stabalized by the wedge created by the little finger behind the head.

Sitting in meditation after headstand is very powerful.

Different Leg Positions for Headstand

Have plenty of open space around you, and especially in front of you because you want to be able to roll forwards onto your back without landing on or crashing into something.

Lotus Headstand Sequence

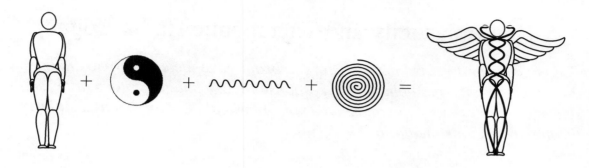

Pain and Suffering

To a nurse, pain is often broadly defined as whatever the experiencing person says it is, existing whenever they say it does. Pain is a subjective experience.

Pain Is Like Static Electricity

Pain is like static interference in your body and nervous system. Static electricity is an imbalance of electric charges. The charge remains until it is able to move away by means of another electric current or electrical discharge. It is called static electricity in contrast to current electricity, which flows through wires. Static electricity is neutralized when grounded to the earth or brought close to a large electrical conductor like a horse in therapeutic horseback riding or a tree for tree hugging. Connect to mula bandha and ground your pain.

Exhale For As Long As You Can, Hold A Deep Pause. Ground, Let Go Of And Release Your Pain.

Neuroplasticity and Therapeutic Hatha Yoga

The neurons and neural networks of the brain have the capacity to change their connections and behavior in response to new images, information and sensory stimulation. You can reduce your physical pain and mental suffering through conscious mediation!

Meditation and A Focused and Steady Mind Can Shut Off Pain Signals to the Brain.

If you are focused on a principle, project or relationship, if you have a strong sense of purpose or calling in life, interruptions, provocations and distractions like pain cannot take root.
Meditate, breathe and focus on your path. Believe in yourself.

R_x  Daily

Watching Yourself Watch Yourself,
Perceive and Observe Your Pain.
Transform Your Pain Into Information and
Transform Information into Awareness.

Create an image, an intention or visualization for your pain. Give your Inner Teacher-Healer-Guide a moment of stillness to create an image, a scene or picture of what is happening. This will give your metaphysical mind something to work with beyond saying it hurts or it is painful. There is a message in the pain. Bring your conscious yoga practice to witness it and transform pain into information and information into awareness. If the pain feels like it is cutting you with a steal knife, create an image of a knife with a dull blade made of candle wax. Transform acid rain into soft morning dew. Transform shards of glass into soft sand. Visualizations can help you relax into a restful state of awareness for practicing conscious breathing.

Your Mind Is an Antenna for Receiving and Transmitting.

Practice self-observation without judgment.
All too often we are too quick to judge our sensations
as simply bad or painful.
Listen to them.
There is a message in the pain.
Decipher it.
Transform it.
The observer effects the observed.

Inhale and observe your pain.
Exhale and transform and release your pain.

R_x ∿∿∿∿∿ Daily

Inhalations create nerve impulses to the brain inducing a signal and receiving a message. Inhale and witness your pain. Exhalations create nerve impulses from the brain radiating a signal and sending a message. Exhale a healing message to transform and release your pain. Conscious breathing can help transform pain into awareness and awareness into a deeper consciousness. Therapeutic Hatha Yoga is about witnessing and consciously breathing our pain, not backing away from it, nor smashing into it. Witnessing our pain, disease or sorrow with breath awareness creates a foundation for conscious healing.

There is a message in your pain.
Breathe into it.
Tune it in.
Know it. Be it. Love it. Release it.
Transform pain into information
And transform information into awareness.

Visualize your pain.
Describe your pain as an image or picture.
Look for vivid meaningful images.
Still your mind. In the deep pause-stillness-space
allow a new image of health and well-being to emerge.

Meditate and resonate with this new image.

Yoga Is Deliverance from Pain and Suffering

Do you believe in suffering?

Do you believe that you have to suffer to get ahead?
Are you willing to let others suffer to get ahead?
Are you willing to let nature suffer to get ahead?
Be conscious of believing in the divine nature of all beings and all things.

Pain and suffering in the yoga tradition are linked to sense of separation and an ignorance of the eternal dimensions of our being. We suffer when we are disconnected from the source of creativity, love and wisdom. Awaken the divine consciousness in you. There is no need to worship suffering or material things. Suffering is the result of a sense of separation, alienation and loneliness. It stems from a skin en-capsulated ego sense of self, a separate and isolated ME sense of self.

Remember, ME…
Is just a WE turned upside down.

Meditate on the 'we' in 'me' in 'you.' Meditate on the unity of life and being. Focus on celebrating your relationships with others and nature, rather than feelings of suffering and loneliness.

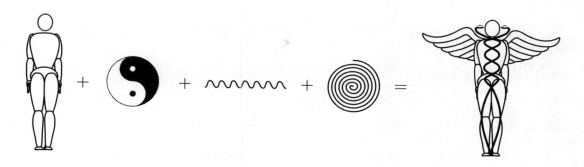

Damaging and Toxic Emotions

Clearing Toxic Emotions and Affirming the Rights the Chakras,

The Psycho-Physical Vortexes of the Body

Clear your mind and body of perceptions and feelings that are damaging and distorted such as fear, guilt, shame, sadness, lying, illusion and attachment. Clear the body of emotional psycho-physical trauma and drama associated with these emotions. Our posture and health are affected and effected by unexpressed and or internalized emotional psychological trauma and drama. Inhale and open yourself to your inalienable rights to be human.

What the Mind Suppresses the Body Expresses!

Conscious breathing can help release damaging and toxic emotions and behaviors. It can strengthen the throat diaphragm and clear your mind. For example we might tend to lie if we feel that we do not have the right to speak and be heard. We might feel sad if we feel we do not have the right to love and to be loved. We might not take action if we feel we will be shamed. Clear your emotions and behaviors of toxic beliefs, and know your rights.

Release Toxic Emotions and Subconscious Beliefs That Cloud Your Vision and Suppress Your Well-Being

Exhale 'aaaaaa' with your mouth open as if you were going to steam up eyeglasses. Release your toxic emotions. Exhale the fog of negative emotions and release any emotions or feelings that distorts and hinders your health and well-being. Exhale and squeeze out any toxic emotions as you squeeze your little finger and ring finger into a tight fist, like you could turn coal into a diamond from the pressure of your little finger. Inhale through your nose, nourishing yourself. Inhale and open to new confidence as you open the hand from the thumb and forefinger. Open your hand, heart and head to emotional and physical well-being.

Exhale and release the fog of fear and anxiety.
Inhale your right to exist and be.

Exhale and release the fog of guilt.
Inhale your right to feel good and virtuous.

Exhale and release the fog of shame.
Inhale your right to act and to do.

Exhale and release the fog of grief and sadness.
Inhale your right to love and be loved.

Exhale and release the fog of lying.
Inhale your right to speak and be heard.

Exhale and release the fog of illusion.
Inhale your right to see clearly without bias.

Exhale and release the fog of attachment.
Inhale your right to know and share joy and happiness.

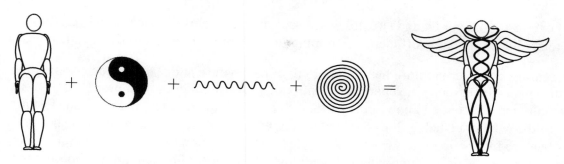

The Feet, Heels, Toes and Soles

Plantar Fasciitis, Bunions, Supination and Pronation

Therapeutic Hatha Yoga has proven very effective in helping dozens of people with plantar faciitis. Plantar fascia is a thin band of fascia (connective tissue) that covers the sole of the foot from the heel to the base of the toes. Plantar faciitis generally refers to a tear or micro-tears in the fascia and the resulting inflammation. It is most often experienced as a dull aching, very sharp or burning pain on the heel or the sole of the foot. Plantar faciitis is the most common cause of heel pain. Its exact cause is not clear. It does, however, seem associated with a number of factors: running, standing for long periods of time, weight gain and weak foot muscles.

Traditional medical treatment for plantar faciitis treatments, include: ice, rest, physical therapy, massage, orthotics, ultra sound, a boot to sleep in and cortisone shots. And while these protocols have proven helpful to my clients and students, they generally have offered only periodic or partial relief from their chronic pain and discomfort. Even good traditional physical therapy for plantar faciitis ordinarily only addresses stretching and strengthening the sole of the foot without any broader connection to the rest of the body, let alone one's breath, feelings, thoughts and beliefs.

The physical therapy my clients have received to strengthen the sole of the foot, prior to my yoga program, have included opening and closing the foot like a fist, gripping a marble with the toes, rolling a round object under the foot, and grabbing and pulling a weighted towel along the floor. Stretching has commonly consisted of flexing the sole of the foot by pressing the toes up the wall in the corner with the heel on the floor and lengthening the calf and back of the leg while leaning into the wall. These are excellent foot exercises to contract and stretch the muscles in the sole of the foot. However, these exercises have proven insufficient in stopping the chronic pain endured by my students.

For centuries Western culture has sought to dominate nature and stand victorious over the earth. This is the essence of separation. I think this sort of belief system promotes a psychological tendency to pound the earth with our feet. In the yoga tradition, our feet are part of the Muladra Chakra, the root chakra, representing the earth element in the body. Our feet are for rooting into the earth. They are our connection to the earth. A true connection, however, is a two-way path and just as the roots of a plant are for holding the plant stable, root are for drawing water and nourishment up from the earth. Energetically, we too are connected to the earth and the earth is connected to us. The soles of our feet need to draw energy up from the earth as well as stand on it.

In order to stand up, we need to root down. The sacrum roots down while the back of the head lifts. The big toes press down while the heart lifts. The soles of the feet can be compared to a trampoline. The inner and outer arches on the sides of the feet, as well as the transverse arch of our feet act like the springs of a trampoline, and plantar fascia stretches out like the fabric of a trampoline. This trampoline. Plantar Faciitis is like a tear in the fabric of the trampoline. To patch the fabric of sole of the foot we need to increase circulation.

To observe the soles of the feet, practice a Supported Bridge Pose and feel the soles of the feet resting on the floor. Roll the weight to the inside and outside, and front and back of their feet and get an inner sense of the position and relative weight on the feet. Visualize the life force (*prana*), rising up through the body on each inhalation and on each exhalation (*apana*) anchoring the body to the earth. Every breath we take can both lift us and ground us, creating a union of opposites, the wisdom of paradox, moving us beyond separation and duality into unity and yoga.

Connect to Your Soles

Bridge Pose / Setu Bandasana

Feel the sole of the foot and all of the toes on the floor. Shift the weight to the heels and press down with the big toe and lift the other four toes. Fully articulate feet can lower only the little toe to join the big toe on the floor.

Coordination and Flexibility in the Soles, Toes, Feet and Ankles

What sort of strength, coordination and flexibility do you have in your foot? These simple movements with the feet immediately let us know how connected or disconnected we are from our feet. *Practice this 7x daily for a great yoga pill for the feet.*

Open the sole of the foot, stretching the hamstrings and the calves as we pull the toes back of the extended leg.

Exhale and push with the ball of the foot while spreading the toes.

Grap onto an imaginary towel or marble with the toes.

Inhale and pull back with the toes grabbing and making a fist with the foot.

Tight hips and or hamstrings might prevent you from sitting comfortably on the floor . You can practice sitting on a cushion or chair.

Rx ∿∿∿∿ Daily

A Simple Way To Stretch and Strengthen the Ankles and Feet

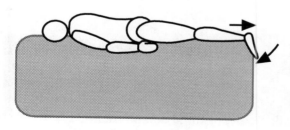

Exhale

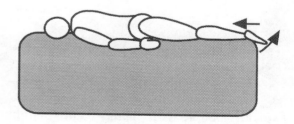

Inhale

Exhale and vigorously press the top of the foot onto the bed. Inhale and firmly point the feet. It is more powerful than it looks, especially if you count out six and nine as you inhale and exhale.

Supported Extended Foot Postures

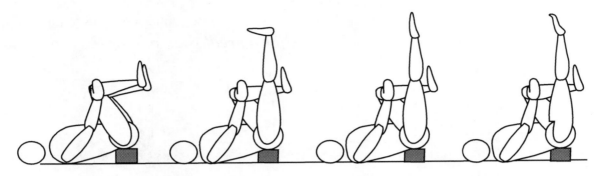

Exhale-Hug The Knees   Exhale-Flex The Foot   Inhale-Point The Toe   Press The Ball

Rotate the foot   Spread legs apart and extend out through the feet.

R$_x$ $\sim\!\sim\!\sim\!\sim\!\sim\!\sim$ Daily

Child's Pose / Balasana bah-lah-sah-nah, bala=child

Techniques: Sit on heels and lower the torso onto the thighs. Let the head rest on the floor, hands or block. Emphasize the exhalation and rooting the sacrum down.

Typically people with plantar faciitis will have difficulty sitting back on their heels in Child's Pose because of tightness in the ankles, knees hips and or thighs. Therefore, one can use a rolled-up yoga mat under the ankles and or a blanket under the seat as needed. Witness the soles of the feet with breath awareness. Supporting the head with a block or bolster will help lower the buttocks to the heels as well. Holding and breathing into this posture is important to create a deep healing.

Inhale   Exhale

R$_x$ ∿∿∿∿ Daily

The ability to exhale and contract the sole of the foot so that the toe nails come off of the floor, even a little, will sensationally strengthen the foot.

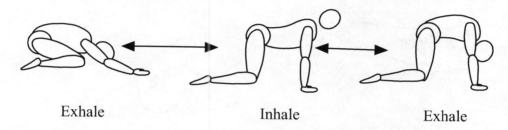

Exhale   Inhale   Exhale

Focus on Pointing Your Toes

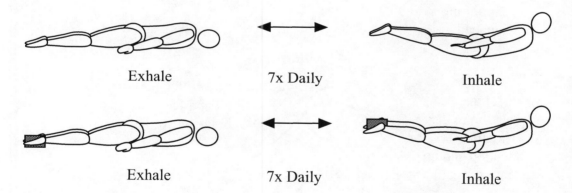

Exhale   7x Daily   Inhale

Exhale   7x Daily   Inhale

Take Your Foot To The Wall

The resistance from a wall offers a clear focal point for connecting to the heel, ball of the foot and the big toe without bearing full weight on it.

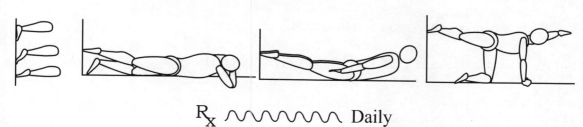

R$_x$ ∿∿∿∿ Daily

One-Foot Downward Dog

Eka Pada Adhomukha Shavanasana

Ideally the calves and the Achilles tendon are stretched out before attempting any serious contraction of the sole of the foot because the calf will contract and cramp before the foot. One Foot Downward Dog is an good posture to stretch the calf, ankle and heel.

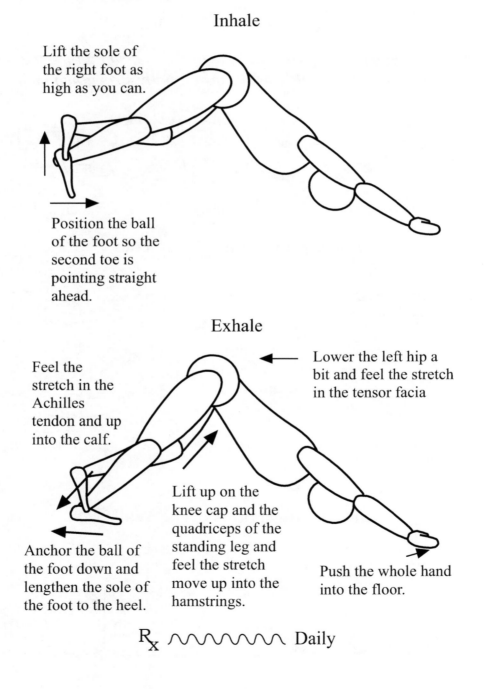

Inhale

Lift the sole of the right foot as high as you can.

Position the ball of the foot so the second toe is pointing straight ahead.

Exhale

Feel the stretch in the Achilles tendon and up into the calf.

Lower the left hip a bit and feel the stretch in the tensor facia

Lift up on the knee cap and the quadriceps of the standing leg and feel the stretch move up into the hamstrings.

Anchor the ball of the foot down and lengthen the sole of the foot to the heel.

Push the whole hand into the floor.

R̩x ∿∿∿∿∿ Daily

Yoga Marble Therapy

Therapeutic Hatha Yoga "Yoga Marble Therapy" has had the single most profound effect on contracting the sole of the foot and reducing the pain of plantar faciitis. It is quite common to build foot flexibility and strength by having people pick up a marble with their toes. However, many of my clients have been able to pick up marbles with their feet and yet not reduce their pain. Yoga Marble Therapy is different in that you incorporate more of your entire being with the marble. Instead of just contracting the toes around the marble, you pick up the marble while contracting the entire backside in a posture like Supported Bridge Pose, which creates an arch in the lumbar spine.

While in a Supported Bridge Pose, place a marble or something like it under the toes and grab it. Since marbles roll around the room, I use flat glass beads (like those used in flower vases). If it is too difficult to grab a glass bead, you can place a rubber band around the toes to help keep the focus on contracting the foot. Then, extend the leg upward with the foot holding onto the glass bead. Exhale and flex the foot and then inhale and point it. Repeat this several times. Next, with the foot pointed, lower the extended leg to the floor bending the knee slightly so the big toe touches the floor before the heel does. Hold and tap the big toe on the floor, keeping the leg as straight as possible.

For most people, the sole of the foot will cramp holding onto a bead in a Supported Bridge Pose. Virtually everyone's feet will cramp if they touch the big toe to the floor and practice straightening the leg a little and the pointing the foot with more effort. The soles of the foot will typically cramp so intensely that people often drop their marble to the floor. Learning how to take the foot to the point of cramping has been **THE** turning point for people with plantar haciitis. That **"Eureka!"** moment happens the first time the soles of people's feet cramp because they have found a direct connection to their problem. Strengthening the arches of the sole of the foot so cramping does not occur so easily is the first step to being free of pain from plantar faciitis.

Supported One Legged Bridge Pose Holding Onto A Marble With The Toes

Eka Pada Salamba Setu Bandhasana

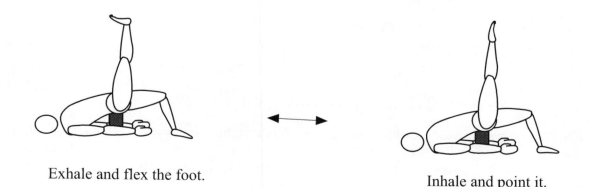

Exhale and flex the foot.   Inhale and point it.

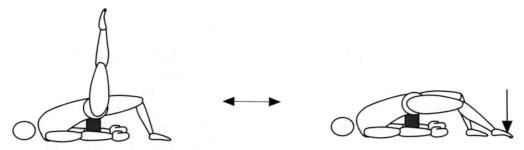

Next, with the foot pointed, lower the extended leg to the floor bending the knee slightly so the big toe touches the floor before the heel does. Hold and tap the big toe on the floor, keeping the leg as straight as possible.

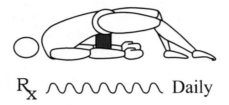

R_x ∿∿∿∿∿ Daily

Extend the leg as much as possible while keeping the heel and the big toe on the floor and then press down with the big toe and lift the heel. The soles of the feet will typically cramp so intensely that people will drop their marble or glass beads from their toes as their foot cramps. The cramping will diminish as the sole of the foot gets stronger.

Touch the big toe and the heel to the floor and then lift only the heel. **Eureka!**

Here is another great way to contract the sole of the foot near the heel. Lying on your back, keep the toe pointed, as you inhale and lift one leg up and exhale it down.

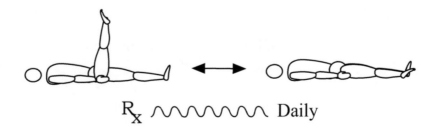

R_x ∿∿∿∿∿ Daily

Calf and Achilles Wall Stretches

After the sole of the foot, calf and back of the leg have been contracted, stretch them out with these postures. Pressing against a wall is a good calf stretch and lifting the front foot will increase it dramatically. Inhale top, middle, bottom, and exhale bottom, middle, top seven times.

Stretching the soles of the feet by pressing the ball of the foot in a corner and having the toes go up the wall is a common therapy for plantar faciitis. However, it has limited ability to stretch the fascia of the heel of the foot as the knee cannot go forward beyond the wall. Placing a block against the wall allows for a deeper knee and ankle bend. Standing on one foot and bending the knee is extremely effective for stretching the fascia over the heel, up the Achilles tendon and into the soleus and the gastrocnemius muscles of the calf. 7x Daily.

    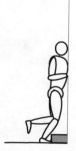

There are many excellent ways to stretch the calf and heel of the foot

R$_x$ ∿∿∿∿∿∿ Daily

Squatting Posture

Squatting is a good stretch for the ankles, yet can be challenging for the knees and thighs. If you are not be able to lower the hips below the knees rest your elbows on your thighs and lower to the best of your ability.

R$_x$ ∿∿∿∿∿∿ Daily

Holding On To The Kitchen Sink Squat

R$_x$ ∿∿∿∿∿∿ Daily

Standing on One Foot

Tree Pose Variations / Vrkshasana

Balancing on one foot is a great way to feel the lifting and grounding muscles of the foot. It is a great way to strengthen the feet, ankles, toes and soles. Tree Pose or Vrkshasana, is a classic pose to "root" down.

Tree Pose Variations Vrkshasana

All balancing postures strengthen the feet.

R$_x$ ∿∿∿∿∿∿ Daily

The soles of the feet are for rooting into the earth. Roots are for pulling water and nourishment up from the earth, as well as offering stability to the plant. Grounding is not only connecting you to the earth it is also the earth connecting to you. Our heels are pounding the pavement and our big toes are hardly touching the ground.

Connect the big toes to the earth's electromagnetic field.

Point The Toes
Practice keeping the toes pointed as you breathe.

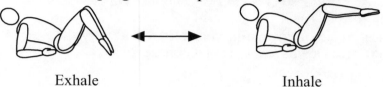

Exhale   Inhale

Rx 〰〰〰〰 Daily

Inhale and visualize are drinking water through a straw in the sole of your foot. Inhale and nourish yourself through the sole of your foot.

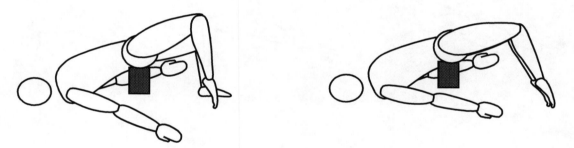

Our big toes are often frozen and no longer point. Practice bridge pose first with the toes of one foot curled under. Then try it with both feet. Slowly stretch the toe tendons and ligaments that have tightened.

Rx 〰〰〰〰 Daily

Ardha-Bhekasana - Half-Frog Pose / Bhekasana - Frog Pose / Assisted Frog

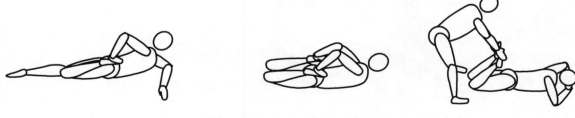

Rx 〰〰〰〰 Daily

Marble Grasshopper Pose

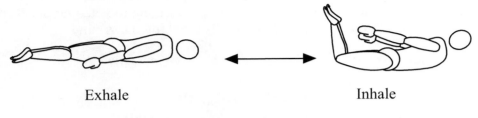

Exhale   Inhale

R$_x$ ∿∿∿∿∿ Daily

You can practice holding a marble in your toes to intensify the pose. Your hamstrings might cramp. Practice Down Dog as a counter pose.

Balancing on the Ball of the Foot

Practice exhaling down the back of the rear leg.

R$_x$ ∿∿∿∿∿ Daily

Super Toes

Roll over the toes onto the top of the feet.

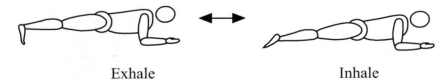

Exhale   Inhale

Once you are comfortable doing this,

practice rolling over your toes going from Down Dog to Up Dog.

Wide Foot Stance / Prasarita Padottanasana

  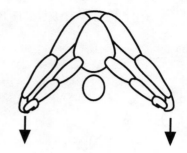

Separate the feet one-leg length or more. Point the feet straight ahead to the best of your ability. Rotate the thighs inward. Hold onto the big toes with your forefinger and index finger and lift the heart forward and up, without jutting the chin forward pinching the back of the neck. Most people will have to bend their knees to hold onto the big toes.

Wide Downward Dog

 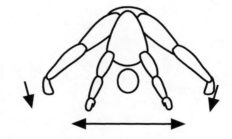

R~x~ ∿∿∿∿∿ Daily

Separate the feet one-leg length or more. Point the feet straight ahead to the best of your ability. Rotate the thighs inward. Walk the hands forward until the heels come up off of the ground, turn the feet totally straight ahead if not a bit pigeon toed. Separate your hands and further lengthen the upper back. Anchor the big toes down and lengthen from the soles of the feet to the top of the head.

THY Yoga Pill for Bunions

Bunions, hallux valgus is a condition which affects the joint at the base of the big toe, which almost never occurs in cultures that do not wear shoes. Japan rarely had bunions before Western footwear was introduced. Virtually every web site about bunions attributed them in part to improperly fitting shoes, though the language used might say the big toe is "forced into position" or "environmental factors." Some say bunions are genetically inherited, though it might be more relevant to say that someone inherited a style of shoe from their parents. However, biomechanically, if the second toe is longer than the big toe there is a tendency for the second toe to bear more weight and big toe to drift out of alignment towards the second toe creating a bunion.

Strap the Big Toes Together

Ground, Strengthen and Keep The Big Toes Facing Forward

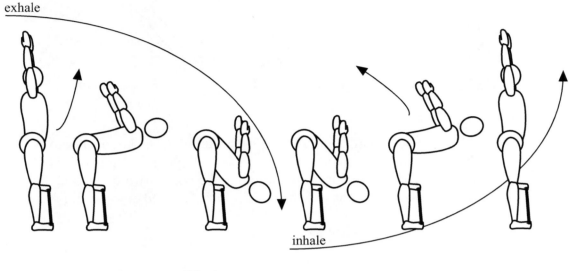

exhale

inhale

R~~x~~ ∿∿∿∿∿∿ Daily

THY Yoga Pill for Supination

The soles of the feet are our connection to the earth, yet most of us wear shoes the majority of our lives. So often it is the pounding of the earth through running, walking and standing on hard surfaces in shoes that restricts the sole of the foot from contracting. Typically, we are not engaging the arches of the sole of the foot when we walk or stand because our shoes are too tight. I recommend wearing shoes with a toe box wide enough so that we can curl our toes down, creating an arch in the sole of the foot, while still wearing our shoes. This way we can practice creating an arch in our foot all day. Taking our shoes off and walking barefoot in nature or rolling a ball under our feet will awaken and strengthen the sole of the foot. Of course by curling the toes and pointing the foot away and you can begin to connect the sole of the foot to the calf through the heel.

Bio-mechanically, we can describe walking as a heel to toe event in which the weight starts at outside of the heel and rolls in about 15 degrees so that the entire foot makes complete contact with the ground and then pushing off from the front of the foot. This is referred to as normal pronation while walking and running.

People with plantar faciitis are typically cautioned against excessive pronation of the foot. Excessive pronation limits the full range of movement of the ankle and foot and often results in collapsed arches.

Supination is the result of the foot not rolling inwardly enough and the body weight isn't transferred hardly at all to the big toe, forcing the outside of the foot to carry the stress. All too often, our big toes hardly engage the ground and push off as we walk. This is in part due to improper tight fitting shoes, which encourage hard heel strikes and squeezes the big toes.

Inhale, and Engage the Big Toe and the Arch of the Foot

Careful! Bend the front knee slowly.

R$_X$ 〰〰〰〰 Daily

Strapping the big toe helps to further strengthen the big toe.

Keep the heart lifted, keep extending out of the inside of the foot.

Therapeutic Hatha Yoga for Pronation

R$_X$ 〰〰〰〰 Daily

Wrap the foot with one end of a strap so that the strap pulls from the outside edge of the foot and high on the arch near the ankle. This helps spread energy out through the toes and keeps the foot from excessively rolling inward or pronating. Exhale and extend out through the outside of the heel and foot.

Bridge Pose with Block for Ankles

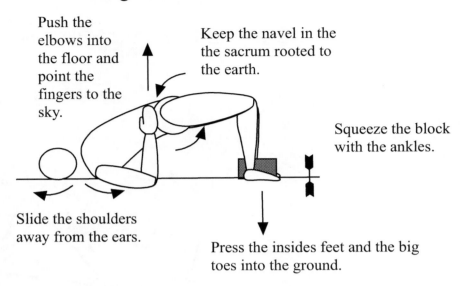

Push the elbows into the floor and point the fingers to the sky.

Keep the navel in the the sacrum rooted to the earth.

Squeeze the block with the ankles.

Slide the shoulders away from the ears.

Press the insides feet and the big toes into the ground.

R$_x$ ∿∿∿∿∿∿ Daily

One Legged Reversed Plank Pose / Eka Pada Purvottanasana

R$_x$ ∿∿∿∿∿ Daily

Place your hands on the floor with the fingers facing forward to the best of your ability. (Fingers facing backward creates hyperextension through the elbow.) With one leg bent and the other partly extended, lift the hips and straighten the extended leg to the best of your ability pressing the foot flat onto the floor.

Then press down with the big toe, see if you can lift the heel.   **Eureka!**

The Reversed Plank Pose / Purvottanasana

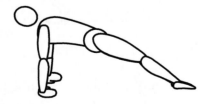

This is a challenging yet excellent pose for strengthening the backside of the body.

The Big Toe Pulling an Elastic Band
Variation of Reversed Plank Pose

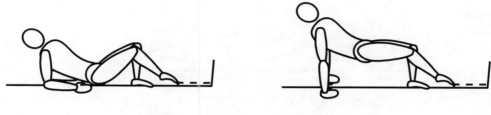

R$_X$ ∿∿∿∿∿∿ Daily

This is a powerful plantar fascia strengthening practice.

Attach an elastic band or something stretchy

to something stable like the leg of a couch or desk.

Three Legged Table

Catuspadapitham / Four Footed Pose is difficult for tight shoulders or wrists.

Reclining Thunderbolt Variations Supta Vajrasana / Virasana

These are intense postures. Start by sitting on a block with one leg underneath you.
Support yourself with your hand as you exhale and sit with just one leg underneath you.

Reclining Thunderbolt

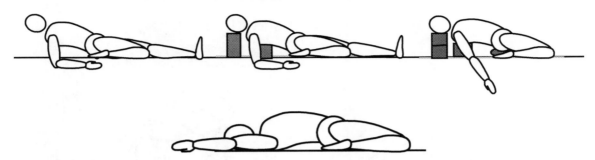

Caution: Not recommended for bad knees or a tight lower back. Supta Vajrasana and its supported variations are excellent postures, but too challenging for most, to improve the arch in the sole of the foot. These postures are ideal for inhaling through the soles of the feet.

Exiting Reclining Thunderbolt / Supta Vajrasana

After staying in any one of these poses for 7 breaths or longer slowly come out of the pose. The knees will need a delicate exit and a good knee straightening counter pose like down dog.

Thunderbolt / Vajrasana Posture Variations

Vajra means both thunderbolt and diamond.

Inhale   Exhale

R~~~~ Daily

Exhale and contract the toes and sole of the foot and lift your toenails off of the floor to the best of your ability. Placing a rolled up yoga mat or foam tubing under the ankles will make it easier to contract the sole of the foot and lift your toenails off of the floor. Place your hands on your legs, lap or anywhere they are comfortable and stable. Inhale from the soles of your feet to the top of your head.

Exhale and contract the soles of the feet and visualize turning coal,

the pain of plantar faciitis, into diamonds

as you contract the soles of your feet.

For those who are able to comfortably sit on your heels and curl your toes cross the arches of your feet as you sit back down on your heels. Then make a fist with your bottom foot by contracting the sole of the foot around the back of the top foot curling the toes. **Eureka!**

R~~x~~ ∿∿∿∿∿ Daily

Meditation Postures For Your Sole

R~~x~~ ∿∿∿∿∿ Daily

THY Metaphysical Healing Mantra For Feet

Smell The Square Red Earth With The Soles Of Your Feet

Mantras and affirmations are also helpful for generating awareness. The feet are contained in the Muladhara Chakra, the Foundation or Root Chakra. This chakra is allied with many qualities including the earth element, the color red, the shape or "*yantra*" of a square and the sense of smell. The message Plantar Faciitis seems to be trying to tell us is that we need to be more connected to the earth. Instead of perceiving the earth as a sordid and dirty thing, not to be touched, let us instead embrace her with the soles of our feet.

Practicing a seated Thunderbolt postures visualize a diamond / vajra body. Diamonds are created through extreme pressure exerted on coal. Contracting the sole of the foot as you breathe in a variation of vajrasana, visualize a transformation of the black coal of plantar fasciitis into the brilliance of a diamond, yet with the softness of a flower petal.

Strap Your Big Toes Together

Restful awareness with the big toes strapped together is another way to bring greater awareness to your feet and toes directing consciousness to any bunions, supination or pronation.

R$_x$ ∿∿∿∿∿ Daily

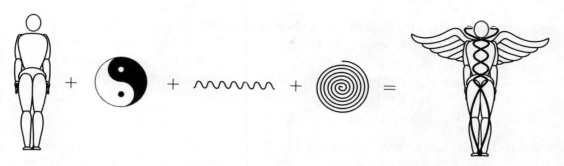

The Low Back

A truly healthy back is not just a strong or flexible back. It is a resilient back that is elastic and hardy. All muscles are connected and functioning together in a giant whole body fascia web. Individual muscles are directly paired with other muscle and lines of energy along the web. Your back is working with your abdominal muscles to create an upright posture. This practice will include lower abdominal work, hip flexor openers and back strengthening postures.

To Reduce Low Back Pain and Stiffness
Lengthen Down the Back of the Body
Focusing on these Areas.

Lengthening down the back half of the body reduces pinching in the low back and often frees nerve flow. To lengthen down the back half of the body, focus on standing down rather than standing up. Shoulder blades slide down and in. The tailbone anchors the pelvis. The buttocks root the legs and hips while the calves lengthen down to the heels releasing tension behind the knees. Triceps straighten the elbows and arms down through the fingers.

The spine is divided into a series of curves. These curves function as shock absorbers. Standing up straight is about aligning the curves of your neck, upper back and lower back in relation to your skull and tailbone. The curves of both the neck and the low back move into the center of the body, while the curve of the upper back rounds away from the center of the body. Low back pain is typically the result of engaging the muscles of the low back without the rest of the skeleton –muscle-fascia web. Typically this means neglected abdominal pairing with the low back. This would include the deep psoas muscles. Remember the breath is a giant wave that organizes all of the muscles, tissues, organs and bones of the body. You do not have to know the names of each muscle and nerve of the body to connect to them with your breath.

Conscious Breathing for the Low Back

Inhale to the heart and draw the breath down to the pubic bone.
Feel the tailbone tilt to the floor.
There should be a small arch in the small of the back.

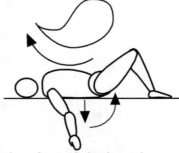

Exhale to the navel and expel the breath up and out of the body.
The navel moves toward the spine and the spine towards the floor.
The pelvic floor contracts as the tailbone anchors to the pubic bone.

R$_x$ $\sim\!\sim\!\sim\!\sim\!\sim\!\sim$ Daily

Conscious Breathing Practices for the Low Back

Inhale (lift back off of hand) Exhale (Press back onto hand) Hold for 7 breaths

Inhale Exhale Hold for 7 breaths or more.

Inhale Exhale Hold for 7 breaths or more.

Deep Rest for the Low Back... 5, 10, 15 Minutes

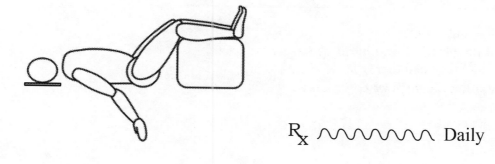

R$_X$ ∿∿∿∿∿ Daily

Happy Baby or Dead Bug Pose for the Low Back

Apanasana: apana = out-breath or downward breath

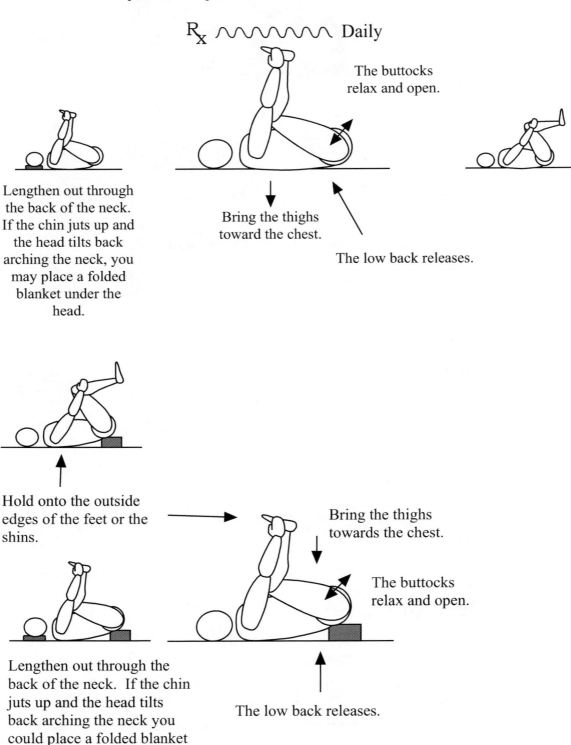

R~~~~~~~~~~~ Daily

The buttocks relax and open.

Bring the thighs toward the chest.

The low back releases.

Lengthen out through the back of the neck. If the chin juts up and the head tilts back arching the neck, you may place a folded blanket under the head.

Hold onto the outside edges of the feet or the shins.

Bring the thighs towards the chest.

The buttocks relax and open.

The low back releases.

Lengthen out through the back of the neck. If the chin juts up and the head tilts back arching the neck you could place a folded blanket under the head.

Low Back and Piriformis Releasing Postures

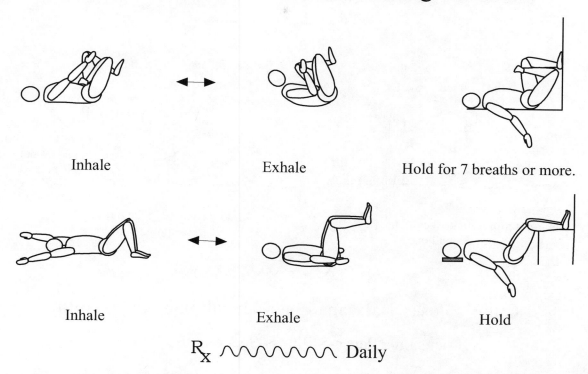

Inhale   Exhale   Hold for 7 breaths or more.

Inhale   Exhale   Hold

R$_X$ ∿∿∿∿∿ Daily

Practice restful awareness with your legs on a chair, footstool or cardboard box, anything that is not too high so the legs and low back can deeply relax. Hold the pose for five, ten, fifteen minutes consciously breathing and releasing any stress or tension.

One Leg Up the Wall

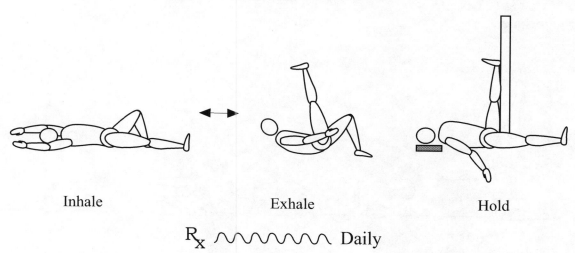

Inhale   Exhale   Hold

R$_X$ ∿∿∿∿∿ Daily

Hold one leg up the wall for three to five plus minutes. The hips can be further away from the wall with the leg at more of an angle. A folded blanket or small block behind the head will help keep the head level and the neck from over arching.

Cat and Dog Tilts for the Low Back

Bidalasana • bidal=cat

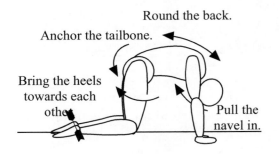

Round the back.

Anchor the tailbone.

Bring the heels towards each other.

Pull the navel in.

Exteriorly rotate the thighs toward the tailbone.

Lift the tailbone.

Arch the back.

Let the heels separate.

Lift the heart and do not let the belly drop and sag.

Interiorly rotate the thighs toward the pubic bone.

R$_x$ ∿∿∿∿∿ Daily

Child's Pose / Balasana - bah-lah-sah-nah / bala~child

Focus on a Pause-Stillness-Space in the Breath

exhale   inhale   exhale

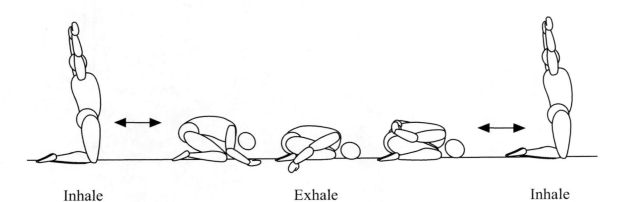

Inhale   Exhale   Inhale

Hands can go in front, beside or behind you depending on individual ability.

R$_x$ ∿∿∿∿∿ Daily

Breathe into Child's Pose for a Couple of Minutes

Sit on heels and lower the torso onto the thighs. Let the head rest on the floor, hands or block. Place a blanket under ankles if the feet are not comfortable. Emphasize the exhalation rooting the sacrum down to start.

Exhale and Contract the Ribs
Exhale and Pull the Navel in and Up
Exhale and Contract the Pelvic Floor

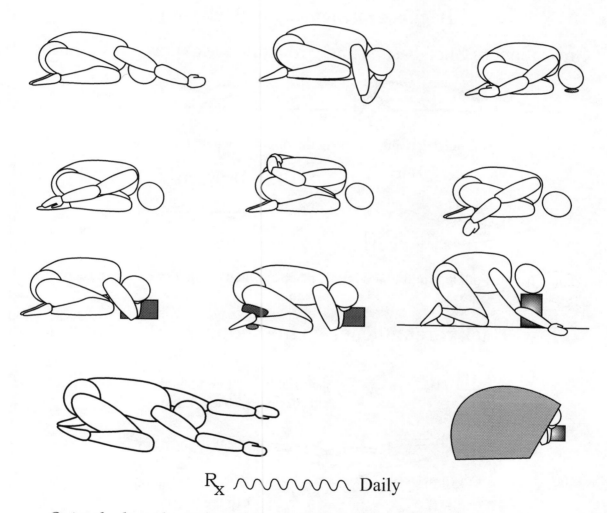

R$_x$ ∿∿∿∿∿ Daily

Quiet the breath, and hold the pose for a couple of minutes or more.

Sooth Low Back Pain. Calm the Body and the Mind.

Throw a blanket over your child's pose variation and practice conscious breathing for three to ten minutes. Let the breath, body and mind quiet down. With the rib cage pressing on the thighs, the chest will not expand very much. The breath will become almost still. In that calm and centered space, practice inhaling a small puff of air into your lower back and release any chronic or acute pain.

Building Strength in the Low Back

It is paradox that even though back extensions feel like they are aggravating the low back, they are critical for witnessing and strengthening it.

Begin to Strengthen the Back with

Grasshopper / Shalabasana and Crocodile / Makarasana Variations

Lift one leg, while pressing the opposite leg and hip down.

R$_x$ 〜〜〜〜〜 Daily

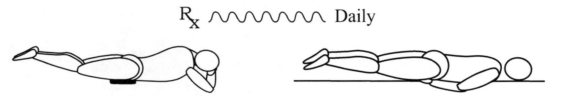

To help lift the both legs at the same time, place a folded blanket or both hands under the thighs and hips.

Low Back Strengthener – Grasshopper / Shalabasana

Feel the low back stable and strong.

Lengthen the back of the neck.

Gaze down and front.

Lift the legs.

Lift the heart.

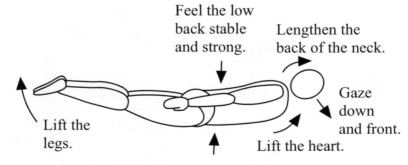

Straighten the arms and slide the shoulder blades down the back.

Inhale and lift legs, chest and arms. Hold For 7 Conscious Breaths.

R$_x$ 〜〜〜〜〜 Daily

Exhale and press down with the feet, pelvis and arms.

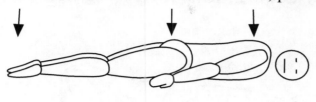

Rest

One Arm Variation

Inhale and lift the opposite arm and leg.

Lift the leg without lifting the hip off the floor.

Feel the muscles of the low back strong and stable.

Extend the opposite arm.

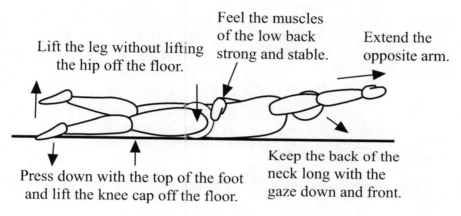

Press down with the top of the foot and lift the knee cap off the floor.

Keep the back of the neck long with the gaze down and front.

Hold for 7 long slow breaths.

R_X ∿∿∿∿∿ Daily

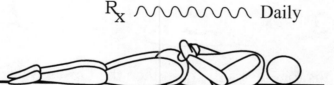

Rest the forehead or side of the head down. The hands can be behind your back or at your side. Rest and change sides and repeat for 7 slow breaths.

Grasshopper / Shalabasana Variations

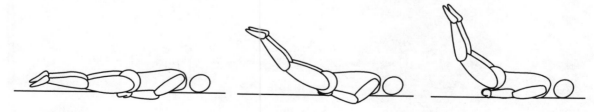

These poses involve a serious contraction of the low back muscles. Down Dog is a good counter pose.

Cobra Pose Variations for Low Back Pain

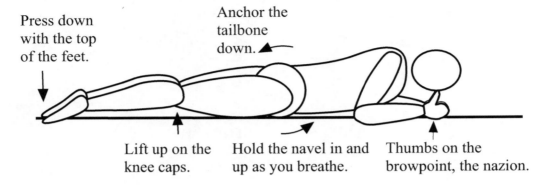

Press down with the top of the feet.

Anchor the tailbone down.

Lift up on the knee caps.

Hold the navel in and up as you breathe.

Thumbs on the browpoint, the nazion.

Lifting the navel in and up takes strain off the low back. People with intense low back pain can benefit from a modified cobra with the heart and head not lifted so high as to pinch the low back.

R_x ∿∿∿∿∿ Daily

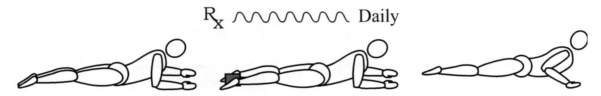

Keep the hips on the ground and the navel in to the best of your ability.

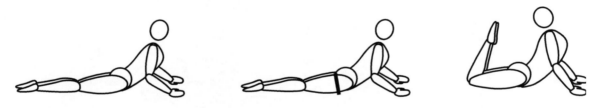

Strapping the thighs together will strengthen the hips and deepen the anchoring of the sacrum lengthening the low back curvature.

Down Dog is a great counter pose after cobra for lengthening the low back.

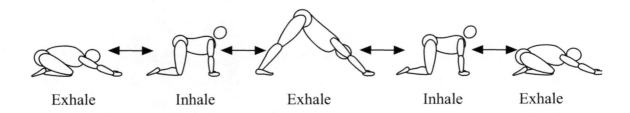

Exhale   Inhale   Exhale   Inhale   Exhale

When your lower back feels strong and flexible and you are ready to fly, practice holding this posture for a sensational experience in the low back.

Deep Low Back Contraction Occurs When the Legs Are Separated

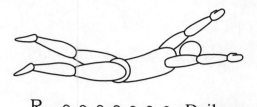

R$_X$ ∿∿∿∿ Daily

Deep Low Back Stretch – Seated Postures

These are intense stretches for the low back, legs and hips. Lift the heart and straighten the spine before you come forward, otherwise you might over stretch the low back.

Seated Forward Folds for the Low Back and Hamstrings

*Seated floor postures can over stretch the low back,
If the hips are too tight to tilt the pelvis forward, sit on a blanket, block or rolled up yoga mat.*

Since seated floor postures require so much flexibility in the legs and hips, using a strap will help many people lengthen out of the low back by rolling the thighs inward and pulling the flesh away from the sitz bones.

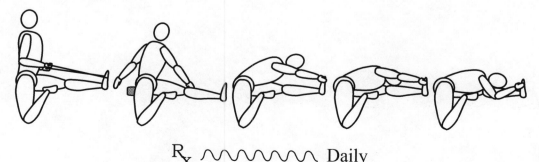

R$_X$ ∿∿∿∿ Daily

Marichyasana Variations

R$_X$ ∿∿∿∿∿ Daily

Seated Forward Folds

Lengthen the Back Side of the Body

With the Mind∞Body Infinity Loop

Paschimottanasana

R$_X$ ∿∿∿∿∿ Daily

These are more challenging variations of paschimottanasana.

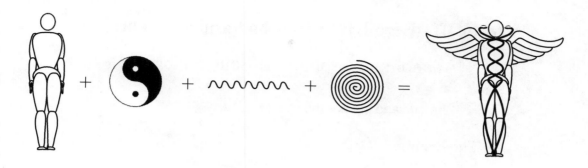

The Legs: Hamstrings, Piriformis and
The Illiotibial Track (IT Band)

Sciatica

Sciatica is the general term for most pain in the low back, hips and legs and as such is second only to the common cold in its effects on people. Sciatica is a pain cause by pressure on the sciatic nerves. The sciatic nerves are the largest nerves in the body. They are about as round as your little finger. They start in the lower spine, pass behind the hip joint, and go down the buttock and through the back of the legs to the feet. Sciatic nerve pressure can be the result of any number of reasons, the most common is muscle tightness in the low back, hips, buttocks, piriformis and or hamstrings.

Therapeutic Hatha Yoga addresses the issue of sciatica as a core issue of our body, breath and mind. When we are out of alignment with our center, our core, we hold onto muscular tension elsewhere in the body, whether it is the result of poor posture, daily routines or cooler weather. The most common areas of holding onto tension are the large muscle groups of the gluteus maximus, hamstrings and the low back. Therapeutic Hatha Yoga focuses on specific postures that can lengthen and relax these muscles that put pressure on the sciatica nerve. People who are very 'up tight' often have sciatica. They stand tall holding too much tension in their back and buttocks. They need to exhale and be a little bit more grounded as well as up right. In a fundamental way healing sciatica pain is a dynamic between being lifted and rooted so that the nerve flow keeps moving.

Warrior III / Hero III / Vira Bhadrasana III Variations

Anchor and Ground the Sciatic Nerve.

Exhale and anchor the standing leg.

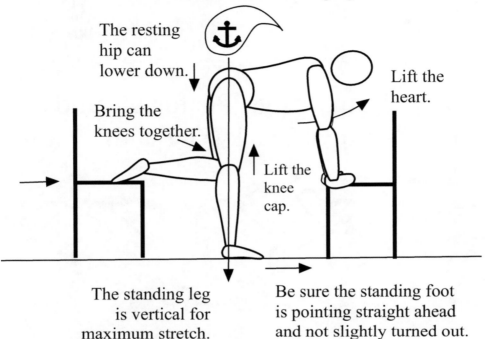

The resting hip can lower down.↓

Bring the knees together.

Lift the knee cap.

Lift the heart.

The standing leg is vertical for maximum stretch.

Be sure the standing foot is pointing straight ahead and not slightly turned out.

Hold for 7 smooth conscious breaths and then exhale for the count of 30.

Pain is like static electricity. Ground it!

R$_x$ ∿∿∿∿∿ Daily

Traditional Warrior III

Revolving Half Moon Pose Variation for Sciatica and IT Band

The IT Band, illiotibial track, is a longitudinal fibrous reinforcement of the fascia late on the outside of the thigh. The action of the IT Band and its associated muscles is to extend, abduct, and laterally rotate the hip.

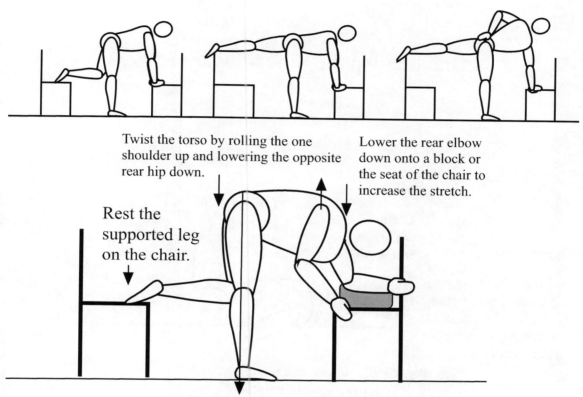

Twist the torso by rolling the one shoulder up and lowering the opposite rear hip down.

Lower the rear elbow down onto a block or the seat of the chair to increase the stretch.

Rest the supported leg on the chair.

Keep the standing leg vertical.

Hold for 7 smooth conscious breaths and then exhale for the count of 30, and pause. Ground your pain.   *Find the Variation that Works for You!*

R$_x$ ∿∿∿∿∿∿ Daily

R$_x$ ∿∿∿∿∿ Daily

One Leg Up the Side of a Door Way

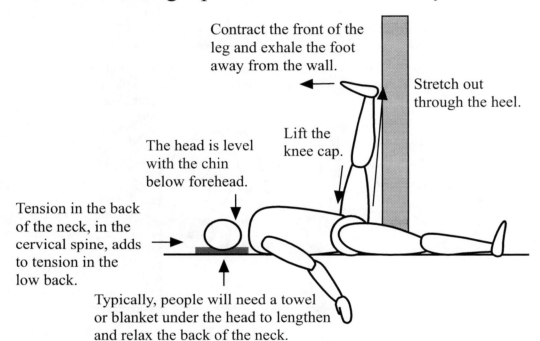

Contract the front of the leg and exhale the foot away from the wall.

Stretch out through the heel.

Lift the knee cap.

The head is level with the chin below forehead.

Tension in the back of the neck, in the cervical spine, adds to tension in the low back.

Typically, people will need a towel or blanket under the head to lengthen and relax the back of the neck.

R$_x$ ∿∿∿∿∿ Daily

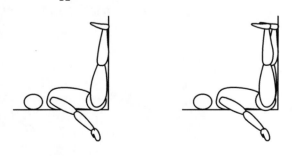

Both legs up the wall is a great pose to
release the low back and the sciatic nerve.
Practice exhaling and lifting one leg away from the wall.

Asymmetrical Forward Fold

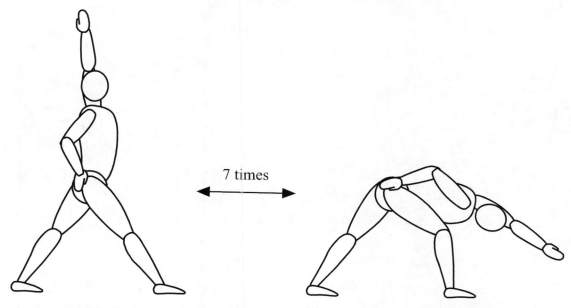

7 times

Step the right foot forward and place the right hand on your hip or behind the back. Raise the left arm over head. The elbow can be bent if the shoulder is stiff. Exhale and extend forward out and down over the right leg. Inhale to the heart and press with the right big toe as you return to standing. Keep the chin in on the way up. Do not try to lift yourself by contracting and straining the back of the neck.

Count Out 20 Slow Conscious Exhalations.

Activate the rear left leg and tighten the buttock driving the left hip forward an inch.

Yield into the right hip and leg and release the hip back an inch.

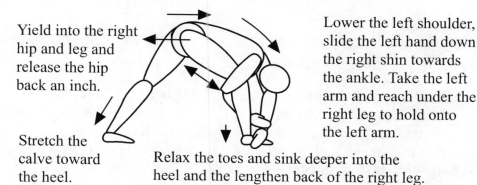

Lower the left shoulder, slide the left hand down the right shin towards the ankle. Take the left arm and reach under the right leg to hold onto the left arm.

Stretch the calve toward the heel.

Relax the toes and sink deeper into the heel and the lengthen back of the right leg.

On the last exhalation, breathe everything out, and hold the pause-stillness-space, connect your front leg to the earth, and ground your sciatica pain.

R$_x$ ∿∿∿∿∿ Daily

THY Wall Piriformis Stretch

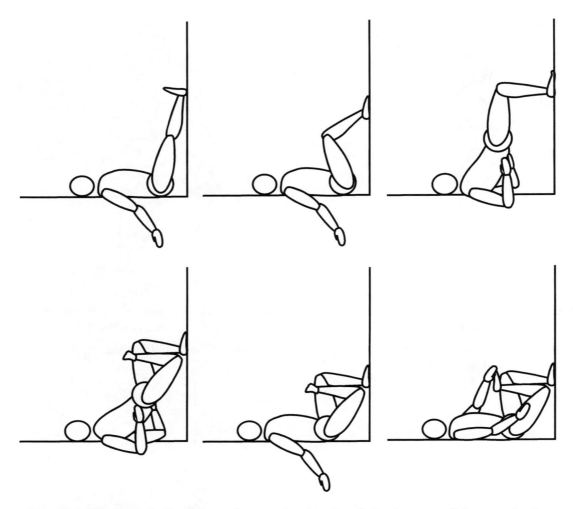

Ground the lines of energy down the back of the legs and buttocks by extending out through the heels and flexing the feet as you exhale.

Lie down on the floor with your legs up the wall. Be about 6 inches from the wall. The closer to the wall you are the more difficult the stretch will be, while a position further away will be less intense. Bend your knees and place your feet on the wall. Push your feet into the wall and lift your hips as high as you can. Cross the foot and ankle of the leg with the tight piriformis over the thigh of the other leg. Gently lower your hips down. The hips can rest on the floor or even be just a couple of inches off of the ground. Breathe. Extend out through the heels. Use your hand to help flex the foot and extend the lines of energy down through the leg.

R$_x$ ∿∿∿∿∿ Daily

Support and adjust the posture with your hands. One hand can help flex the foot and other hand on the thigh can help adjust the piriformis and hip release. Breathe into it for two minutes to fully release it.

The piriformis muscle is a small, band-like muscle located deep in the buttocks near the top of the hip joint. This muscle is important in lower body movement because it stabilizes the hip joint and lifts and externally rotates the thigh away from the body. This enables us to walk, run, shift our weight from one foot to another, and maintain balance. The sciatic nerve is a thick and long nerve that passes alongside or goes through the piriformis muscle, goes down the back of the leg, and eventually branches off into smaller nerves that end in the feet. Nerve compression can be caused by spasm of the piriformis muscle.

Piriformis syndrome is a condition in which the piriformis muscle becomes tight or spasms, compressing or strangling the sciatic nerve beneath it. This causes pain, which you could visualize as static nerve flow in the buttocks region; and may even result in referred pain. Piriformis tightness or syndrome can be the result of a history of trauma to the area, repetitive, vigorous activity such as long-distance running, or prolonged sitting.

Lying Twist / Jathara Parivartanasana Variations

jathara = belly, parivartan = turning, rolling, turning round

Lying twists are great for stimulating the organs of digestion and releasing the muscles around the sciatic nerve in the low back and hip, along IT Band and back of the leg.

It is simplest to bend the knees to begin with.

R$_x$ ∿∿∿∿∿ Daily

To help open the chest and rotate the torso, bend the elbows and put one hand on the rib cage and lower that elbow to the floor, rather than extend the arm out with the shoulder floating off of the floor.

Place the other hand on the extended thigh and lower that bent elbow toward the floor. Once you can lower the shoulders to the floor, straighten your arms out to the side.

A block and or a strap are effective props for lying twists.

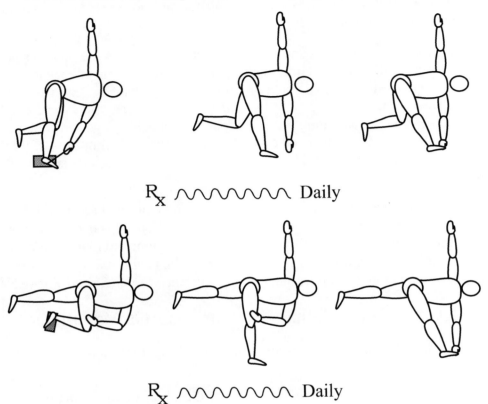

R$_x$ ∿∿∿∿∿∿ Daily

Blanket Under The Hips   **Eagle Leg Twist**   **Bound Twist**

R$_x$ ∿∿∿∿∿ Daily

Raising the hips a little with a blanket or another rolled-up yoga mat, will deepen the twist in the low back. Eagle Leg Twists   are intense and generally require a block, or your fist, under the knee to stablize the pose and even then, it is difficult to keep both shoulders down. For a Bound Twist, hold onto the bottom leg with palm facing up, as you extend the other leg out.

Lying Twist with Movement and Breath
Can be practiced with both knee bent

Inhale   Exhale   Inhale   Exhale

In this rigorous twist, inhale the legs to the sky, press the hands into the floor as you exhale the legs down to one side, inhale center and exhale to the other side. Hold. Take 7 breaths. See if you can extend your legs towards your hand and hold onto your feet. Only practice what you can breathe into.

LyingTwist with Both Legs

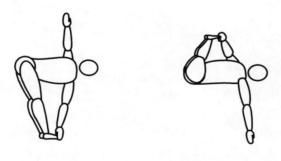

R_x ∿∿∿∿∿∿∿ Daily

A Quick Review of Some Postures for Sciatica

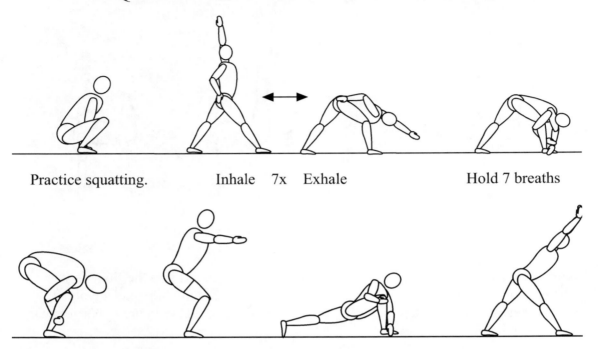

Practice squatting.　　　　Inhale　7x　Exhale　　　　Hold 7 breaths

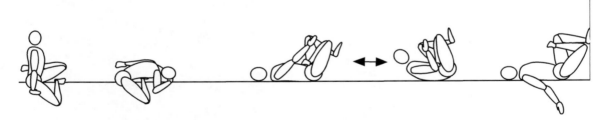

Bring the knees towards the midline of the body, internally rotating the thigh and release the flesh away from the buttocks. Breathe.

Yoga is sensational. Extend out through the heels of the feet and release your sciatica.

R$_x$ ∿∿∿∿∿∿ Daily

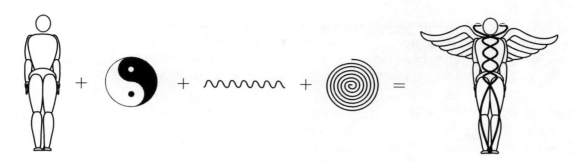

The Neck, Throat, Jaw, and Thyroid

Getting Your Head in the Right Place

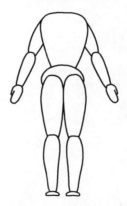

What might it mean to have your head in the right place, both mentally and physically? The neck is the physical connection between mind and body. When your head is not in the right place, your neck has to strain to maintain the connection. The relationship between your body and your mind is through your neck for breathing, eating, speaking and moving. The tension we carry in our necks is in part related to the tension in the between what we think in our head and feel in our hearts and body. We have chronic neck pain in part because our heads and thoughts, are out of alignment with our body and feelings.

Posture – Is your head thrust forward when you stand?
Breathing – Can you inhale to the heart without tensing the shoulders?

Eating – Can you swallow with the navel out?
Speaking – Does your voice resonate in your head and or your body?
Movement – Do you initiate basic movement from your core and or head?
Life – Can you be guided from your heart as well as your head?

Tension and or pain are static information on your radio dial to the infinite. Tune it in. Bring it into alignment. Healing is a conscious as well as a physical activity. Nothing seems more challenging to understand in this context than to heal the neck.

Breathe Through The Mind∞Body Infinity Loop To Relieve Neck Tension

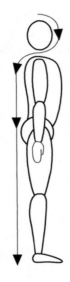
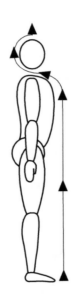

Exhale and contract the abdominal cavity.	*Inhale and expand the heart cavity.*
Exhale to the navel.	*Inhale to the heart.*
Exhale to the navel and anchor the sacrum.	*Inhale to the back of the head.*
Exhale into a pause, a moment of stillness.	*Inhale into a pause, a moment of stillness.*
Exhale and keep the back of the neck lifted.	*Inhale and keep the sacrum anchored.*
Exhale from the top of the head	*Inhale from the soles of the feet*
To the soles of the feet.	*to the top of the head.*
Exhale and keep the back of the neck long.	*Inhale and keep navel in.*
Exhale from your third eye to your sacrum.	*Inhale to your heart to your third ear.*
Exhale and be spiritually grounded.	*Inhale and be spiritually lifted.*

R$_x$  Daily

Standing / Tadasana / Mountain Posture / Samasthiti

Good posture to relieve neck pain and tension is about bringing our heads level and centered with the rest of our bodies, so that lines of energy flow smoothly. To have your head in the right place is to have your head sitting squarely on your shoulders, literally and figuratively.

Practice the Mind∞Body Infinity Loop in these Postures

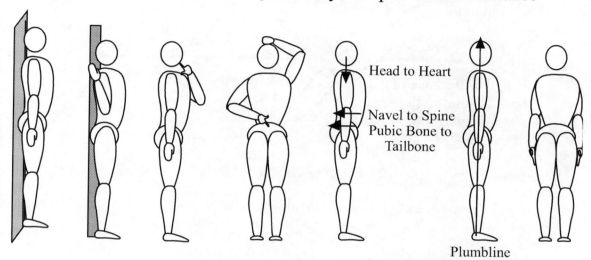

Head to Heart

Navel to Spine
Pubic Bone to
Tailbone

Plumbline

When we stand with our backs against the wall, it is often difficult for to have the backs of our heads touching the wall, with the tip of the nose below the middle ear. The chin is ideally positioned when it seems as if it was resting on a shelf. Take a fist, exhale and press down on the top of your head as if you were carrying something heavy on top of your head. Nod your head up and down and find a sturdy shelf for your chin.

Restful Awareness Postures for Neck Pain

The edge of a foam wedge or triangle piece of foam just below the occipital ridge is a perfect place to witness and release neck tension. At first, the sensation might seem too great. Breathe. Focus, relax and breathe into it for 3 to 5 or more minutes.

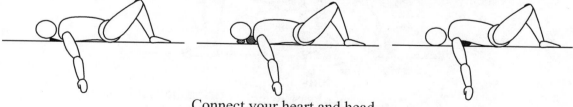

Connect your heart and head.

Small round pieces of foam or fabric can also be placed under the occipital ridge at the back of the head. Many types of rolls can be put behind the neck for several minutes to help balance the curvature of the neck. Placing a small roll or blanket under the shoulder blades will open the heart and help root the shoulder blades down the back.

Strengthening the Neck, Throat, Jaw, and Thyroid
Strengthen Your Connection Between Your Head and Your Heart.

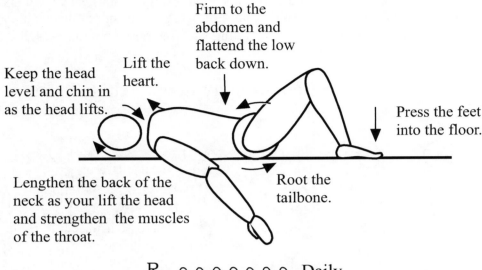

Keep the head level and chin in as the head lifts.

Lift the heart.

Firm to the abdomen and flattend the low back down.

Press the feet into the floor.

Lengthen the back of the neck as your lift the head and strengthen the muscles of the throat.

Root the tailbone.

R$_x$ ∿∿∿∿∿ Daily

When we lift heavy objects, we often try to pull them up by pulling our-neck and heads back and up, which can create vertigo.

This posture helps us focus on engaging the muscles along the front of the body, including the front of the neck to lift objects.

Bridge Pose or Two Footed Desk Pose Variations

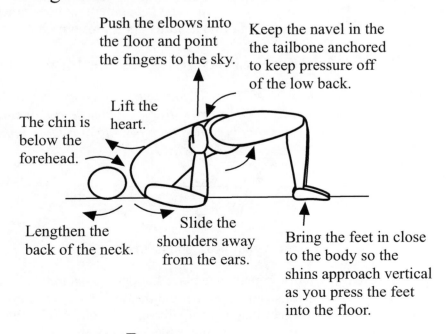

Push the elbows into the floor and point the fingers to the sky.

Keep the navel in the the tailbone anchored to keep pressure off of the low back.

The chin is below the forehead.

Lift the heart.

Lengthen the back of the neck.

Slide the shoulders away from the ears.

Bring the feet in close to the body so the shins approach vertical as you press the feet into the floor.

R$_x$ ∿∿∿∿∿ Daily

Bridge Pose With Movement and Breath and Arms Over Head

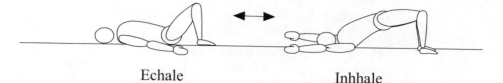

Echale   Inhhale

Opening the Back of the Neck
Opening the "Windows to the Sky"

The 'windows to the sky' are acupressure points at the base of the occipital ridge along the back of the neck. Inhale into the back of the neck and open your windows to the sky, lengthen the nape of the neck Expand the back from the sacrum to the cranium.

Exhale and spiral your face in towards your navel. Exhale to the first resistance. Pause, and then inhale, lengthen and expand the back. Exhale and spiral in a bit more. Breathe into your edges: do not force the pose. Lower the elbows only to the point where you can breathe into it. Take 7 breaths.

Plow and Should Stand Postures Help Release Neck Tension

Take the weight of your burdens off of your neck and shoulders.

The Crocodile Twist Pose For A Stiff Neck

Turn your head to the side and relax.

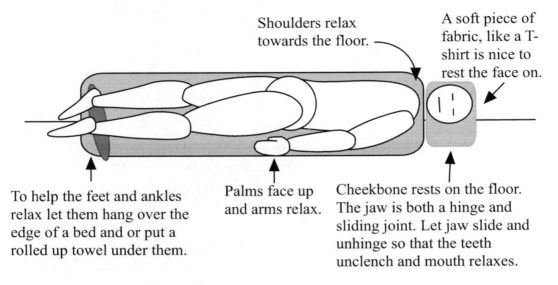

Shoulders relax towards the floor.

A soft piece of fabric, like a T-shirt is nice to rest the face on.

To help the feet and ankles relax let them hang over the edge of a bed and or put a rolled up towel under them.

Palms face up and arms relax.

Cheekbone rests on the floor. The jaw is both a hinge and sliding joint. Let jaw slide and unhinge so that the teeth unclench and mouth relaxes.

Let go and let the breath flow for two to five to ten minutes.

Try this pose on your bed with the tops of your feet on the edge of the bed and the covers nice and flat to lie on. Turn your face to one side. This pose stimulates a parasympathic relaxation response in the body.

Back Extensions - Grasshopper / Salabahasana Variations

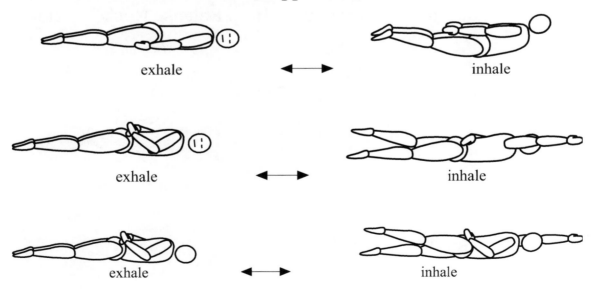

exhale ↔ inhale

exhale ↔ inhale

exhale ↔ inhale

R_x ∿∿∿∿∿ Daily

Fly Like Superman or Superwoman

And Strengthen the Muscles Between the Shoulder Blades

Viewed from the side.

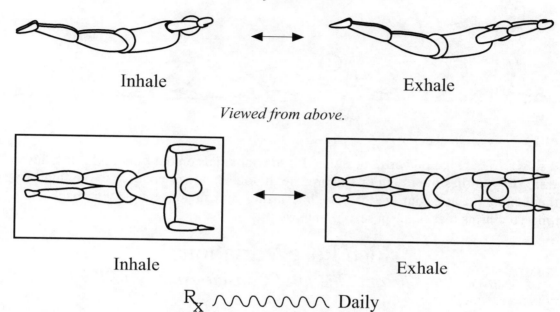

Inhale   Exhale

Viewed from above.

Inhale   Exhale

R_X ∿∿∿∿∿ Daily

Inhale and expand the chest, and bring the arms back with the elbow bent and the palms facing out and thumbs pointing down. Exhale and dive into the space in front of you like Superman extending the arms out straight, while turning the palms inward and pointing the thumbs up. You can also practice this keeping the legs down.

Deep Neck Releases

Rotated Head Child Pose /Parivrrita Sirsa Balasana

Take a couple slow conscious breaths to lower down and turn the head into any of these variations. Lower the ear to the block. Release the jaw. Listen to your Inner Teacher-Healer-Guide.

Deeper Neck Releases

Go slowly. These are powerful postures. Place your hands on the floor and gently lower the side of your head to the floor and breathe. If you can lower your ear to the floor, try straightening the arms out to each side. Interlacing your fingers behind your back and lifting your arms makes the pose very intense.

Fish Pose Variations
Float on the Vibrant Ocean of Consciousness in Fish Pose.

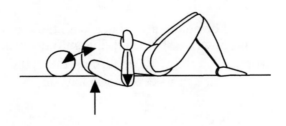

R$_x$ ∿∿∿∿∿ Daily
Legs Extended Fish Poses
Keep the connection between the heart and head.

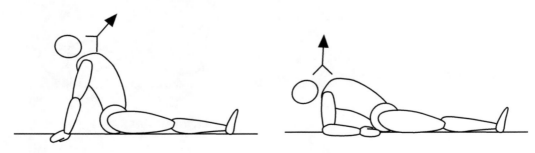

Open and close the mouth.
Vocalize, say aloud, "Aaaa Uuuu Mmmm."

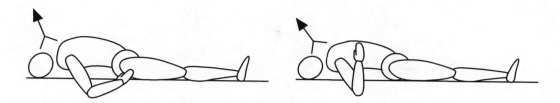

Look behind you. Press the back of the head and arms down. Open the heart.

Bring the palms together. Breathe. Extend the legs and arms out.

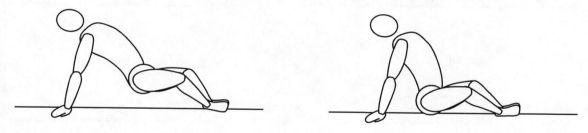

Extend the arms over head. Interlace the fingers and press the palms away.

R~~~~~~ Daily

Soles-Of-The-Feet Together Fish Pose Variation

Lift the hips off of the floor, look behind and focus on a spot. Hold your eyes fixed on the spot and slowly lower the hips down. Feel the front of the body and hips openning. Keep the connection between the heart and head.

R~~~~~~ Daily

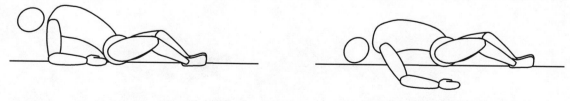

Lower to the elbows and then lower the back of the head to the floor.

Stablize the head on the floor. Lift the elbows and bring the palms together.

R$_x$ ∿∿∿∿∿∿ Daily

Thunderbolt Fish Pose Variations

Only for people with flexible knees.

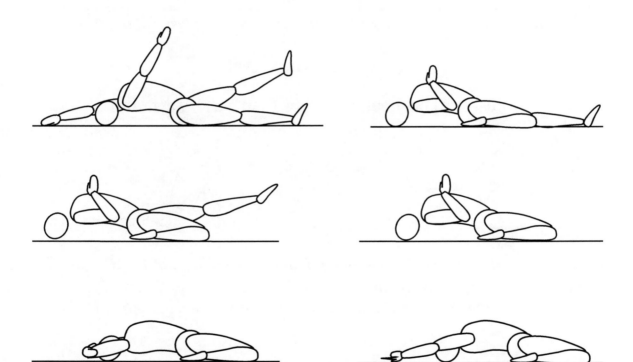

R$_x$ ∿∿∿∿∿∿ Daily

Inhale and Float Your Heart.
Practice the Mind∞Body Infinity Loop

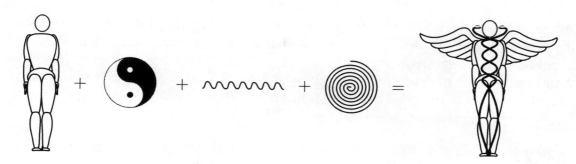

Dizziness and Vertigo

Be Conscious of How You Come To Standing.

Many people get dizzy when they stand up from lying, sitting and or kneeling. This is generally caused by too much blood pressure in the brain. Tension in the back of the neck restricts veins in the back of the neck, which reduces blood flow out of the brain. The woozy dizzy feeling is attributed to an increased blood pressure in the brain. To help prevent dizziness or light headedness keep the head down and the chin in when standing. So often people initiate movement leading with their heads, as if they were pulling their bodies up with their heads. Separating the head from the heart and leading the movement with the head creates lots of tension in the back of the neck.

Integrate, Assimilate and Acclimate to a Higher State

When sitting up lean forward and press down with your legs. Root down and stack the vertebrae one by one, keeping the head down as you come to standing. Roll the shoulders back and down. Place your hands on your thighs and walk your hands up your legs, as you come to standing. Come all the way to standing with the shoulders over the hips, with the head down and the chin in. Raise your gaze first, and then finally slowly level and center the head on the shoulders.

When we lift heavy objects, we often try to lift them up by pulling it up with our neck and head instead of our whole being. This tightens the muscles of the spine and back of the neck and
can be a source of low back pain as well as dizziness and vertigo.

Keep Body and Mind Together and The Head Connected To The Heart When Standing or Picking Something Up.

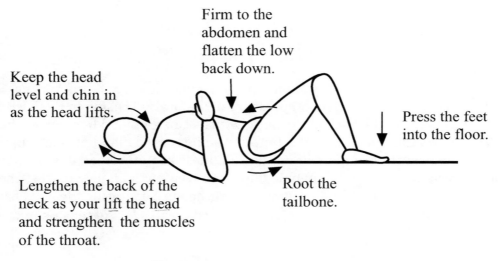

Firm to the abdomen and flatten the low back down.

Keep the head level and chin in as the head lifts.

Press the feet into the floor.

Lengthen the back of the neck as your lift the head and strengthen the muscles of the throat.

Root the tailbone.

R$_X$ ∿∿∿∿∿ Daily

Strengthen the Front of the Neck

To help Reduce Tension in the Back of the Neck,

Which will help Keep the Blood Flowing Out of the Brain.

All of the neck practices
will help prevent dizziness and
help keep the head level and centered on the shoulders.

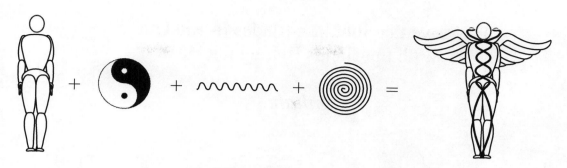

The Shoulders

We Are Vessels for Spirit

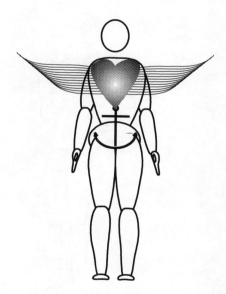

Our bodies are like ships for our spirit to explore wisdom and compassion. Our shoulders are like masts and yards for our arms to open and unfurl as we inhale. Our shoulders are directly connected to the air element in the Heart Chakra. Let us spread our wings and set sail onto the ocean of consciousness, and at the same time be able to anchor down.

Move the Shoulder Blades In and Out
With the Hands Behind the Head

Inhale

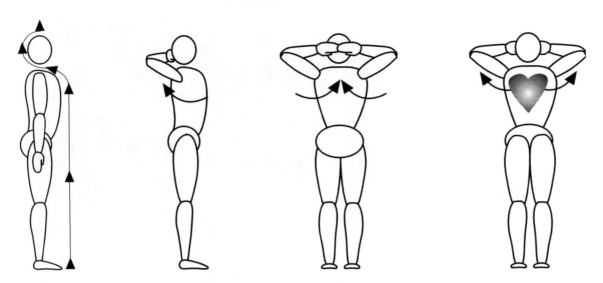

Inhale and feel lifted, open the arms and press the shoulder blades back and in toward each other. Inhale, unfurl your sails and feel the wind at your back and your heart open.

Exhale

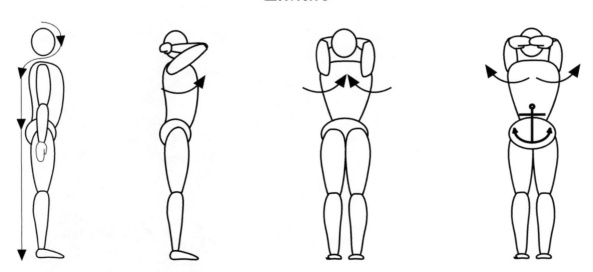

Exhale and feel grounded, close the arms in together and separate the shoulder blades. Fold your sails in and anchor down in a safe harbor. This is an excellent practice kneeling and sitting too. *It is easier to feel the tailbone anchor down while exhaling and separating the shoulders, if it is practiced kneeling.*

Palms Facing Out and In

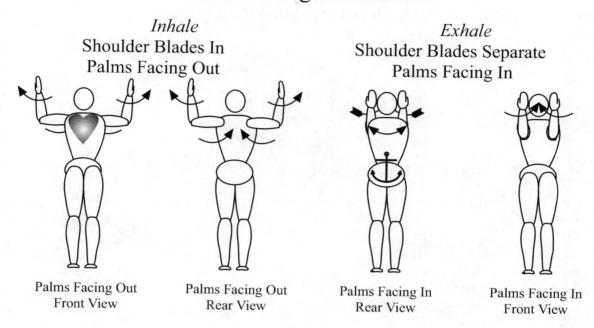

Inhale
Shoulder Blades In
Palms Facing Out

Exhale
Shoulder Blades Separate
Palms Facing In

Palms Facing Out
Front View

Palms Facing Out
Rear View

Palms Facing In
Rear View

Palms Facing In
Front View

Shoulder Push Ups

Establish a neutral straight spine with the middle ear, shoulder and hip in alignment.

Inhale with a straight spine and draw your upper back towards the floor.

Exhale with a straight spine press down with the arms and slightly round the upper back and move the shoulder blades away fronm each other.

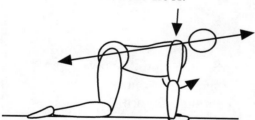
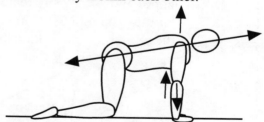

Inhale Shoulder Blades Down and In
Exhale Shoulder Blades Up and Apart.

R_x  Daily

Focus the breath in the heart cavity. Hold the pelvis neutral. Inhale and draw the shoulder blades onto the back and towards each other. Exhale and separate the shoulder blades, contracting the chest.

Align the Spine
Root the Neck Down Between the Shoulder Blades

More Challenging Variations of Shoulder Push Ups

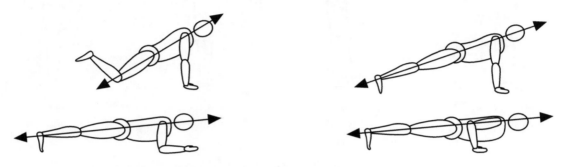

Inhale Shoulder Blades Down and In.
Exhale Shoulder Blades Up and Apart.

R$_X$ ∿∿∿∿∿ Daily

Down Dog Variations for Stiff Shoulders

Release the sitz
bones and
buttocks up into
the air.

Create a neutral
spine with a
lumbar, low
back, arch.

Straighten the elbow
and extend out
through the arm.

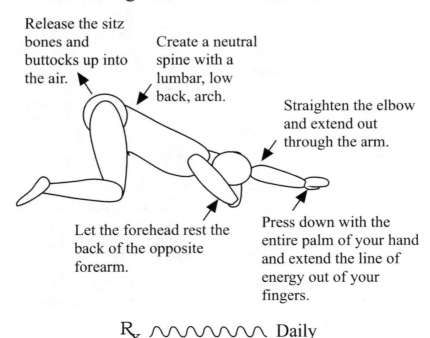

Let the forehead rest the
back of the opposite
forearm.

Press down with the
entire palm of your hand
and extend the line of
energy out of your
fingers.

R$_X$ ∿∿∿∿∿ Daily

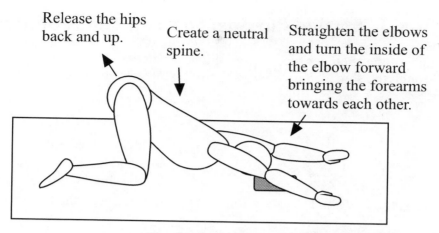

Release the hips back and up.

Create a neutral spine.

Straighten the elbows and turn the inside of the elbow forward bringing the forearms towards each other.

The forehead can rest on a block, blanket or floor.

Hands wider than shoulders will be easier for stiff shoulders.

Bend the Knees and Lift the Heels

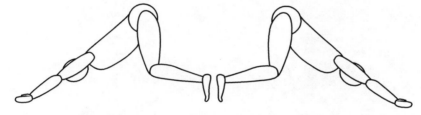

Bend the knees and lift the heels of the feet to reduce tightness in the back of the legs. This also enables a more natural lumbar arch and helps flatten the upper back. 7x Daily.

Lying Twist

Lying Twist, with a block under the knee, and arm movement with breath.

Inhale the arm along the floor up towards the ear. Exhale it down.

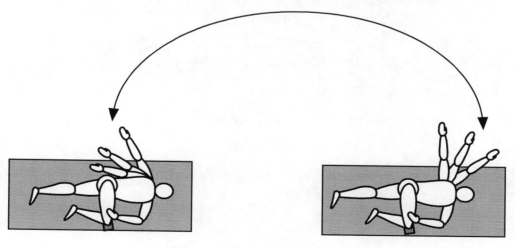

Lateral Bends for the Shoulders and the Sides of the Body

Exhale and anchor the shoulder blades from the little finger down through the elbow and triceps through the shoulder and down the back while breathing into lateral bends.

Adjust the angle of your arm, or bend the elbow if needed to keep the shoulder blades sliding down the back, and keep the heart open.

Standing

Kneeling

Seated

Lying

R_x ᗺᗺᗺᗺᗺᗺᗺ Daily

286

Reduce Stiffness in the Shoulders
Plow and Shoulder Stand Variations

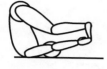  

People with delicate necks can place a folded blanket under the arms and shoulders.

R$_X$ ∿∿∿∿∿ Daily

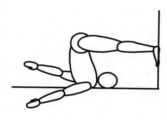 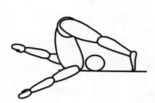 

Interlace your fingers behind your back and rocking side-to-side straighten your arms.

Supported Shoulder Stand / Shalamba Sarvangasana

Unsupported Shoulder stand / Niralamba Sarvangasana

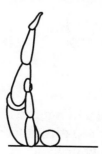 

R$_X$ ∿∿∿∿∿ Daily

287

Strap The Shoulder Down
Release Neck and Shoulder Tension

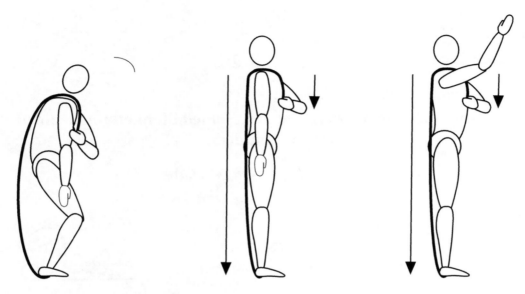

Stand on the end of the strap with the heel of one foot. Drape the strap over the shoulder and hold onto it with the opposite hand. Pull the strap down in front as you stand up drawing the strap tight pulling the shoulder down the backside of the body. Lengthen the calves toward the heels and root the tailbone. Explore the feeling while consciously breathing. *Move the head side-to-side and release any neck tension.* Keeping the shoulder down away from the ears, raise the arm with the elbow lightly bent.

R$_x$ 〰〰〰〰 Daily

Open Hearted Hero Pose

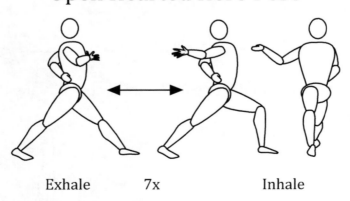

Exhale   7x   Inhale

Place your hand over your heart. Inhale, open your arm and expand the heart cavity. Inhale open to a new day. Keep the heart lifted as you exhale, gathering in creativity, love and wisdom as you bring your hand back to your heart. Keep the heart lifted and open, extending out through the arm, wrist, hand and fingertips. A collapsed heart cavity brings the shoulders forward and out of alignment.

288

Side Bow / Parsva Dhanurasana Variations

Inhale and Expand the Heart Cavity.

Slowly extend one arm along the floor as you lie down on your side supporting yourself with the other arm.

Start with a hand on the hip.   Raise the arm.   Reach back for the top leg.

Move slowly. Consciously breathe into your edges.

R𝗑 〰〰〰 Daily

Side Bow

Start on your stomach and reach back and grab both feet for bow pose and then roll over onto one side and take seven conscious breaths.

Open and expand the chest. Feel the contraction between the shoulder blades.

R𝗑 〰〰〰 Daily

Wide Leg Stance / Prasarita Padottanasana Variation

With a Strap in Your Hands Behind You Release Tension in Your Neck and Shoulders

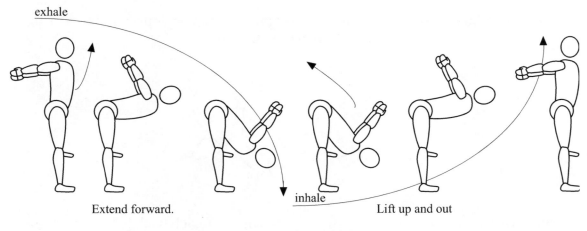

exhale

Extend forward.

inhale

Lift up and out

R꙰ ∿∿∿∿∿ Daily

Make the strap into a giant loop, and take the loop behind you, otherwise just hold onto the strap shoulder width or greater. Hold onto the strap and lift your arms up off of your back. Your feet are wide apart with the outer edges parallel to each other or even slightly pigeon toed inward. Take a deep inhalation and hinge forward leading with your chest and keeping the back of your neck long and your chin in. Inhale and lift, coming up with a flat back. Use the insides of your legs to lift and extend the torso forward, out and up. Repeat six times and then hold the downward position. Keep your chin in, dropping the top of your head towards the floor. The shoulders will hunch up by your ears, and release coming to standing.

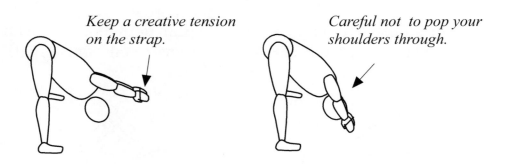

Keep a creative tension on the strap.

Careful not to pop your shoulders through.

Some people with loose shoulders can take their arms all the way over to the floor. Be careful! Do not carelessly or violently roll your shoulders open. Keep a creative tension on the strap. You might want to shorten your giant loop if your shoulders are free of tension and your arms easily roll over to the ground.

Eagle Posture Variations to Open the Upper Back

R$_X$ ∿∿∿∿∿ Daily

Exhale and Inhale, and Open the Upper Back

Repeat on the other side.

Cow Face Posture / Gomukasana

R$_X$ ∿∿∿∿∿ Daily

Gomukasana is one of the most challenging yoga postures for stiff shoulders. By combining a static prop, a strap, with dynamic movement and conscious breathing, you can create a powerful opening in the shoulders, neck and arms.

Half Bound Wide Mountain Pose for Tight Shoulders

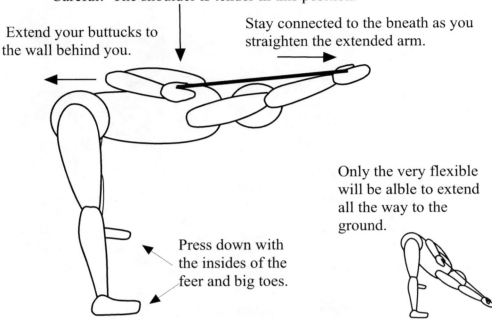

Careful! The shoulder is tender in this position.

Extend your buttucks to the wall behind you.

Stay connected to the bneath as you straighten the extended arm.

Only the very flexible will be alble to extend all the way to the ground.

Press down with the insides of the feer and big toes.

Many people have difficult time scratching behind their backs. With one arm strapped behind your back, and the other extended forward, the interplay between the shoulders and the back in lifting and lowering the torso can really open and work the shoulder. As your shoulders gets looser and looser you can reach it up further between the shoulder blades. Beginning with a bound wide mountain stance, bend the left arm and extend the right arm up. Keep the chin in and the back of the neck long. Using the same principles as we have practiced before, exhale, hinge at the hips. Shift more weight onto your heels to help extend further forward. Inhale and come up and change sides. *An easier option is to stand with the feet hip distance apart and bend the knees as you come forward.*

R_x ∿∿∿∿∿ Daily

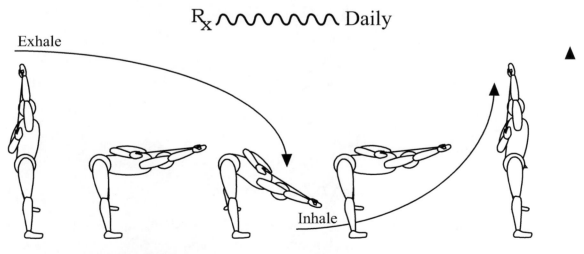

Exhale

Inhale

Extend before you bend.

Lift the chest before the chin

Pendulum Variations - Lolasana

Hands, Arms and Shoulders Press Down, While the Abdomen Lifts Up.

First place your hands either side of your shins and lift your knees off of the ground. Then try lifting one foot off of the ground. Lifting both legs off of the ground requires a lot of wrist and abdominal strength. Placing a couple of blocks or a foam wedge under the wrists will help.

Exhale and connect to your core of grounded energy and lift off. Exhale your shoulders down away from your ears. Straightening the arms down helps us stand up straighter.

R𝗑 ∿∿∿∿∿ Daily

Staff Pose / Dandasana

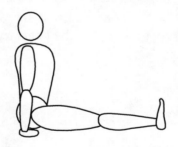

Straighten the arms down and roll the shoulder blades down the back while lifting the heart. Extend the legs and point the toes towards the sky. Pointing the fingers straight ahead can be challenging. Turning the hands out to the side a little will help open the chest and straighten the arms. *Lifting the hips up can be very difficult for stiff shoulders.*

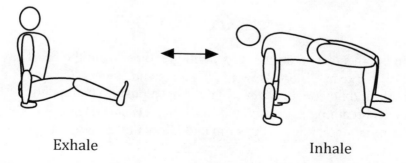

Exhale   Inhale

Hold the lifted position for a few conscious rhythmic breaths.

Open Hearted Restful Awareness for the Shoulders Pose

Inhale and expand the heart cavity.

Exhale and keep it lifted.

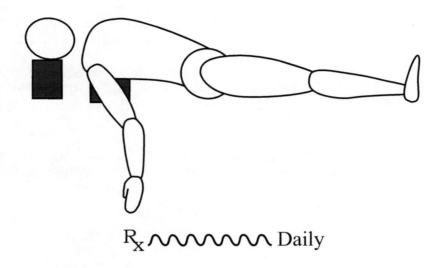

R$_x$ ∿∿∿∿∿ Daily

The block under the shoulder blades supports a lifted and open-heart cavity. The block behind the head is generally a little higher than the heart rest block so the neck does not over arch.

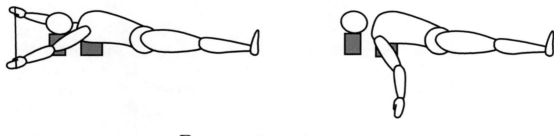

R$_x$ ∿∿∿∿∿ Daily

Holding a strap overhead for a minute or so will greatly expand the heart cavity, and eventually cut off nerve and blood flow to the hands and fingers. Dosage is the difference between medicine and poison, between what makes a posture therapeutic or toxic. Practice conscious breathing and listen to your Inner Teacher-Healer-Guide, when you feel pinching or numbness, release the strap and allow the arms to rest out to the side.

Wall Practice for Shoulders

Inhale, open the heart, press with the inner thumb mound of the palm of hand, flatten the upper back and feel the shoulder blades moving in together.
Exhale, draw the navel in, press with the outer little finger mound of the palm of hand and feel the shoulder blades move slightly apart and down.

R$_x$ 〰〰〰〰〰 Daily

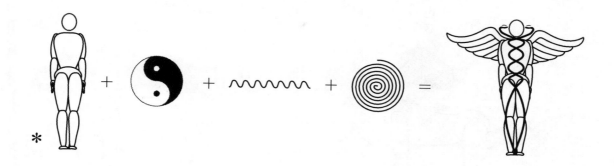

The Hands, Wrists, Thumbs and Fingers

Carpal Tunnel and Hand Arthritis

Carpel tunnel syndrome and related neck, forearm, wrist and finger pain is very common with repetitive motion such as typing, but also aging in general. Pregnant women, computer users, musicians, overweight people and people with thin delicate wrists often suffer from carpal tunnel syndrome. Typically this is the result of a combination of overuse and fatigue. We need to rest and rebalance our hands and wrists periodically. Here is a series of postures to increase the range of movement and circulation in our hands and fingers. Becoming aware of how often you unconsciously habitually use your wrists and hands for things like getting up out of a chair, pushing a door open, sitting at computer or pushing a button is critical to addressing chronic conditions. Everyone seems to develop a bit of hand arthritis and a variety of wrist, thumb and finger issues as they age and so everyone can benefit from these postures, regardless of age.

Medicine or Poison

In martial arts, the attacking pressure points are the same as the healing points. What makes one harmful and the other helpful is the intention with which the pressure is applied. Dosage is the difference between medicine and poison. These postures can strengthen the wrist and can aggravate carpal tunnel syndrome. The secret is to use breath as a biofeedback loop. If you cannot breathe into it, back out of it.

Cat and Dog Tilt Variations for the Wrists

Inhale   Exhale

R$_x$ ∿∿∿∿∿∿ Daily

Coordinating movement and breath on your hands and knees is an ideal way to witness your wrists, palms, thumbs and fingers. Begin with your palms on the floor.

If you look at your palms, you will see two mounds of flesh at the wrist separated by a couple of deep lines in the skin. Not only do you want to keep the weight distributed evenly on these mounds, you also want to distribute the weight onto the whole hand. This way the energy flows through the wrist and into the whole palm and fingers and especially during more intense weight bearing postures.

Be sure not to collapse onto just the outside mound of the palm while practicing hand balancing asana, as in the sequence below, or even with the simplest of weight-bearing postures on the hands.

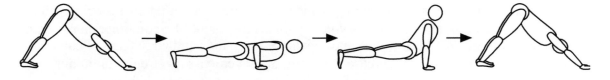

Lines of Energy on the Hands Connect
To Lines of Energy on the Front and Back of the Body.

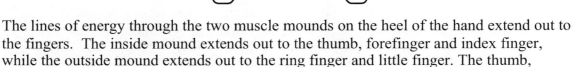

The lines of energy through the two muscle mounds on the heel of the hand extend out to the fingers. The inside mound extends out to the thumb, forefinger and index finger, while the outside mound extends out to the ring finger and little finger. The thumb, forefinger and index finger line up on the front side of the plumb line and the little finger and ring finger line up on the back side of the plumb line while standing.

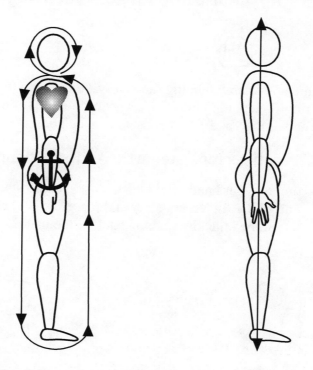

The lines of energy on the front of the body
Flow through the thumb, forefinger and index finger.

The lines of energy on the back of the body
Flow through the ring finger and little finger.

The inhalation expands and opens the heart cavity out through the chest, opening the bicep, palm, thumb, forefinger and index finger. The lung meridian in acupuncture begins with the space between the thumb and forefinger.

The exhalation contracts and anchors the body down the backside of the body down through the back of the arm, elbow, ring finger and little finger.

Inhale and Open Your Hands
Starting With Your Thumbs and Forefingers

Inhale and focus your intentions on releasing any stiffness or tightness in the hands. Make the letter 'L' with the forefinger and thumb. Open the space between the thumb and the forefinger to 90 degrees. Take seven conscious inhalations.

Exhale and Make Fists
Starting With Your Little Fingers and Ring Fingers

Exhale and contract the body, straightening the elbows, tightening the triceps and closing the little fingers and ring fingers tight into fists. Anchor the lines of energy run that down the back of the body and arms. Take seven conscious exhalations.

THY Practices for Osteoarthritis in the Fingers

You can begin by starting on your hands and knees, or you could stand and place your hand on a table. Bring all of the fingers together and place the heel of one hand on top of the fingers but not on top of the knuckles and the back of the hand.

Inhale   Exhale

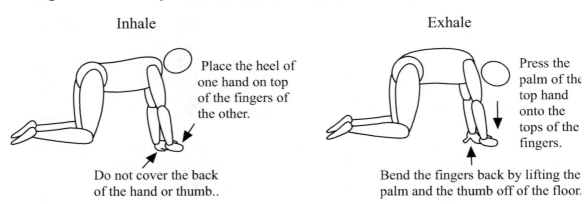

Place the heel of one hand on top of the fingers of the other.

Do not cover the back of the hand or thumb..

Press the palm of the top hand onto the tops of the fingers.

Bend the fingers back by lifting the palm and the thumb off of the floor.

Inhale to the count of six, exhale to the count of nine and press down on top of the fingers with the heel of the other hand. At the same time lift the palm of the bottom hand and press the ball of the hand that is underneath into the floor. Your knuckles might crack at this moment. Open the palm of bottom hand further by lifting the thumb up, out and away. Hold the pose. Consciously extend lines of energy and awareness through each of the knuckles and finger joints out to the fingertips. Release. Look at the palm of the bottom hand. It should be pink with fresh blood pouring into it.

Some people's wrists are so stiff that they cannot bear weight on the palm of their hands. They have to use their fists or fingertips with one hand to support themselves while practicing different positions with the other hand.

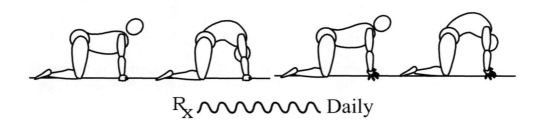

R$_x$ ∿∿∿∿∿∿ Daily

Carpal Tunnel 1A / Cat and Dog Variation

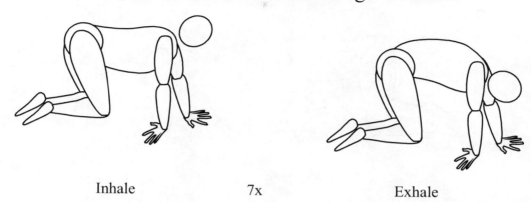

Inhale   7x   Exhale

Delicately place the back of the hand on the floor. This is an intense posture to release tightness in the backside of the wrist, hand and fingers. Remember there is no inherent difference between medicine and poison. It is the dosage or the amount of pressure, which makes positions therapeutic or toxic. Take six conscious rhythmic breaths and on the seventh one, inhale for the count of six and exhale for the count of nine or longer. Hold the pause and witness the joint, ligaments, tendons and bones. If you cannot breathe into it, back out of it. Keeping the back of the hand on the floor and then touch your thumb to each of your fingertips.

Carpal Tunnel 1B / Cat and Dog Variation

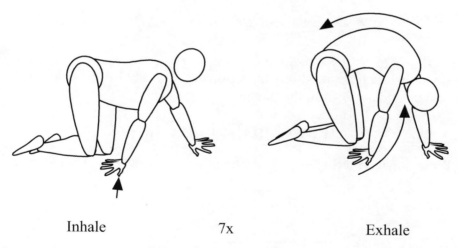

Inhale   7x   Exhale

Turn one palm on the floor so the fingers are pointing towards the knee and the thumb is pointing out to the side stretching the forearm and the inside of the wrist. Place the hand on the floor underneath the shoulder if possible. If the wrist is tight and stiff place the hand near the knee to take some weight off of the wrist. Inhale and lift the heart forward and exhale and look within and feel the stretch down the front of the forearm. Press down on the turned hand and stretch out the wrist and forearm. Inhale and back off for a total of 7 times. Hold the pause on the seventh exhalation and consciously focus on releasing any tightness in your wrist and forearm.

Stretch both Wrists and Forearms at the Same Time

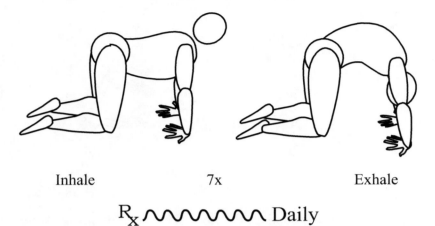

Inhale   7x   Exhale

R$_x$ ∿∿∿∿ Daily

Exhale for the count of nine on the seventh breath and witness your limit, edge and healing in the pause in the stillness, in the space between the breaths.

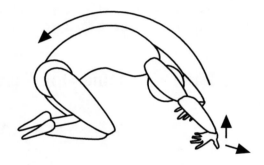

If you are very flexible practice sitting back on your heel and lift the palm of the hand up and the thumb up and away from the fingers.

Power in the Fingertips

Press down with fingertips and lift palm as you sit back on you heels.

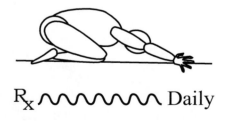

R$_x$ ∿∿∿∿ Daily

Balance the strength and coordination between the fingertips of the left and right hands in elbow plank pose or kneeling elbow plank pose.

Exhale and press your fingertips together from the core of your being. Exhale for the count of five and hold the space for your fingers to strengthen.

Peacock Pose / Mayurasana

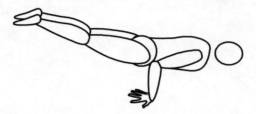

The peacock pose is for those who seek excellent wrist strength and flexibility.

Pressing the backs of the hands together is an excellent counter pose for peacock, crow and handstands.

Lion Pose

In Lion Pose the fingers are to resemble claws, the eyes look up into the third eye and the tongue extends all the way out and down towards the chin. Exhale vigorously through the mouth with the tongue out. Lion Pose activates the emotional psyco-physical side of our face and hands. Practice exhaling the negative emotions that are gnarled in your hands and fingers. Through your eyes, togngue and hands exhale vigorously and release fear, guilt, shame, grief, lying, illusion and attachment.

Anjali Mudra – Namaste - Postures

Anjali mudra, the palms together in front of the heart, the hand gesture traditionally associated with the expression *namaste*. Namaste means to honor, bow, acknowledge and or salute you. It is often translated as the divinity in me honors the divinity in you. Anjali mudra is an excellent psycho-biofeedback loop for how our hands express reverence and gratitude. Anjali mudra can be incorporated into many yoga postures.

R$_X$ 〜〜〜〜〜 Daily

Anjali mudra is an excellent mudra for meditation. Feel the presure of the heel, ball and fingertips of your hands touching. Focus on how the left and right sides of your body are resonating and communicating together as you meditate. Is there more presure on the wrists, and not enough on the on the ball of the hand? Is one hand holding the other up? Is one hand warmer than the other? Is one hand moister?

Having only the finger tips touch with the hands in anjali mudra,
and lowering the position of the hands
helps keep the heart and chest open, and the shoulders relaxed.

Handstands - Adho Mukha Vrksasana / Downward Facing Tree

People often think that you have to hold yourself perfectly still to balance while doing a handstand, like you would hold the steering wheel of a car perfectly still while driving on a straight road. The truth of the matter is that we make constant small adjustments with the steering wheel while we are driving down a straight road. We need to make constant small adjustments with our hands to maintain balance while practicing handstand.

Shift your weight from the fingertips to the heel of the hand and back again. Lean forward and shift your weight onto the fingertips. Press down on the fingertips and shift your weight onto the heel of the hand. Balance your weight between the heel of the hand and the fingertips to maintain a dynamic balance.

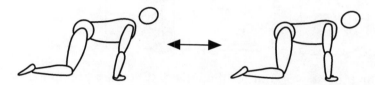

Shift the weight from the fingertips to the heel of the hand to maintain balance.

Focus Your Eyes

Focus your eyes on a point between your hands. Keep you eyes on the point. I like to use an actual object as a focal point like a pebble or crystal that I can clearly see and stay focused on while hopping up into a handstand.

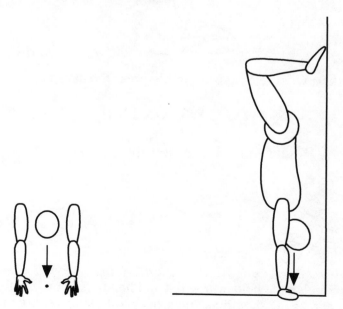

Handstands are an intense workout for the wrists. If you are practicing only practice it a few times before taking a break and let the wrists recover.

Wrist Releasing Postures After Handstands And In General

The simplest and quickest wrist release is to lightly press the backs of the hands together.

R_x ∿∿∿∿∿ Daily

Release and Lengthen the Wrists

Hold onto one wrist and relax the held arm, wrist and hand. As you breathe feel the expansion of the body across the shoulders and arms gently lengthening the space in the wrists. Take seven conscious breaths in any of these postures.

Stand on the Palms Pose / Padahastasana

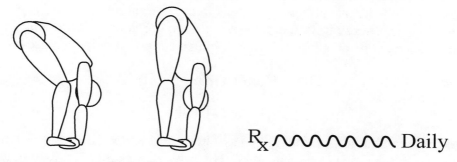

R$_x$ ∿∿∿∿∿ Daily

Stand on your hands with the palms facing up. Bring the toes all the way up to the wrists and lift up on the arms, lengthening the wrist joint. Feel the pressure of the big toe pressing on the base of the thumb. Legs can be bent or straight. Take 7 conscious breaths.

Upward Facing Hands

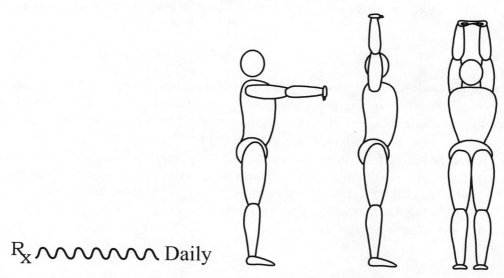

R$_x$ ∿∿∿∿∿ Daily

Interlace the fingers and press the arms straight out in front. Inhale the arms overhead to the best of your ability. Take seven conscious breaths.

Strap Work for Shoulders, Arms and Hands

Inhale up. Exhale forward out and down 7x daily.

Wrap a strap around each hand, inhale and lift the strap off of your back, and exhale forward out and down. Inhale back up to standing. Wrapping the strap around your palm can connect you to different subtleties of joints in the thumbs and fingers. The strap connects the lines of energy from our core out through our hands. Combining full body movement and conscious breathing while grabbing a strap will help increase our grip.

Get a Better Grip on Life

Get Bigger Handles

I remember my grandfather's carpal tunnel syndrome. Grandpa Glenn was a hard workingman from the Great Depression era. He was a remarkably handy man with neat rows of tools in his workshop. When he retired he managed an apartment complex where he put his skills to work making all of the repairs needed. As he grew older, his busy hands started to fail him and he could not grip onto small pliers and screwdrivers. He created special thick handles for his tools so he could get a better grip on them. Eventually he had surgery on his wrist, which helped some, though he was slowly forced to let go of his handyman lifestyle. On the other hand, he became an avid reader in his later years.

Hold On Loosely. Practice Being As Well As Doing.

In our materialistic and mechanistic culture our 'grip on life,' our sense of worthiness and happiness is often based on our possessions and property, and our good works and deeds. As a result, our modern culture focuses on things to get a better grip on life. The emphasis in life is to acquire things and do things to feel happy and useful. Our compulsion to be productive is often stressful. In yoga our sense of self worth is intrinsic in that it is the yoga belief that happiness comes from within, and each of us carries a spark of the divine cosmic flame. If your arm is burning with pain, maybe all you really need is to stop trying to do everything and relax and start being the creativity, love and wisdom that shines through you as you.

R℞ ∿∿∿∿∿ Daily

Close your eyes, open your hand, heart and head, and let your consciousness, intentions and visualizations for health and well-being flow out through your arms and hands.

308

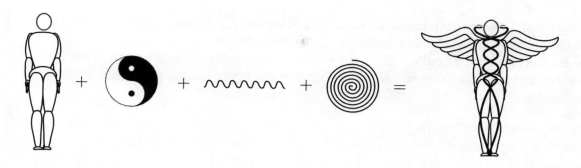

The Knees

Knees are a hinge joint and sensitive to lateral movement and trauma. Part of the reason they are so delicate is that the thigh bone is not in a straight line with the shin, so we need to be conscious of not putting lateral stress on the joint. Whole body integration is the best way to improve the health and well-being of the knees.

There are a large number of postures oriented towards the knees. There are 17 muscle groups that cross the knee. We each have different ranges of motion and unique muscular development so there is a need for a wide variety of therapeutic postures to create the right "recipe" of key postures. Depending on the severity of the issue and where you are in your healing, different key postures for the same issue will present themselves over time. Therapeutic Hatha Yoga is not about toughing it out. It is about loving it out.

Years ago, while putting up holiday lights, I tripped over a kid's bicycle and fell to the pavement with a severely twisted knee. I knew immediately that I had traumatized the tendons, ligaments and fascia at the knee. I was able to walk. I sought out compression for the knee. I cut the sleeve off of a sock and put it around my knee for support, warmth and protection. That made it possible to function the rest of the afternoon. Arnica essence, oil and or aloe gel helped too. Then I headed to the couch with an ice pack on top of the knee and a pillow under the calf and foot. Reclining postures are postures to get you in touch with your inner healer. I have had dozens of students with knee trauma, surgery and replacement over the years. *The classic recommendation for knees is RICE. RICE stands for Rest, Ice, Compression, and Elevation*

Deep Healing Knee Postures

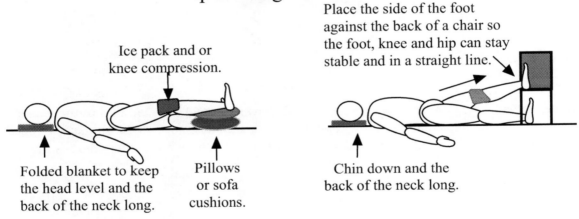

Ice pack and or knee compression.

Place the side of the foot against the back of a chair so the foot, knee and hip can stay stable and in a straight line.

Folded blanket to keep the head level and the back of the neck long.

Pillows or sofa cushions.

Chin down and the back of the neck long.

Breathe long slow even exhalations.
Inhale and witness your pain, exhale and release it.

Bridge Pose with movement and Breath

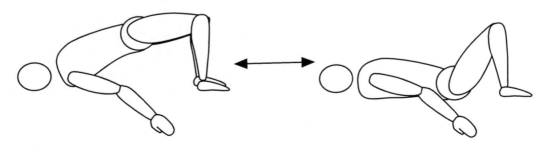

Exhale and lift the hips up rooting the tailbone underneath. Inhale with the hips lifted. Exhale and lower the hips slowly. Inhale with your back on the floor. Exhale and slowly raise your hips. Inhale and expand the heart cavity with the hips raised. Exhale and lower them. Focus on developing the quadriceps, which support the knees.

Consciously Strengthen, Straighten and Stabilize the Knee Joint

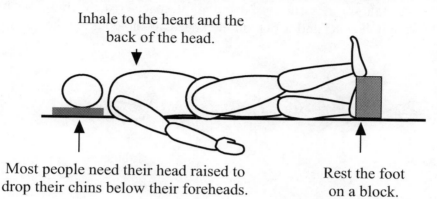

Inhale to the heart and the back of the head.

Most people need their head raised to drop their chins below their foreheads.

Rest the foot on a block.

The knee is happiest when it is straight with the quadriceps engaged and kneecap lifted creating a 'smiling kneecap'.

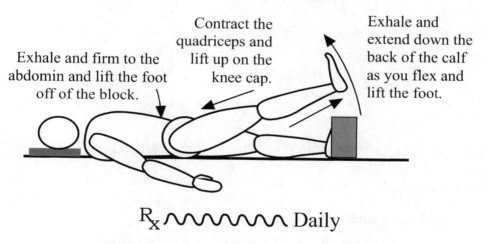

Exhale and firm to the abdomin and lift the foot off of the block.

Contract the quadriceps and lift up on the knee cap.

Exhale and extend down the back of the calf as you flex and lift the foot.

R$_x$ ∿∿∿∿∿ Daily

See if you can exhale for the count of 30 and consciously connect to your knee in the space, in the pause, at the bottom of the exhalation.

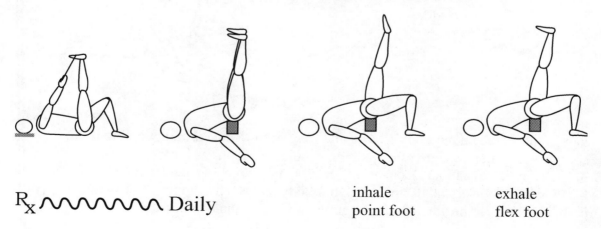

R$_x$ ∿∿∿∿∿ Daily

inhale point foot

exhale flex foot

Bend, Straighten and Strengthen the Knee

The knee is a hinge joint. Bend and straighten the knee pressing through the inside and the outside of the foot and knee equally. Repeat for seven conscious rhythmic breaths and on the last one exhale for the count of 30 and in the space create a conscious healing. Extend out through the heel and lift up on the knee cap and contract the quadriceps.

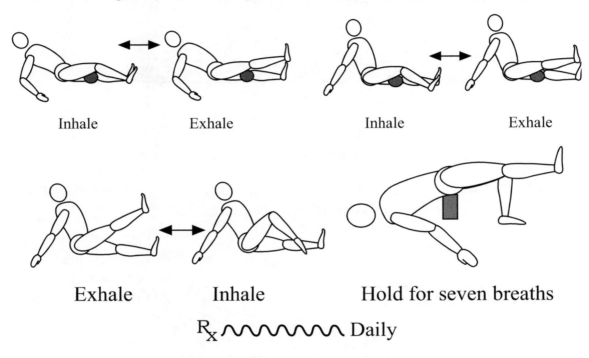

Inhale   Exhale   Inhale   Exhale

Exhale   Inhale   Hold for seven breaths

R$_x$ ∿∿∿∿∿ Daily

Add Resistance to the Extended Leg.

Add a sand bag, shoe or an ankle weight to build more strength. Hold and stay present with the breath. Be careful to maintain the connection between the navel and the spine so as not to strain the low back.

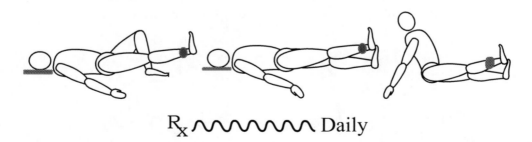

R$_x$ ∿∿∿∿∿ Daily

Pain is like static on our body's radio dial. We need to tune it in, not ignore it. To complicate matters, we are often judging simple sensations as hurtful and bad. There is a message in the sensation. Decipher it! Are the muscles above the knee weak? Knowledge is power and deciphering your body's messages empowers you to not only participate in your health, but also to grow in wisdom and compassion.

Hyperextension and Water Behind the Knee Poses

Focus on Contracting the Muscles Behind the Knee. You could use elastic resistance.
Also practice standing in a forward fold with the knees bent for three minutes!!

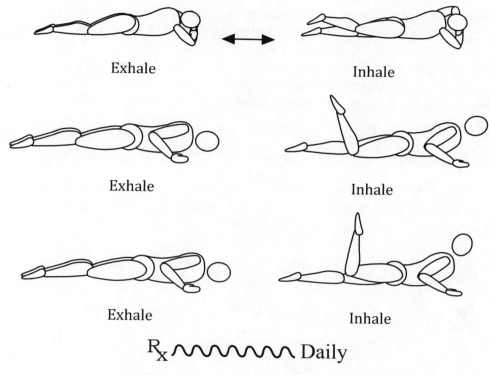

Exhale   Inhale

Exhale   Inhale

Exhale   Inhale

R_x ∿∿∿∿∿∿∿ Daily

Patella Tracking and Knee Alignment

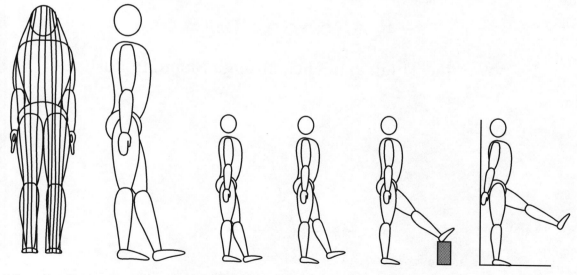

Visualize lines of lines of energy, anatomy trains or kinetic chains running up and down
the whole body. Patellar tracking disorder occurs when the kneecap (patella) shifts out of
place as the leg bends. In most cases, the kneecap shifts too far toward the outside of the

leg. This could happen while bending the knee bicycling or sitting in meditation. The knee joint is a complex hinge that joins the lower leg bones (tibia and fibula) with the thigh bone (femur). The kneecap is held in place in the front of the knee joint by tendons on the top and bottom and by ligaments on the sides. A layer of cartilage lines the underside of the kneecap, helping it glide along the groove at the end of your thighbone. The kneecap can slide off track if the groove is too shallow or if the cartilage is damaged. Ligaments, tendons, or muscles that are too loose can allow the patella to slide out of the groove. Strengthening and improving the lines of energy in the leg and especially the lines of energy moving up the front of the knee connecting to the thigh muscles (quadriceps) is recommended. Consider the patella in the context of the whole body including relative hip rotation, alignment in the knee hinge joint and how the feet are turned.

Chair Pose Variations for the Knees, Hips and Legs

Coordinating movement and breath in Chair Pose with a block between the knees with help center the knee joint in relation to the leg. Strapping the thighs together helps keep tight hips from pulling the knee out of alignment.

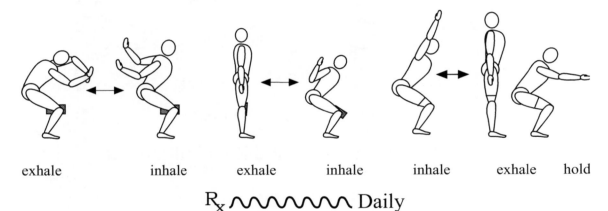

| exhale | inhale | exhale | inhale | inhale | exhale | hold |

R_x ∿∿∿∿∿ Daily

Empower the Thigh and Knee through Standing Postures.

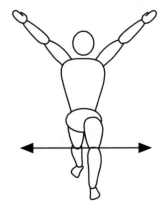

Be Sure the Knee Is Tracking Straight Over the Front Foot and Not Drifting Out or In while Standing, Walking and Cycling.

Strap Your Big Toes Together!

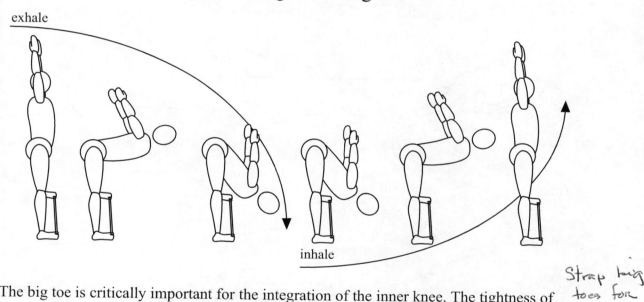

The big toe is critically important for the integration of the inner knee. The tightness of the outer thigh, which pulls the patella off track, can be balanced with good big toe integration. Think of the energy of a torus vortex moving from the toes up through the body towards the top of the head. The grounding energy of the big toe helps to strengthen the inside of the knee providing greater support and stability, thus providing for better tracking for the patella.

There is no need to make the strap too tight and make us wince as we practice. The body will not readily accept what it cannot breathe into.

Visualize your core with lines of energy, running from the toes to the head.

R$_X$ 〰〰〰〰〰 Daily

Adductor Strengthening Poses for the Knee Cap

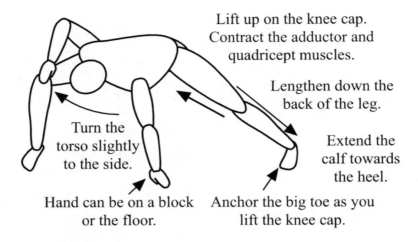

Lift up on the knee cap.
Contract the adductor and
quadricept muscles.

Lengthen down the
back of the leg.

Extend the
calf towards
the heel.

Turn the
torso slightly
to the side.

Hand can be on a block
or the floor.

Anchor the big toe as you
lift the knee cap.

Child's Pose / Balasana bah-lah-sah-nah

Child's Pose lengthens the quadriceps just above the knee adding mobility to the knee.

Exhale   Inhale

Exhale

R$_x$ ∿∿∿∿∿ Daily

316

Thunderbolt / Vajrasana Variations for Thighs and Knees

As your knee heals, you can practice bending it more.
Pressing the palms together helps stabilize the posture. Resting the hands on the thighs is more relaxing. Bringing the thumb and forefinger together (jnana mudra, the wisdom seal) is also powerful.

R$_X$ ∿∿∿∿∿ Daily

THY Blockhead Yoga Knee Practice

inhale   exhale

inhale
point foot

exhale
flex foot

R~~~~~ Daily

Lotus Postures

Sitting in padmasana, the lotus posture, is a great challenge for most of us, yet it is one of the iconic postures we associate with Yoga. It is the typical pretzel pose we want to attempt. The lotus posture requires very flexible ankles, knees and hips to be performed safety and comfortably. The basic problem with full lotus is that if your ankles and or your hips are tight and uncomfortable the stress is usually felt in the knees. In fact, without proper lines of awareness and attention through the feet, knees and hips, the knees will experience pain and injury.

Knee injury from practicing full lotus and half lotus is all too common. In an effort to get a taste of the lotus posture, one can lose sight of function of the posture for exterior physical form. The Lotus Posture is an iconic posture not because of its pretzel nature, rather because it is one of the most stable postures for meditation. Any stable seated posture is great for meditation. You do not have to be a pretzel to meditate.

My Knees And Full Lotus

My knees were really strong after three years of roller-skating in Venice, California. When I started practicing meditation and yoga I didn't have any pain or discomfort in my knees, though I could only hold full lotus for a couple of seconds. I heard stories about people hurting their knees, though my knee never hurt. They were just stiff.   I kept practicing yoga and meditation though I stopped roller-skating. This was not a problem and in a couple of years of daily practice I was great at full lotus and was able to sit for up to a half an hour though I practiced sukha or siddhasana most of the time. Then I stopped practicing intensely and the years went by. One cool morning in November, I thought I would sit for 20 minutes of meditation and I pulled my legs up into full lotus without much thought! I damaged the inside of my right knee and probably tore medial collateral ligament and or cartilage of my right knee. I had to practice therapeutic yoga for 18 months before I felt comfortable in full lotus again. That was over dozen years ago and I have perfected safe ways of entering and exiting lotus for the knees.

319

It is extremely important to warm up hips, knees and feet completely before moving into lotus. It is important to remember that what truly attracts us to the lotus posture are the principles and benefits of stillness and meditation, not contortionism Furthermore, we must remember that we do not need to master lotus to reap the benefits of stillness and meditation and that we meditate primarily with our hearts and heads not our legs.

Lotus is one of the most important postures in the ancient and modern yoga texts. "The yogi seated in the padmasana posture, by steadying the breath... becomes liberated. There is no doubt about this." according to the *Hatha Yoga Pradipika*. Eric Schiffmann lists padmasana as the most important posture, and shavasana as second because they offer the most stable postures for meditation. A unique number of lotus petals are associated with each of the seven major chakras. The lotus is commonly referred to as symbolic of human's spiritual evolution, with its roots in the mud representing our lower nature, the stem rising through the water symbolizing our spiritual search and the flower blossoming in the sunlight symbolizing our self-realization.

Our toes are what really snuggle into the mud and they are the final destination of the lines of energy, which connect the hip, knee and ankle. The toes are the seed of the lotus posture and without incorporating them first you run the risk of damaging your knees if your hips or ankles are too tight.

Preparation for Half Lotus and Full Lotus Postures

Connect the lines of energy and awareness out through the hips, knees, feet and toes.

Exhale and bring your face towards your knee.

R$_x$ ∿∿∿∿∿ Daily

Hold onto the sole of the foot with the palm of one hand. Flex the foot, extend out through the heel and exhale it towards your face. Repeat the movement six times, then hold the foot towards the face for the seventh breath. Change sides.

See if you can bring your heel to your buttocks as you exhale.

Rock The Baby

R_x  Daily

Cradle your leg in your arms. Extend out through the heel and dorsiflex the foot pulling your toes back. Lift your heart as you hug the leg to your chest and take seven deep breaths. Sitting on a cushion, foam block or folded blankets helps level the pelvis and maintain a natural curve in the low back. You can rock your leg, though just holding steady and lifted is good. Pretend that your leg is a baby, and your knee is the baby's head and kiss your knee. Can you nibble on your baby's toes?

A Lotus Seated Twist

Extend through the ball of the feet and the heel. Practice turning the head left and right.

Lotus Fish Pose Variations

Inhale and lift the heart. Exhale and extend out through the legs.

Extend out through the sole of the foot, heel and toes.

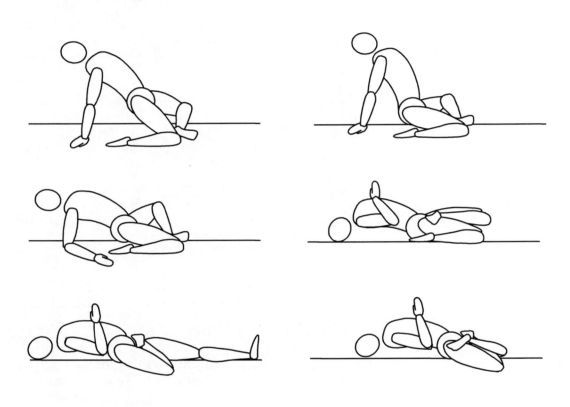

Half Lotus Sequence

The Lotus Knee Posture
Janu Padmasana

A Half Frog Posture
Ardha Bhekasana

The Lotus Seed Posture
Bija Padmasana

The Sleeping Lotus Bud
Ardha Padma Savasana

The Waking Lotus Bud
Urdva Ardha Padma Savasana

The Lotus Breeze Pose
Ardha Padma Pavanamuktasana

The Single Half Lotus Leg Lift
Urdhva Ardha Padma
Ekapadasana

The Half Lotus Staff
Ardha Padma Dandasana

The Half Lotus Boat
Ardha Padma Navasana

The Half Lotus Opens to the East
Ardha Padma Purvottanasana

The Half Lotus Bridge
Setu Bandha Ardha Padma
Sarvangasana

The Half Lotus Desk
Ardha Padma Dvipada
Pithamasana

The Half Lotus Shoulderstand
Ardha Padma Sarvangasansana

The Half Lotus Plow
Ardha Padma Halasana

Half Lotus Fish
Ardha Padma Matsayasana

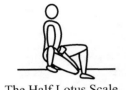

The Half Lotus Scale
Ardha Padma Tolasana

Lotus
Padmasana

Scale Pose
Tolasana

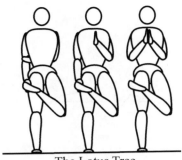

The Lotus Tree
Ardha Padma Vrikshasana

R~~~~~~~ Daily

Om Mani Padme Hum

(OM MAH-NEE PAHD-MEY HOOM)

The Jewel of the Mind Rests in the Lotus of the Heart.

The Jewel of Consciousness is in the Heart's Lotus.

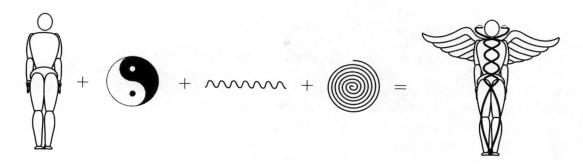

The Pelvic Floor, Urinary Incontinence
And the Prostate

Women and men have a urinary sphincter.
Men have a prostate gland wrapped around it.
What is good for the goose is good for the gander.

This practice is ideal for urinary incontinence, the prostate and the vagina. It is a conscious integration of body, mind and breathe that goes beyond the commonly prescribed Kegel exercises. In traditional Kegel exercises, you simply contract the pelvic floor muscles and hold the contraction of three seconds and repeat it several times. Therapeutic Hath Yoga postures for urinary incontinence and prostate and vaginal health are chosen to connect to the urinary sphincter, pubococcyeal muscle and other muscles of the pelvic diaphragm similar to traditional Kegel exercises. However, there is a huge difference. Therapeutic Hatha Yoga postures incorporate conscious breathing and visualization. Lots of research has been done around Kegel exercises for women and men. Many studies identify Kegels with the PC muscle and pelvic diaphragm, yet they make no mention of how the pelvic diaphragm is involved with the breath. Even though abdominals and buttocks are "separate" muscle groups from the PC muscle they are all woven together with connective tissues and all participate in a deep, full, diaphragmatic breath. The commonly suggested way of to find and become ware of your puococcygeal muscles is to stop your flow of urine. Another way to find them is to put your finger in your anus and feel the muscles used to contract the pelvic floor.

Posture Chart for the Pelvic Floor, Urinary Incontinence and the Prostate

Some advice for men practicing Therapeutic Hatha Yoga: start simple. Inhale to the heart exhale to the navel seven times. This is a highly structured practice integrating body, breath and mind. No need to worry about whether you are accomplishing anything as long as you keep taking deep conscious rhythmic breaths.

R$_x$ 〰〰〰〰 Daily

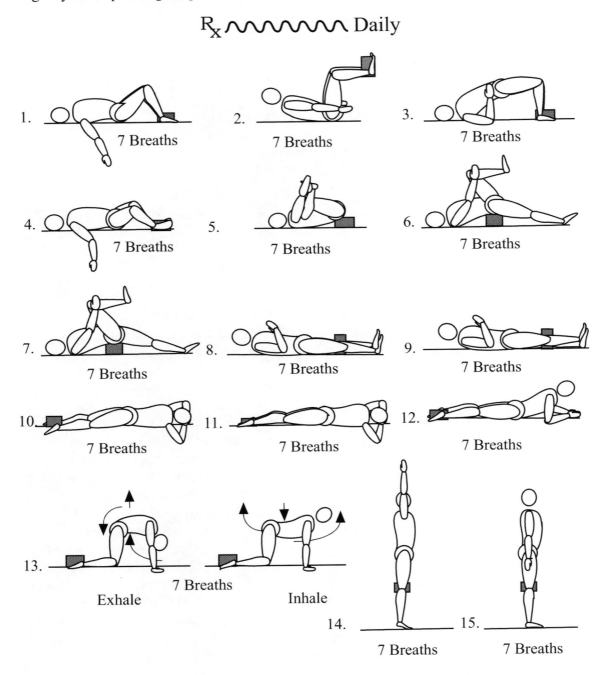

1.   7 Breaths

2.   7 Breaths

3.   7 Breaths

4.   7 Breaths

5.   7 Breaths

6.   7 Breaths

7.   7 Breaths

8.   7 Breaths

9.   7 Breaths

10.   7 Breaths

11.   7 Breaths

12.   7 Breaths

13.   7 Breaths   Exhale   Inhale

14.   7 Breaths

15.   7 Breaths

1. Pelvic Floor - Corpse Pose Variation

Shavasana • *shava* = corpse and a*sana* = pose in Sanskrit

Center yourself.

In total stillness and silence,

close your eyes and look within.

Create some space and time to connect to your Inner Teacher-Healer-Guide.

Exhale and contract your body. Inhale and expand your body.

Exhale to the navel and inhale to your heart.

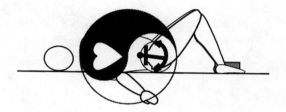

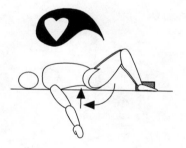

Connect movement
with breath.

7 Breath Cycles

Inhale to the heart. Draw the breath down
to the navel, to the pubic bone. Feel the
tailbone on the floor and an arch in the low
back. Inhale all the way into the prostate.

Exhale to the navel, the navel to the
spine and the spine to the floor and
lightly tuck the the tailbone. Exhale
all the way to the prostate and anchor
the body to the earth.

R_X  Daily

2. Pelvic Floor - Leg Extension Variations

Ardha Urdhva Prasarita Padasana

ardha = half, urdhva = raised or elevated, prasarita=extended, pada = foot or leg

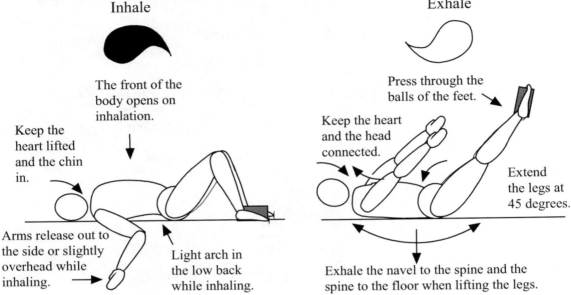

Inhale

The front of the body opens on inhalation.

Keep the heart lifted and the chin in.

Arms release out to the side or slightly overhead while inhaling.

Light arch in the low back while inhaling.

Exhale

Press through the balls of the feet.

Keep the heart and the head connected.

Extend the legs at 45 degrees.

Exhale the navel to the spine and the spine to the floor when lifting the legs.

Leg extensions are ideal for integrating movement and breath, and building abdominal strength.

R̲x̲ ∿∿∿∿∿ Daily

Bend your knees, if your legs and abdomen are not strong enough to keep your low back neutral or on the floor while you exhale.

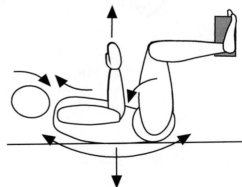

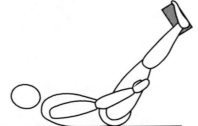

Hold onto the thighs for the most support.

3. Pelvic Floor - Bridge Pose Variation

Setu Bandhasana setu = bridge, bandha = support

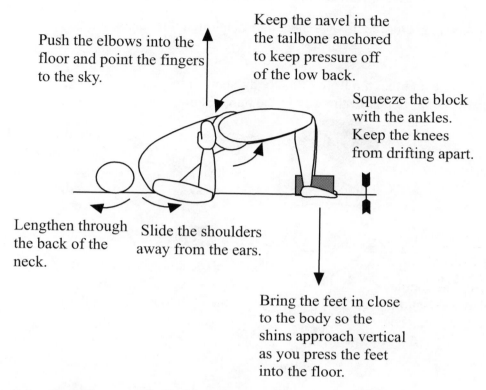

Push the elbows into the floor and point the fingers to the sky.

Keep the navel in the the tailbone anchored to keep pressure off of the low back.

Squeeze the block with the ankles. Keep the knees from drifting apart.

Lengthen through the back of the neck.

Slide the shoulders away from the ears.

Bring the feet in close to the body so the shins approach vertical as you press the feet into the floor.

Exhale, tighten the buttocks and tone the pelvic floor. Inhale and lift the heart.

Our lifestyle dominated by sitting in chairs has adversely affected our pelvic floor health. We drive for hours sitting in bucket seats. We relax on overstuffed sofas. We watch television in reclining chairs. No wonder the webbing of our pelvic diaphragm is sagging, contributing to urinary incontinence, prolapsed uterus, enlarged prostate and hip degeneration. This pose is ideal for reversing a lifestyle of sitting in chairs. Lift your bottom up and out of the seat!

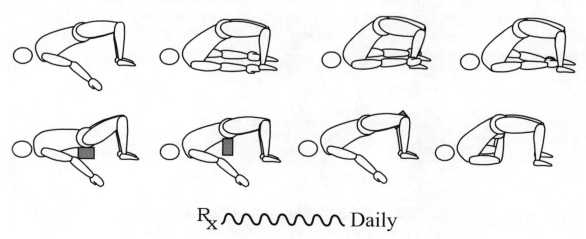

R$_X$ ∿∿∿∿∿∿ Daily

4. Pelvic Floor - Lying Butterfly Pose

Supta Konasana • supta = lying down, kon = angle

Lying Butterfly posture facilitates three part diaphragmatic inhalations.

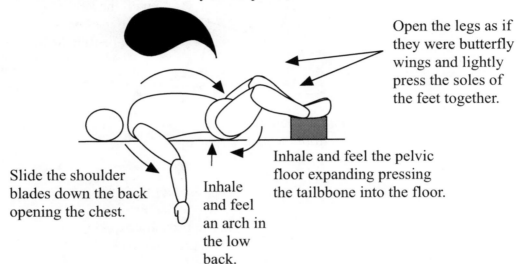

Inhale and feel the front of the body open from the collar bones all the way to the pubic bone.

Open the legs as if they were butterfly wings and lightly press the soles of the feet together.

Slide the shoulder blades down the back opening the chest.

Inhale and feel an arch in the low back.

Inhale and feel the pelvic floor expanding pressing the tailbbone into the floor.

An incomplete inhalation to the pelvic floor diminishes

the circulation of both awareness and blood to the pelvic floor

contributing to urinary retention and incontinence.

R$_X$ ∿∿∿∿∿ Daily

It is important to be able to inhale and completely release and relax our abdomen, buttocks, pelvic diaphragm and legs, as well as to exhale and completely contract the abdomen, buttocks, pelvic diaphragm and legs. This is important so our life energy reaches all corners of our bodies.

Place the feet either side of the block on the floor if it is too much for the back and or hips to have the feet on the block.

5. Pelvic Floor - Happy Baby or Dead Bug Pose

Apanasana • apana = out-breath or downward breath

Here is a real union of opposites to have a posture referred to as Happy Baby or Dead Bug. In Happy Baby we focus on releasing the backs of the legs, buttocks and pelvic floor releasing downward flowing energy, *apana*. This is a great pose to feel the webbing of the pelvic diaphragm.

So often, we use the secondary muscles of the buttocks in an effort to contract the pelvic diaphragm and do not fully engage the true muscles of the pelvic floor, the perineum and the pubococcygeus muscle. In this posture, the buttocks muscles are lengthened, making it virtually impossible to fully engage them and thus making it easier to feel the muscles of the pelvic diaphragm separately when exhaling.

R$_X$ ∿∿∿∿∿∿ Daily

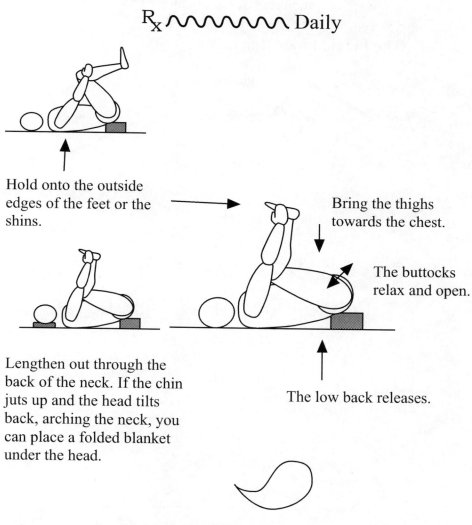

Hold onto the outside edges of the feet or the shins.

Bring the thighs towards the chest.

The buttocks relax and open.

Lengthen out through the back of the neck. If the chin juts up and the head tilts back, arching the neck, you can place a folded blanket under the head.

The low back releases.

Lengthen your exhalations and feel the pelvic diaphragm contract.

6. Pelvic Floor - Hug Left Leg

Eka Pada Apanasana • eka = one, pada = foot or leg

Hold onto the shin and gently hug the knee to the chest while exhaling.

Extend the energy out the leg. The more you pull the left knee in the more the right leg will lift off of the floor.

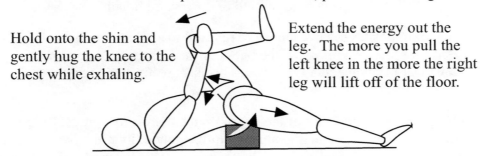

Root the tailbone underneath. You can try tightening and releasing the buttock muscle on the right side to connect to the pelvic floor and increase the opening of the right hip.

The Pelvic Floor Hammuck

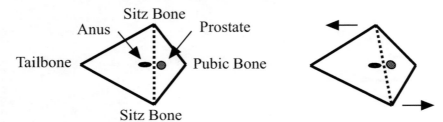

This pose creates lateral shearing of the pelvic floor as you pull one leg in and extend the other out.

R$_x$ ∿∿∿∿∿∿ Daily

7. Pelvic Floor - Hug Right Leg

Eka Pada Apanasana • eka = one, pada = foot or leg

Notice the difference between your right and left sides. Count 7 Exhalations

R$_x$ ∿∿∿∿∿∿ Daily

8. Pelvic Floor - The Nutcracker / Left Leg On Top

The famous yoga master B.K.S. Iyengar in his seminal work, *Light on Yoga,* listed Eka Pada Sirsasana, one leg behind your head, as a curative posture for the pelvic floor and prostate. The problem is that most people cannot do this pose. Here is a pose that most of us can do.

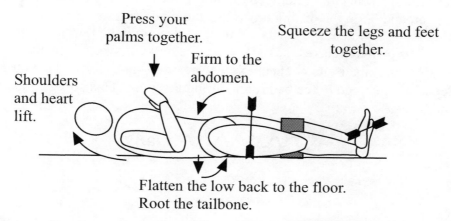

Press your palms together.

Firm to the abdomen.

Squeeze the legs and feet together.

Shoulders and heart lift.

Flatten the low back to the floor.
Root the tailbone.

Exhale and vigorously contract the abdominal cavity.
Inhale and relax back down to the floor 7 times
Rx ∿∿∿∿ Daily

Exhale the navel to spine and spine to the floor. Exhale and squeeze the legs together as if they were the handles of a nutcracker. Contract the abdominal and buttocks so tightly that the legs begin to lift off of the floor. Exhale and tighten the buttocks and drive the tailbone to the pubic bone. Keep the legs on the floor if the low back comes off of the floor. Experiment without the block between the legs.

Exhale and squeeze, 'crack', your walnut shaped prostate gland.

9. The Nutcracker / Right Leg On Top

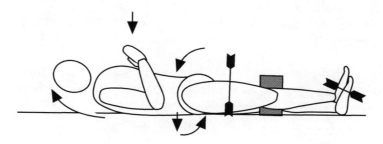

Exhale and vigorously contract pelvic floor and hold the pause 7 times.

10. Pelvic Floor - The Resting Crocodile Pose

Makarasana • makara = crocodile

Connect to the water element in your body.

The 2nd Chakra represents the water element in the body. The animal symbol of the 2nd Chakra is the crocodile. In the resting crocodile, the rib cage rests on the floor restricting the inhalation to the heart cavity. Focus on inhaling deep into the lower abdomen and bladder area. This posture relaxes the parasympathic nervous system. Inhale and feel the fluidity of the body. Inhale and connect to the water element of the body. You will probably feel the urge to go to the bathroom during this pose. This pose is good for urinary continence.

R$_x$ ∿∿∿∿∿∿ Daily

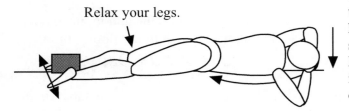

Relax your feet and let your ankles fall away from the block.

Relax your legs.

Rest the forehead on the back of your hands. Inhale and soften your forehead. Let go of any tension in your brow. Let go of any fear or worry.

Relax your brow.

Let any tension melt away.

Let go of any worry.

Let go of any anxiety.

Let go of any fear.

Be like a sleeping crocodile with no worries. No one is going to disturb you. Relax with your belly flat on the floor. Take an inhalation all the way down to the pubic bone and let the tailbone slightly lift. Take a deeper, longer inhalation.

Research that shows that perceived stress and anxiety reduce blood flow and even impair the ability of genes to repair their DNA on a cellular level.

Count 7 Inhalations

11. Pelvic Floor - The Alert Crocodile Pose

Makarasana • makara = crocodile

The Alert Crocodile dams the body's water back. Urinary issues are literally and figuratively connected to the water element. Anchor your tailbone to the floor and make your pelvic basin watertight. Practice this so when you do go to sleep your urinary sphincter is still water tight.

Press down with the tops of the feet.

Focus on rooting the tailbone down and anchoring the pelvis to the floor. Exhale and drive the tailbone through the prostate or the vaginal walls into the pubic bone.

Rest the forehead on the back of your hands. Keep your brow and face soft as you activate your trunck and legs.

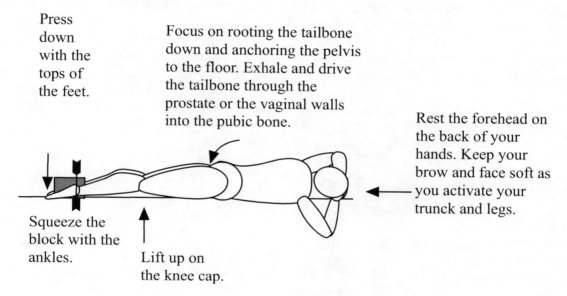

Squeeze the block with the ankles.

Lift up on the knee cap.

Rediscover the pelvic floor with Yoga Kegels!

In traditional Kegel exercises, one simply contracts the pubococcygeal muscle, or PC muscle, and other muscles of the pelvic floor and holds the contraction for a few seconds and repeats it several times. Therapeutic Hatha Yoga Kegels incorporate stylized postures for maximum effect and include specific breathing cues for even more effectiveness. Lots of research has been done around Kegel exercises and they have been shown to help achieve greater control over the flow of urine. I am sure research will show that Yoga Kegels with stylized postures combined with breathing techniques, is very effective for improving the urinary tract and strengthening the pelvic floor.

Make your pelvic basin watertight!

Urinary issues are literally and figuratively connected to the water element. Anchor your tailbone to the floor and make your pelvic basin watertight. Exhale for the count of 9 and root the exhalation from tailbone through the urinary sphincter and into the pubic bone sealing it tight.

Count 7 Deep Inhalations, Deep Exhalations and

A Deep Healing Pause-Stillness-Space that is Watertight.

12. Pelvic Floor - Cobra Pose Variation

Bhujanasana • bhujanga = snake or serpent

Connect to the earth element in your body.

The cobra's habitat is on the earth and between the roots of plants. Snakes are connected to the earth element and the root chakra in the yoga tradition. The Cobra Pose is ideal for making your pelvic basin, your earthen bowl watertight. **No urinary incontinence here.**

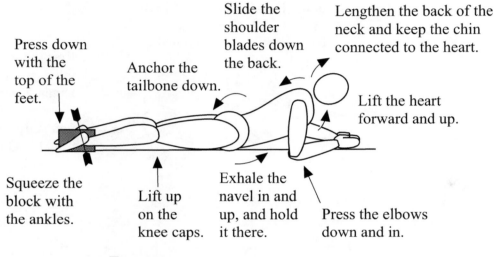

Press down with the top of the feet.

Anchor the tailbone down.

Slide the shoulder blades down the back.

Lengthen the back of the neck and keep the chin connected to the heart.

Lift the heart forward and up.

Squeeze the block with the ankles.

Lift up on the knee caps.

Exhale the navel in and up, and hold it there.

Press the elbows down and in.

R$_x$ ∿∿∿∿ Daily

Hold the pause at the end of the exhalation and engage the Triple Lock.

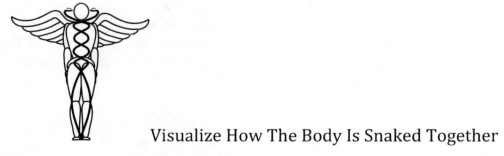

Visualize How The Body Is Snaked Together

Press the right big toe into the floor and inhale *prana* from the right big toe up through the pelvic floor to the left nostril, through the ida nadi. Exhale *apana* back down through the ida nadi removing toxins and disease. Inhale from the left big toe up through pelvic floor to the right nostril through the pingula nadi. Exhale back down the pingula nadi. Press both big toes into the floor and inhale *prana* up your legs and cross the midline at the urinary sphincter and then up to each nostril. Exhale down through the ida and pingula nadis crossing the midline at the urinary sphincter. Breathe fresh life force into the pelvic floor.

13. Pelvic Floor - Cat & Dog Tilts

Find a balance. Find a neutral pelvis, as if you were standing with a plumb line running through your middle ear, shoulder, pelvic floor and hip. Feel your pelvic floor. Contract and release your puboccygeal muscle without engaging your buttocks.

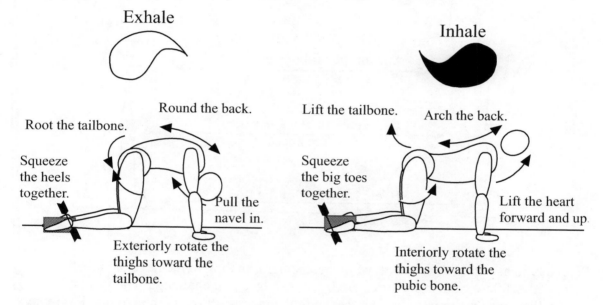

Exhale
Inhale

Round the back.
Root the tailbone.
Squeeze the heels together.
Pull the navel in.
Exteriorly rotate the thighs toward the tailbone.

Lift the tailbone.
Arch the back.
Squeeze the big toes together.
Lift the heart forward and up.
Interiorly rotate the thighs toward the pubic bone.

Exhale and contract the prostate, shut off the urinary sphincter and open the prostate gland ducts for a more powerful orgasm and ejaculation. Inhale and expand the body, adding pressure to the bladder and opening the prostate/urinary sphincter valve for easier urination.

R$_x$ ⌇⌇⌇⌇⌇⌇ Daily

Focus on the pause at the top and the bottom of the breath.

14. Pelvic Floor - Raised Hand Posture Variation

Urdhva Hastasana • urdhva=raised, hasta = hand

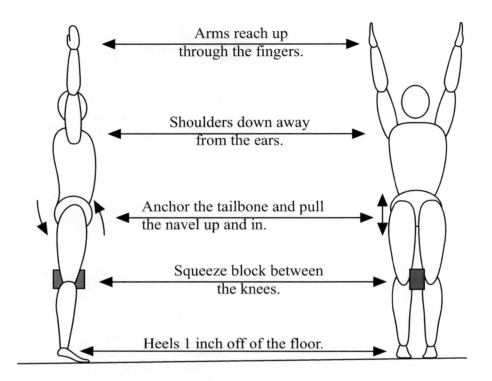

Arms reach up
through the fingers.

Shoulders down away
from the ears.

Anchor the tailbone and pull
the navel up and in.

Squeeze block between
the knees.

Heels 1 inch off of the floor.

People typically hold their breath while balancing. Exhaling to the navel and feeling grounded, while the heels and arms are lifted, can be a real challenge. The weight generally falls to the outsides of the feet and the big toes lift off of the ground. Keep the big toes grounded and the shoulders relaxed.

R$_x$ ∿∿∿∿∿ Daily

Arms can be positioned wider to keep shoulders relaxed & down.

15. Pelvic Floor - Even Standing Pose / Mountain Pose

Samasthiti / Tadasana • sama = even or equal, sthiti = standing, tada = mountain

As you lower your heels to the ground and your arms by your sides you will be able to feel the tailbone ready to root and anchor down.

R$_x$ ∿∿∿∿∿ Daily

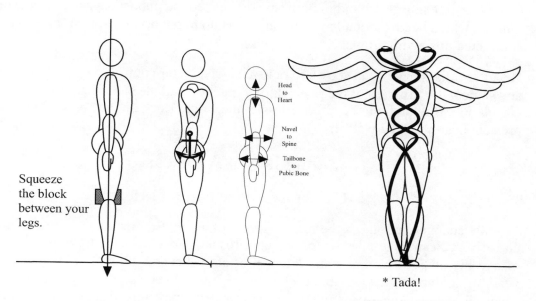

Squeeze the block between your legs.

Head to Heart

Navel to Spine

Tailbone to Pubic Bone

* Tada!

The arms straighten down as you straighten up.

You might think of the interjection "Tada!" in this posture exclaiming that you are now consciously connected to your prostate gland.

The Prostate

The prostate gland is a partly muscular body functioning as both a urinary sphincter and a partly exocrine glandular body that secretes an alkaline viscous fluid, which is a major constituent of the semen. The prostate gland is a vital center for male vitality, urine flow, sex drive and overall health. The prostate gland is about the size of a walnut or kiwi that

encircles the neck of the bladder and the tube that carries urine from the bladder to the penis. A complex system of valves in the prostate sends semen into the urethra during ejaculation and the prostate muscle called the sphincter seals the bladder. The prostate adds the alkaline fluid to sperm just before ejaculation.

The Ultimate Pelvic Floor Pose is The Triple Lock Or The Great Seal
(See Super Yoga Healing Powers)

The prostate is located just above the pelvic floor muscles, or pelvic diaphragm, a hammock-like sheath of muscle webbing. You can visualize the pelvic floor as a spreader-bar hammock having two firm anchor points at the tailbone and the pubic bone with a spreader-bar between them, attached to the left and right sitting bones. This hammock-like muscle, found in both sexes, is called the pubococcygeus muscle or PC muscle, which begins around the anus and runs up to the urinary sphincter, and is contracted during traditional Kegel exercises.

Kegel exercises have been shown to help achieve greater control over the flow of urine and semen, the firmness of the penis during erection and the shooting power of the ejaculation. Research on the effctiveness of the Triple Lock on the pelvic floor and prostate health will be welcome.

Aging Is Not A Disease.

Cancer Cells Are Part Of Life.

Prostate changes are one of the many aspects of aging. Studies indicate that many men at an early age can have microscopic, latent prostate cancer. By the time a man is 50 years of age his odds of having some latent prostate cancer is 30-40%. If you live to be 90 years of age your odds are about 99% that you will have some prostate cancer. Prostate cancer is major concern for men. The cancer cells may spread out to other parts of the body, particularly the bones and lymph nodes. Prostate cancer may cause difficulty urinating, difficulty starting and maintaining a stream and painful urination. Secretions from the prostate gland are included in semen content. Prostate cancer may also cause problems during sexual intercourse or erectile dysfunction. In most cases, prostate cancer is slow-growing and treatable. If you have BHP you do not necessarily have prostate cancer though the odds are greater. Many factors, including diet, toxins, high pH levels, genetics, parasites, nutrition, saturated animal fat and sedentary lifestyle have been implicated in the development of prostate cancer. Traditional allopathic treatments vary and include surgery, radiation, proton therapy, hormonal therapy, chemotherapy and ultrasound. There are a variety of natural treatments which include, but are not limited to saw palmetto, beta-sitosterol, zinc, nutrition, diet, lowering the body's pH, exercise and lifestyle changes.

The all-too-common practice of surgically removing the prostate gland is the equivalent of the unnecessary reproductive surgeries often performed on women, such as cesarean births and hysterectomies. Men are now where women were 30-40 years ago in terms of taking charge of their own reproductive health. Men and women need to become more educated about their bodies, and to do their own research to find out about the wide variety of health-promoting healing approaches available to them.

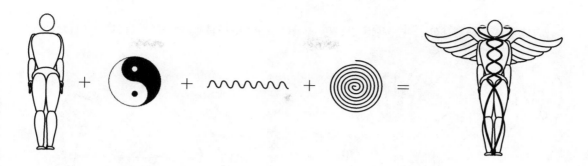

The Sinus Passages, Eyes and Face

Sinus Passages, Eyes and Face Posture Pressure Points1

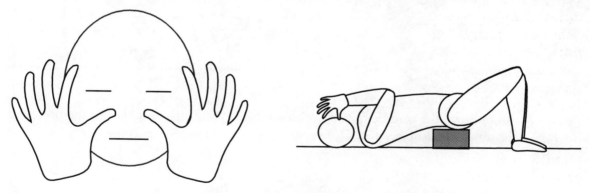

Place your thumbs either side of your nose on the bottom rim of the orb of the eyes.

Lift the hips up and connect your thumbs into your nasal cavities and count out seven conscious actively-yielding exhalations through your nasal passages. Lower the hips down and focus on your sinus passages for seven more breaths.

Sinus Passages, Eyes and Face Posture Pressure Points 2

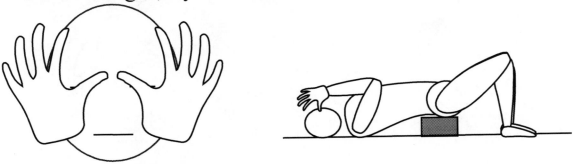

Place your thumbs on the inside corners of your eye sockets, at the nasion and either side of the bridge of the nose.

Lift the hips up and connect your thumbs into your nasal cavities and count out seven conscious exhalations through your nose. Lower your hips and take seven more breaths.

R~~~~~~ Daily

Sinus Passages, Eyes and Face Posture Pressure Points 3

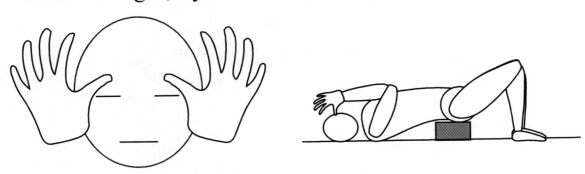

Place your thumbs on the middle of the eyebrows. Lift your hips and deepen the pressure on the eye brows and nasal cavities. Lower your hips and take seven more conscious breaths.

R~~~~~~ Daily

Jala Neti and Sutra Neti

Traditional hatha yoga practices for cleansing nasal passages would include the use of Jala Neti and Sutra Neti. Jala Neti uses a small funnel shaped neti pot for pouring warm lightly salted water into one nostril and out the other irrigating the nasal passages. Traditionally Sutra Neti involves inserting a string coated with bees wax into nasal passages. I tried it, but the string was too thick for my nasal passages. I now use thin, clean, smooth and unscented dental tape. It is perfect for that ultimate nasal cleaning.

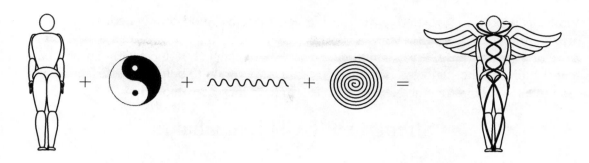

Sleep Apnea,

Throat, Tongue and Baldness

Sleep apnea is a disorder where there is a temporary suspension of the breath during sleep that is primarily due to the tongue and palate falling backwards in the throat and blocking the airway. Sleeping on one's side often helps. Many people are told to avoid alcohol and sleeping pills, which can relax throat muscles contributing to the collapse of the airway at night. Therapeutic hatha yoga for sleep apnea brings strength and structure to the throat, tongue and soft palate.

For moderate to severe sleep apnea, that does not improve with changing sleeping position and or diet, the most common treatment is the use of a continuous positive airway pressure (CPAP) or Automatic Positive Airway Pressure (APAP) device, which 'splints' or 'supports' the patient's airway, open during sleep by means of a flow of pressurized air into the throat. It is important to note that the air we breathe is already pressurized due to the weight of the 6 miles of atmosphere above us. The weight of the air above us actually continuously supplies us with constant positive air pressure.

The patient typically wears a plastic facial mask, which is connected by a flexible tube to a small bedside CPAP machine. The CPAP machine generates the required air pressure to keep the patient's airways open during sleep. CPAP therapy is effective at 'fixing' the problem yet it does not resolve the root of the problem. CPAP only masks the symptoms literally and figuratively.

Baldness is primarily related to diminished hair follicles, and is not genetically predetermined. The weakness in the throat associated with sleep apnea is related to an overcompensation of tightness in the back of the neck, which reduces circulation to the hair follicles in the scalp. As postures strengthen the throat to help prevent sleep apnea, they relax and lengthen the back of the neck to help increase blood flow.

Strengthen the Throat Chakra

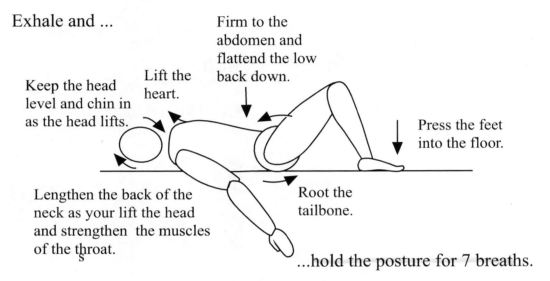

Exhale and ...

Keep the head level and chin in as the head lifts.

Lift the heart.

Firm to the abdomen and flattend the low back down.

Press the feet into the floor.

Lengthen the back of the neck as your lift the head and strengthen the muscles of the throat.

Root the tailbone.

...hold the posture for 7 breaths.

R$_x$ ∿∿∿∿ Daily

Bridge Pose for Sleep Apnea

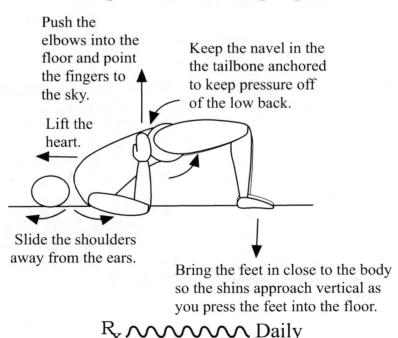

Push the elbows into the floor and point the fingers to the sky.

Keep the navel in the the tailbone anchored to keep pressure off of the low back.

Lift the heart.

Slide the shoulders away from the ears.

Bring the feet in close to the body so the shins approach vertical as you press the feet into the floor.

R$_x$ ∿∿∿∿ Daily

344

Rabbit Pose Variations for the Tongue and Sleep Apnea

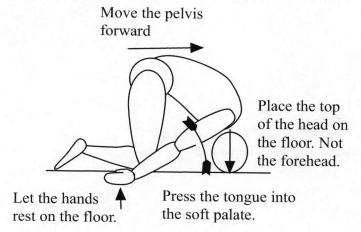

Move the pelvis forward

Place the top of the head on the floor. Not the forehead.

Let the hands rest on the floor.

Press the tongue into the soft palate.

Feel the tongue on the roof of the mouth and the soft palate,

The chest the and front of the body are compressed.

Breathe into the sides of the and back of the body.

Inhale and expand the back of the neck and scalp.

Follow the Infinity Loop

Into the throat and up the back of the head as you breathe.

R$_x$ 〜〜〜〜〜 Daily

Listen to the smooth even flow of the breath.

Listen to the sound of the ocean of consciousness in your breath.

The Metaphysical Meditation For Healing In The Throat Chakra

Listen to Blue Ether with Your Third Ear.

Shoulder Stand and Plow Pose Variations for Sleep Apnea

Shalamba Sarvangasana / Supported Shoulder stand and Halasana / Plow
Shalamba = supported; Sarva = all, whole, entire, complete; anga = limb

R$_x$ ⌇⌇⌇⌇⌇ Daily

Folded blankets under the shoulders, not under the head, can help people with stiff necks to come onto the top of the shoulders. These postures are great for listening to the soft sound of rhythmic ujjayi breathing.

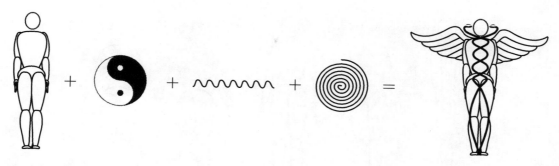

Memory Loss, Alzheimer's, ADD and ADHD

The Mindfulness Standing Posture – Standing at Attention

With the chin in and the back of the neck long, adjust the back of your head onto the wall and tune in to your mind, to your inner space.

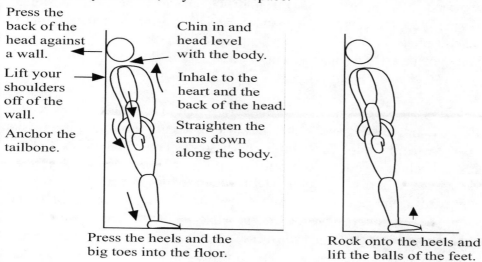

Press the back of the head against a wall.

Lift your shoulders off of the wall.

Anchor the tailbone.

Chin in and head level with the body.

Inhale to the heart and the back of the head.

Straighten the arms down along the body.

Press the heels and the big toes into the floor.

Rock onto the heels and lift the balls of the feet.

To stand at attention is to stand aligning the head with the body. To stand at attention is to be present. It is to be mindful. I would like to see research on the effects of aligning the position of the head in relationship to improved memory, mental focus, lack of attention, Alzheimer's, ADD and ADHD. Do we have better neurological connections when our head is better aligned with the rest of the body?

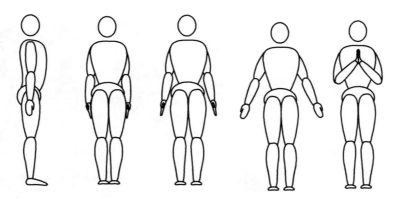

There are several good arm positions to help align the spine while leaning the back of the head onto the wall. Consciously breathe into the mindfulness posture for a couple of minutes.

Yoganautasana / Inner Space Traveler

I created this posture to help people better align their heads on their bodies to increase the flow of energy to the brain. The word *astronaut* includes the root *naut*, from *nautes*, the Greek word for "sailor." This suffix can be used to create many travel-specific words. For example, the Argonauts were mythical Greek sailors on the ship named the Argo. *Astronaut* gets the *astro* from the Greek word *astron*, meaning, "star" making an astronaut a "star sailor." Russian space explorers took the title *cosmonauts*, with the *cosmos* part coming from the Greek word for "universe," *cosmos*. Yoga means union with the infinite 'space', *naught* means sailor from the Greek and asana means posture. Yoganautasana is the space traveler pose. Yoganautasana is a posture to connect you to the space that is above, below and in you. Yoganautasana is like floating in space without any gravity holding you down. Yoganautasana is a great pose to float on the ocean of consciousness.

90% of the population in our modern society has their head too far forward. We are preoccupied with our sense of sight and how things look. Our culture is full of expression like, "I will believe it when I see it." Or "I am from Missouri, show me." It is as if our feelings, thoughts and beliefs do not really matter to our vision. The truth is that you will 'see it' when you believe it. In psychology, the term cognizant dissidence is used to describe our inability to accept and even see things that go totally against our beliefs and paradigm of reality. If we do not believe that it is possible we literally don't see it because our minds cannot accept it. Consciousness is primary and matter is secondary. Everything only looks separate, and distinct to us. This illusion of separateness leads to loneliness and alienation, which ultimately could result in madness or schizophrenia. It is a paradox that we are separate, yet inseparatable.

The body is intelligent. Just as the mind can help the body, the body can help heal the mind. These postures are good for the throat chakra, neck, jaw, inner ear, sleep apnea and baldness.

Yoganautasana for Sleep Apnea, Neck and Throat

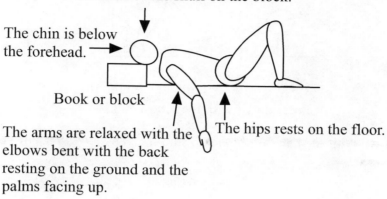

The head is level with the inion or the back of the skull on the block.

The chin is below the forehead.

Book or block

The arms are relaxed with the elbows bent with the back resting on the ground and the palms facing up.

The hips rests on the floor.

Lower the chin to the chest and lengthen the back of your neck as you slowly lift the hips.

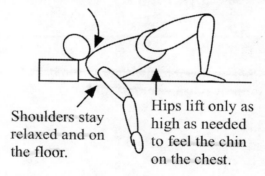

Shoulders stay relaxed and on the floor.

Hips lift only as high as needed to feel the chin on the chest.

Take 7 conscious breaths and slowly lower the hips. Rest a moment.

Inhale and Lift the Shoulder Blades Off the Floor

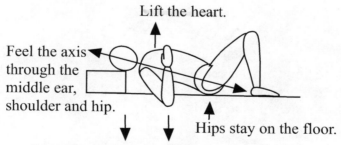

Lift the heart.

Feel the axis through the middle ear, shoulder and hip.

Hips stay on the floor.

Press down firmly with the back of the head and elbows so the shoulders and upper back lifts off the floor.

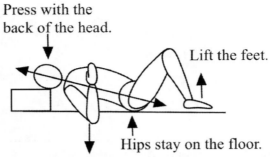

Firmly press down with the back of the head, stabilize, and slowly see if you can lift the elbows off the floor.

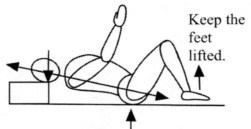

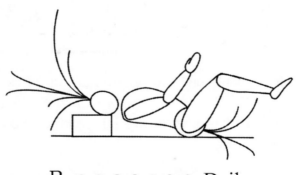

Ŗx ∿∿∿∿∿ Daily
Connect to the core energy
radiating through your central nervous system encased in bone.
Tune into your inner space of feelings, thoughts and belief.
Resonate with the fields of energy in and around you.

Put your thumbs over your ear flaps and listen to the sound of the breath.

Tune in to the Inner Space of Thought, Time and Mind.

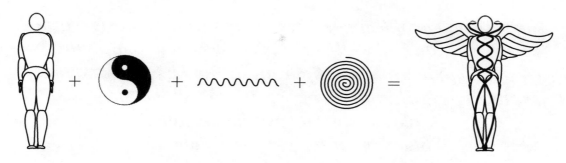

Scoliosis

The word "scoliosis" is derived from the Greek word *skol*, which means twists and turns. In scoliosis, the spine has a variety of twisted, turned and collapsed vertebrae in the lumbar, thoracic and cervical spinal curves that effect our ribs, hips and our ability to stand up. It affects the entire being.

Scoliosis Is The Inability To Stand Up Straight.

The backbone is weakened and the heart center tweaked. Physiology is woven into psychology and psychology is woven into physiology. In order to stand up straight, we have to have "backbone" and an open heart.

To heal scoliosis we must ultimately build

strength and flexibility in spine and character.

Careful!

Do we have to let a metal rod be our "backbone"?
To stand up open heartedly
And to have "backbone" to heal scoliosis
We must structurally, functionally, socially and mentally
Integrate our body, mind and breath.

It is important to note that

The percentage of teenage boys to girls with scoliosis is 1 to 8.
Our health and well-being is connected to our ability
To stand up, literally and figuratively, and have "backbone."
It is critical for girls and young women to feel that they are able to
physically, and psychologically,
Stand up in society, family and life.

Your body is curved and round. Your head is round. You stand on the balls of your feet. Your spine is a series of curves. Your shoulders and hips are referred to as ball and socket joints. Large exercise balls are perfect for lengthening and balancing the natural curves of the spine. I suggest starting with a ball 55cm. in diameter. This is a profound workout for the entire body. Do not underestimate this prop in its effectiveness for strengthening your core, upper back, strengthen the lower back, treat sciatica, improve posture, release your neck tension and strengthen your arms. These balls are often referred to as stability balls because they force you to center and balance yourself.

This practice is perfect for the youth and the young at heart.
It features a big bouncy ball that you can have a fun time rolling around on.

Roll through the curves of the spine vertebra by vertebra.
Even and strengthen the curves of the spine.

Healing Scoliosis Is A Process.

Start with a few postures and build your practice.
Make it enjoyable.
Practice a little every day.

R$_X$ $\sim\!\sim\!\sim\!\sim\!\sim$ Daily

Have a Ball Consciously Healing Scoliosis Practice

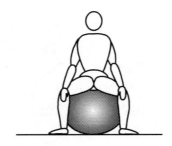

Back Bend on the Ball

Bounce up and down and then find a stable seat. Walk your feet forward until the upper back is on the ball. See if you can put the back of your head on the ball as you inhale and straighten your legs as you swing the arms overhead.

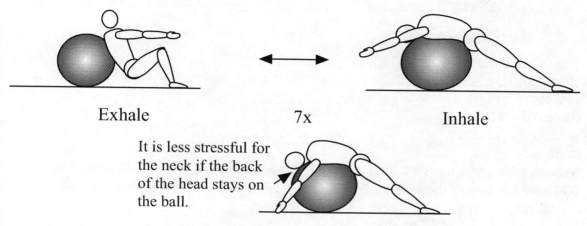

Exhale   7x   Inhale

It is less stressful for the neck if the back of the head stays on the ball.

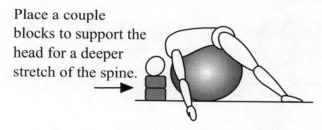

Hold for at least seven breaths or up to three minutes.

Place a couple blocks to support the head for a deeper stretch of the spine.

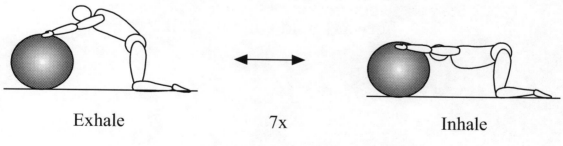

Cat and Dog Tilts on the Ball

Exhale   7x   Inhale

Push Ups on the Ball

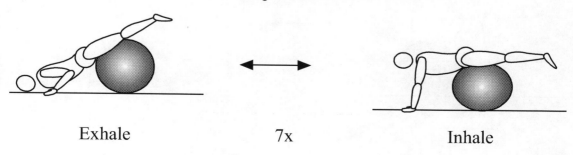

Exhale   7x   Inhale

Child's Pose on the Ball

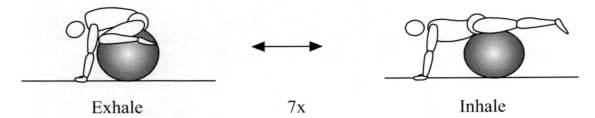

Exhale   7x   Inhale

Side Rib Cage Strengthener

Breathe into the sides of the and back of the body.

Even the sides of your body with this pose. All of us have a little imbalance and in scoliosis one side of the spinal column will be substantially longer. Practice contracting the longer side of the body.

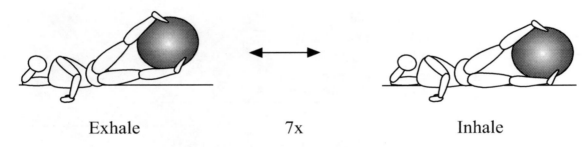

Exhale   7x   Inhale

Repeat on the other side.

Forward Fold with the Ball

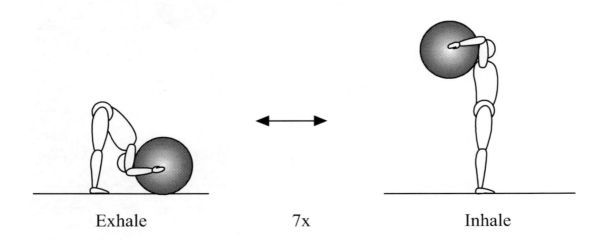

Exhale   7x   Inhale

Down Dog Variation with the Ball

Hold for 7 breaths.

Asymmetrical Forward Fold Variation with the Ball

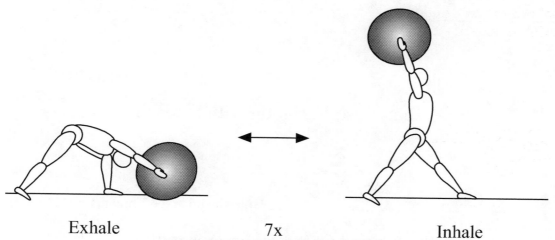

Exhale   7x   Inhale

Repeat with the other leg in front.

Warrior I Pose with the Ball

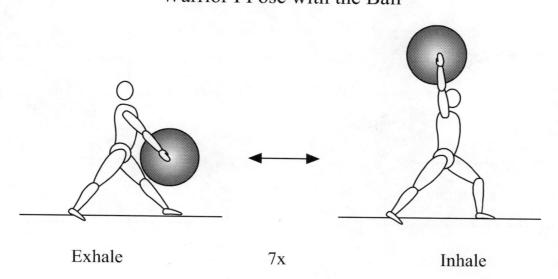

Exhale   7x   Inhale

Low Abdomen Postures with the Ball

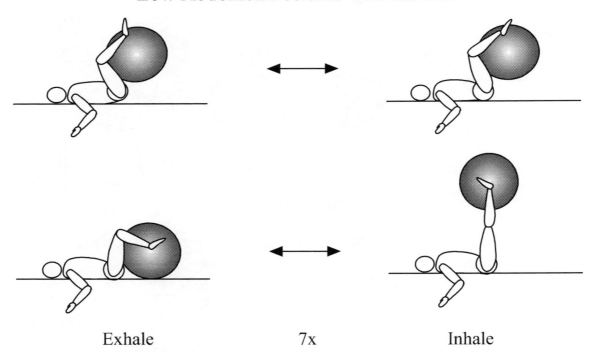

Exhale   7x   Inhale

Boat Pose Variation with the Ball

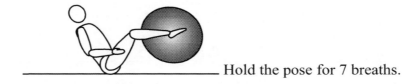

_____ Hold the pose for 7 breaths.

Shalabasana and Cobra Variations with the Ball

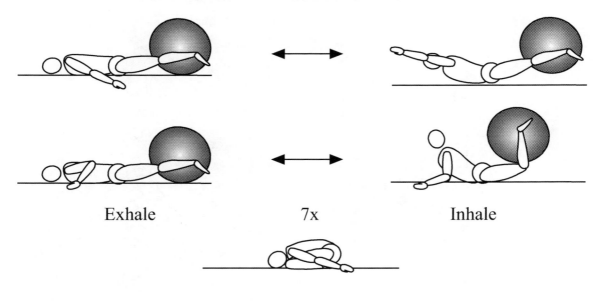

Exhale   7x   Inhale

Seated Practice on the Ball

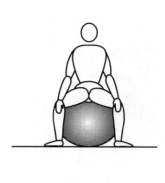  

Practice the posture that speak to you for 7 breaths. Repeat on the other side.

Seated Twist With the Ball

Turning to the torso and head to the right front and side views.

Hold for 7 breaths. Twist to each side.

Chair Pose with the Ball

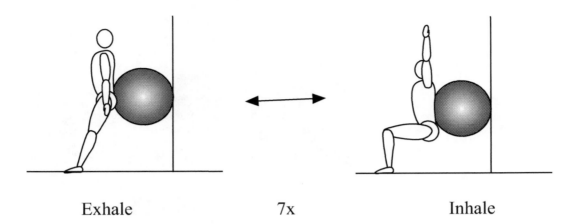

Exhale   7x   Inhale

Seated Forward Fold on the Ball

Hold any variation for 7 breaths. Repeat with the other leg.

Back Arches with the Ball

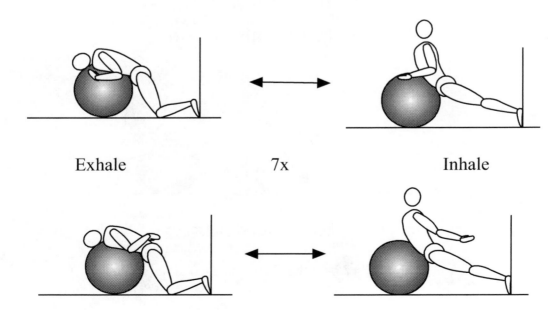

Exhale   7x   Inhale

Vajrasana Variations with the Ball

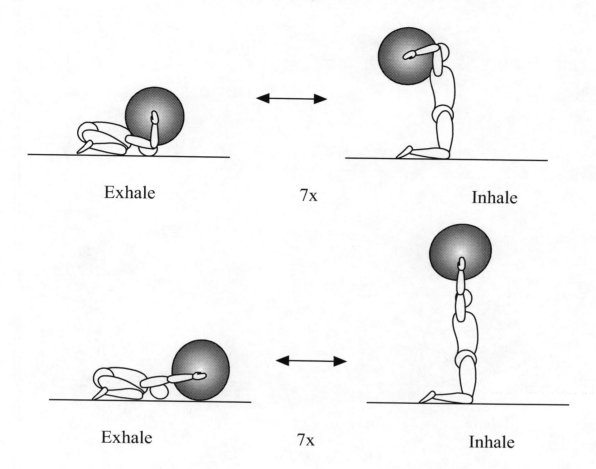

Exhale   7x   Inhale

Exhale   7x   Inhale

Camel Pose Variations with the Ball

R$_x$ ∿∿∿∿∿∿ Daily

Shoulder Stand Variations with the Ball

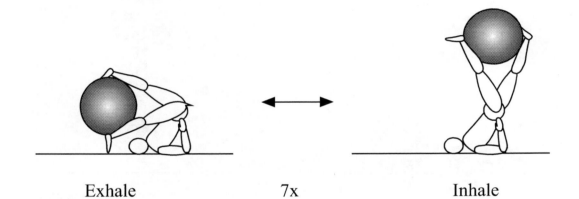

Exhale   7x   Inhale

R$_x$ ∿∿∿∿∿ Daily

Savasana Variation with the Ball

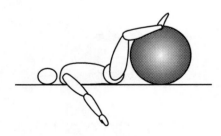

Restful Awareness

R$_x$ ∿∿∿∿∿ Daily

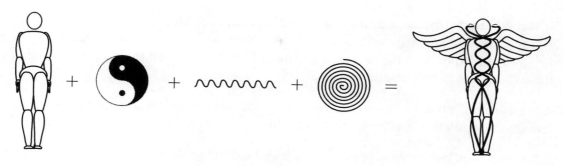

The Hips

The Space...in the Hip

What I refer to as *the space in the hip* is a joint placement where the bones are centered and supported for free range of movement without pinching or grinding. No one is perfectly centered and balanced. Everyone has to compensate for a little misalignment. Are you actively-yielding or are you primarily yielding-actively in the way you hold your postures? There are two common body responses to skeletal-muscular misalignment. The first is to have strong and stiff muscles in order to create stability around the joints. This often results in pressure on the nerves from tight muscles, most notably the sciatica in the case of the hips. The second response is to let the ligaments of the body carry the weight. Here the muscles are generally a little weaker and floppier, and the bones collapse in on each other, resulting in joint deterioration. The goal is to be stable and flexible with good *space in the hip*, not too hard and not too soft. Breathe down and up through a centered and conscious space in the hip socket.

The hip is a ball and socket bone joint with connective tissue, ligaments, tendons and muscles attached all around. The muscles that affect the hips can be grouped into regions to help map the range of motion of the hip.

The first region is the upper groin area, which help with walking and standing up straight. These muscles include the psoas and illiascus muscles, which combine to form the iliopsoas.

The second region, the front groin that includes quadriceps and the tensor fascia latae. These muscles are primarily used to pull the femur towards the body and serve as a pump to bring the blood back to the heart. What are commonly referred to as hip flexors are the combination of regions one and two.

The third region is the lower inner groin, which includes all of the adductor muscles. These muscles pull the thigh toward the midline of the body.

The fourth region has the hip rotators, which include the piriformis and gluteus maximus which when tight, forces you to stand with your toes pointed outwards.

The fifth region includes the hamstrings, which run along the backside of the legs. When tight, these will pull on the lower back.

Even though someone has a large range of motion through their hips, it does not mean they have a healthy flow of bodily fluids through them. For such a state to occur the bones have to be centered and aligned and muscularly supported so that the body can be grounded and lifted. Physiologically, healthy groin muscles facilitate the free flow of fluids between the legs and the torso. Weight gain in the thighs and hips indicate that there is not a free flow of energy or fluid through the muscles connecting the thighs to the torso and strengthening the muscles around the hips would be appropriate.

The *space* in the hip--filled with intelligence, love and the discernment to find the balance between our joint stability and flexibility,
yang and yin, and exhaling and inhaling.

Building Hip Abduction Strength

Weak hip abduction is the most common cause of dull ache and pain in outer hip. You see people with dull pain walking around or standing with their hand on the top their buttock. I often say you can have a choice between a titanium hip and buns of steel. We sit on our butts so much. Rarely do we feel the sitz bones on a firm chair. We sit in bucket seats, sofas and cushions with little awareness of our pelvic floor. We seldom exhale and contract our buttocks and pelvic diaphragm. The muscles grow weak the femur head begins to rub against the walls of the socket. Without practicing self - observation and awareness the sensation of the friction between the ball and socket is experienced only as suffering and pain instead of information and awareness. The pain in the hip is telling you the space in the hip is uneven; pay attention. Create balance.

The hips need to be aligned with the shoulder and the knee to be balanced.

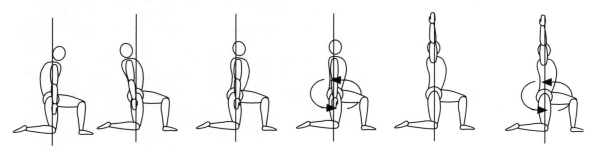

Hold A Leg Out to The Side
Create Stability in and Around the Hip Socket.

Since we spend hours of unconscious time sitting on our buttocks, we will have to practice holding and building muscle memory to create balance in the space in the hip.

Flex the foot.

Extend out through the heel.

Lift up on the knee cap.

Press down with the bottom leg.

A thick mat or a blanket underneath your hips will help you relax and focus on the lifted leg.

R$_x$ ∿∿∿∿∿ Daily

Make circles with the foot as you extend out of the hip.
Make circles in the other direction.
Organize the space in the hip
holding the leg lifted and exhaling for the count of 30.

Hold the pose with the toes pointed in different directions.
Feel the difference in which muscle groups are used for each one.

Maintain your core connection as you extend out of the hips through your legs, feet and toes.

R_x ∿∿∿∿ Daily

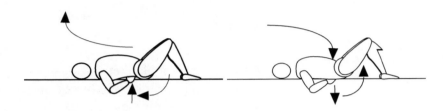

Hold the essence of the heart lifted as you exhale and hold the essence of the navel anchored as you inhale.

Bridge Pose with Movement and Breath

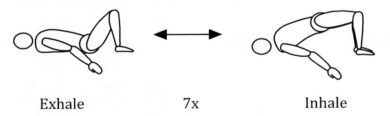

Exhale   7x   Inhale

Holding Bridge Pose Variations

Inhale, lift the heart and press the big toes down.
Exhale, tighten the buttocks and press the heels down. Hold the pause at the end of the exhalation and feel the muscles stabilizing the hip socket.

R_x ∿∿∿∿ Daily

These variations of shoulder stand help strengthen the muscles in and around the hip sockets.

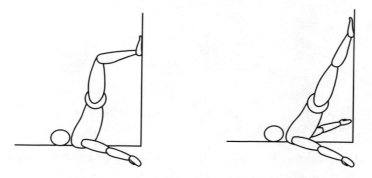

Find Your Rock Bottom

Connect to the earth element, tighten your buttocks and get a rock hard bottom with this cobra variation. If the muscles are too weak to stabilize the hip socket, the bones will start to rub and eventually grind together, and a titanium hip replacement might be needed. Strong and stable gluteus muscles are essential for healthy hips and preventing hip replacement.

You have a choice between getting buns of steel or a titanium hip socket.

Elbow Cobra Pose Your Rock Bottom Pose for the Buttocks

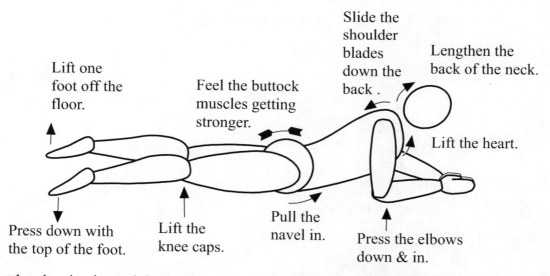

Lift one foot off the floor.

Feel the buttock muscles getting stronger.

Slide the shoulder blades down the back .

Lengthen the back of the neck.

Lift the heart.

Press down with the top of the foot.

Lift the knee caps.

Pull the navel in.

Press the elbows down & in.

People who sit a lot and those who are very flexible in the hips run the risk of wearing out the cartilage as they become less active. This pose is ideal to balance flexibility with strength. Exhale and engage your Triple Lock and find a deep stable ground of being.

R$_x$ ∿∿∿∿∿ Daily

Strengthen Muscles and Ligaments around the Hips

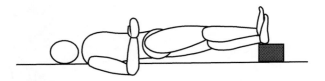

Cross one foot on top of the other, squeeze your legs together, contract the abdominal cavity, press down with the elbows and lift the hips off the floor.

Exhale and push down on the foot resting on the block and raise the hips off the floor. Hold dynamic tension keeping the navel slightly in while you inhale.

R$_x$ ⌇⌇⌇⌇⌇ Daily

Side Plank Variations

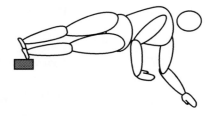

R$_x$ ⌇⌇⌇⌇⌇ Daily

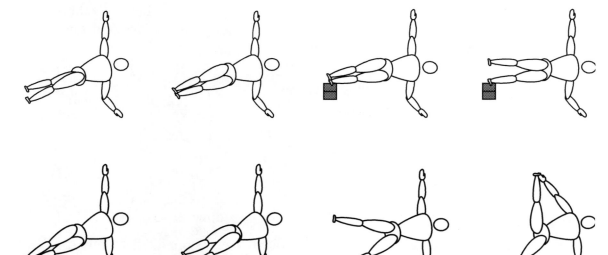

Which posture is best for your conscious rhythmic breathing?

Challenging Hip Flexor Postures

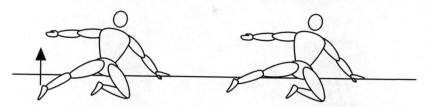

Extend one leg out and lift it pointing the toes down.

Practice stability with extension in the hip socket, leg and foot.

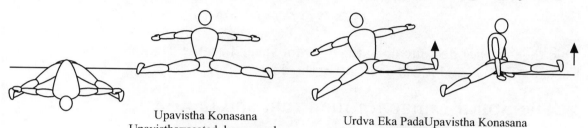

Upavistha Konasana
Upavistha=seated kona=angle

Urdva Eka PadaUpavistha Konasana
One Leg Raised Seated Angle

Extend one leg out and lift it pointing the toes up.

Powerful Hip Abductor Postures

R$_X$ 〰〰〰〰 Daily

First, lift a bent knee to the side and breathe. Try straightening the knee, and holding the leg parallel to the ground. Finally, extend the opposite arm and to the best of your ability, make both your arm and extended leg parallel to the ground.

Psoas, Hip Flexor and Quadricep Lengtheners

After surgery or injury or if you have extremely tight hips, simply lie down on a bed with the feet on the floor or a block and consciously breathe.

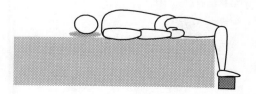
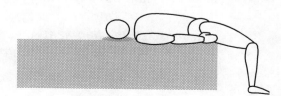

A Basic Hip Flexor Release

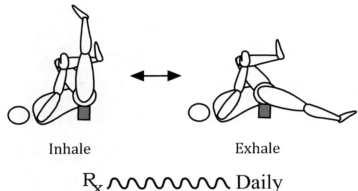

Inhale   Exhale

R$_x$ ∿∿∿∿∿ Daily

Hold the leg extended out along the floor for seven breaths. Tighten the buttock of the extended leg and it will come off of the floor.

The Spiral Lunge for the Front and the Back of the Hip

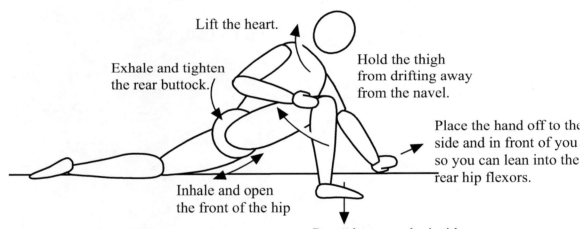

Lift the heart.

Exhale and tighten the rear buttock.

Hold the thigh from drifting away from the navel.

Place the hand off to the side and in front of you so you can lean into the rear hip flexors.

Inhale and open the front of the hip

Press down on the inside of the front foot.

Inhale top, middle, bottom and open the hip flexors of the rear leg.
Exhale bottom, middle, top tightening the buttock.

R$_x$ ∿∿∿∿∿ Daily

Take your right hand behind your back and grab onto your right buttock.
This is a great posture to explore and feel
the muscles and ligaments deep the hip socket with your right hand.
Change sides.

Hip Flexors, Thigh and Psoas Releases

R$_X$ ∿∿∿∿∿∿ Daily

Splits / Hanumanasana

Hanuman is the mythic monkey god and devoted servant of Rama.

R$_X$ ∿∿∿∿ Daily

Pigeon Posture Variations

R$_x$ ∿∿∿∿∿ Daily

Hamstring, Hip Rotator and Low Back Extension

Inhale   Exhale   Hold

Down Dog Variations

Inhale   Exhale   Hold

R$_x$ ∿∿∿∿∿ Daily

Chair Pose Variations For Hips, Hamstrings and Quadriceps

Exhale   Inhale   Hold a variation.

Strapping the thighs together will deepen the hip release.

R$_x$ ∿∿∿∿∿ Daily

Standing Hip and Low Back Releasing Postures

R$_x$ ∿∿∿∿∿ Daily

Tortoise Pose Variations / Kurmasana for Flexible Hips

These postures are openers for both hip and shoulder sockets.

R$_x$ ∿∿∿∿∿ Daily

Deep Hip Rotator, Sacrum and Low Back Releasing Poses

R$_x$ ∿∿∿∿∿ Daily

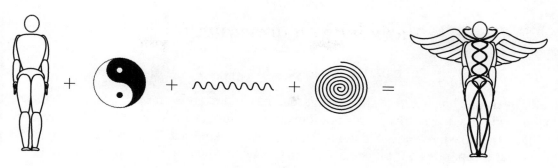

Weight Loss,

A Big Belly and Obesity

The Post-Modern-New Millenial Manifesto for Losing Weight:

Consciousness Is Primary, Diet Is Secondary.

Weight loss is a complex issue. From a holistic perspective our physical form is inseparable from our formless feelings, thoughts and beliefs. Our psychology is woven into our physiology. Consciousness about what is eating us is as important as what we eat. 'Can I lose weight by practicing yoga?' is one question I often hear. This is an interesting question because even though practicing yoga is often equated with exercise and fitness, historically yoga has really been about connecting to higher consciousness, rather than to our physical form. All of the reported health benefits from yoga come from the fact that in order to be more self-aware and self-actualized, you need to be able to integrate your physical, emotional, mental, social and spiritual energies. Therapeutic Hatha Yoga is a path of integrating physiology with psychology, of body and mind moving toward higher consciousness and liberation. It might surprise you how yoga can liberate you from excess weight.

What is eating you is as important

as what you are eating!

Eat Less, Exercise More?

Virtually everyone has heard of the saying, 'eat less and exercise more', as a prescription for losing weight. Clearly this prescription is not working, as most people in America are overweight and obesity is now the number one killer in America. The problem with that saying is that it separates our physical form from our formless feelings, thoughts and beliefs and puts matter before consciousness. The problem telling everyone to eat less and exercise more is that 'eating less' sounds like deprivation and 'exercise more' sounds like punishment. On an emotional and conscious level, it is difficult to follow advice that is experienced as deprivation and punishment, Body and mind are one.

A Sound Body Is the Product of a Sound Mind!

To heal the body, we must also heal our thoughts, beliefs and relationships. Your attitudes toward work, society and the environment affect your attitude toward food and lifestyle. Eating less and exercising more, is a purely materialist approach to health and well-being focusing on numbers of calories in an out. Thus, even though a huge percentage of the population says they are on a diet and/or exercise program at any one time, America is still two-thirds overweight.

Many people point to lifestyle changes as critical for losing weight. Our lifestyle and our beliefs about the world and ourselves shape our appetites. Lifestyle is based on one's concept and perception of life. A modern, materialistic and individualistic approach to life reduces you to a marvelous machine and food to an industrialized convenient commodity. If you have been taught that matter and life are unconscious, why be conscious about what you are eating? A change of lifestyle requires a change of consciousness, feelings, thoughts and beliefs about life, work, play, food and the world. What we are truly hungry for is wholeness, oneness and unity. We must nourish our minds, hearts and spirit as well as our bodies, if we are to heal.

Modern Society Has Created a Culture of Fear,

That Eats at All of Us.

What is eating at modern society is the materialist, monetized and reductionist consciousness and morality of the modern industrial era. This mode of thinking and being creates feelings of stress, fear, separation and scarcity. This modern culture is disconnecting us from our own spirit, each other and nature's abundance. This culture of fear is eating at us, and we are expressing it through destructive addictive behavior with food, pills, tobacco, alcohol, sex, gambling and more to cope and soothe ourselves. I believe that addition to any substance is ultimately a subconscious response to feelings of fear and a fundamental disconnection from the source of creativity, love and wisdom.

Don't succumb to this culture of fear, when you feel something is eating you! Flip the switch. Inhale to your heart through the Mind∞Body Infinity Loop and nourish yourself from the infinite source of creativity, love and wisdom.

Conscious Healing Begins With Conscious Breathing.

Conscious Breathing Begins With Breathing Through Your Nose.

Overweight and obese people have a difficult time moving, exercising and even breathing through their nose. Typically, they are unconsciously breathing through their mouths as they huff and puff their way around. Practicing breathing through the nose is a realistic first step everyone can take on the path to good health. Breathing through the mouth is unhealthy and it creates an alert response in the body, a stress response. We tend to soothe our stress by eating. Consciously breathing through your nose is the first step for losing weight. Practice each of the 25 Conscious Breathing Practices in this book.

Skinny Belly and Lifted Heart Pose

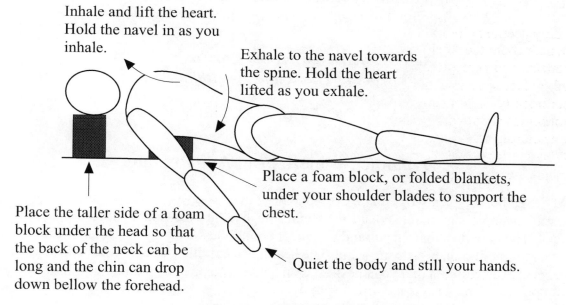

Inhale and lift the heart. Hold the navel in as you inhale.

Exhale to the navel towards the spine. Hold the heart lifted as you exhale.

Place the taller side of a foam block under the head so that the back of the neck can be long and the chin can drop down bellow the forehead.

Place a foam block, or folded blankets, under your shoulder blades to support the chest.

Quiet the body and still your hands.

R~~~~~~~ Daily

People will often pat their bellies and say I have to lose this. The subtext of what they are saying in part is that they are disconnected from this part of their body. For so many men, and women too, the belly is distended and dropping down and out. The navel is no longer connected to the spine. Conscious breathing for the belly begins with contracting the abdominal cavity and exhaling the navel towards the spine. When the belly drops down and out the low back is pulled in and tight adding to the potential of low back pain.

Inhale and expand the heart cavity. Exhale and contract the abdominal cavity.
Hold the navel in, and inhale. Hold the heart lifted, and exhale.
Inhale and float he heart. Don't bloat the belly.
Exhale collapse, condense and contract the belly. Don't collapse your heart.

Gratitude Is the Attitude to Lose Weight

Our understanding of life seems out of balance. It seems that our love of life and an attitude of gratitude has been replaced with a fear of death and an attitude of greed.

Start Loving.
Stop Fearing.
Stop Counting Calories and Feeling Deprived.
Stop Forcing Yourself to Exercise and Feeling Punished.

Add Nutrient Dense Foods to Your Diet.
Practice Conscious Breathing.

R_x ∿∿∿∿ Daily

Dynamic Stillness Is an Active State

At the end of a typical yoga class, everyone lies down in savasana for a meditative, restful awareness moment. What I notice most is that the overweight people fidget the most. They readjust their hands and wiggle out of stillness and any sustained meditative integration of body, breath and mind. The healthiest and fittest people tend to lie as still as stone. The stillness of a yoga posture is an active state, like a spinning top. It looks motionless from afar, yet it is filled with dynamic energy. You can increase your vibration by practicing dynamic stillness and burn calories.

Yoga Has Been Defined As Skillful Living And As Meditation in Action.

Yoga will help you reflect on your actions and lifestyle. People who make a lot of unconscious movements in their yoga postures surely are making unconscious movements in their day-to-day lives. They are often reaching for food in an unconscious manner. You have to be conscious not to overeat. You have to be able to still yourself. People are consuming more than we are expressing. We must express the life essence we consume, or we will take on weight, plug up and fatten with unexpressed feelings, thoughts and spirit, as well as undigested food. This is not the direct fault of an overweight person. We are trained to be materialistic consumers through business and advertising, while the arts and other forms of spiritual nourishment are being dropped from our school's curriculum. Change your mind and change your life. Our labor saving culture has helped give us more time to actualize our own lives, yet we live in a materialistic consumer society. We no longer refresh and celebrate our own lives.

Be More Conscious. Practice Meditation.

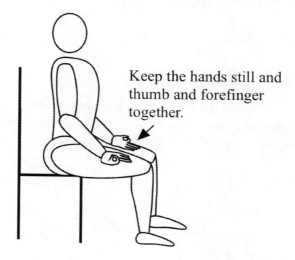

Keep the hands still and thumb and forefinger together.

Maintain Dynamic Stillness.
Create a Feeling of Spaciousness Instead of Emptiness.
Keep the Heart Lifted as You Exhale.
Keep the Navel in as You Inhale.
Hold the Stillness in Your Hands.
R$_X$ ∿∿∿∿∿ Daily

"The Heavy One"

Obesity is a more than a physical phenomenon. Obesity is the result of our consciousness, of our emotional, psychological and social relationships with others, food and nature. When your position in society makes you in charge of decisions, your decisions "weigh" more. As a large person you carry weight literally and figuratively. You can play the role of Mr. Big, and be the 'the heavy one.' It is interesting to note that the yoga word 'guru' literally translates as teacher or the remover of darkness. The term guru has also been translated as the weighty one or the heavy one. Psychologically we often associate being big as a symbol of success, power and influence.

At the same time weight gain and obesity are in part an expression of our need to feel shielded, protected and insulated. These feelings could come from fear of the outside world and or feelings of emptiness from within.

Don't Eat with a Consciousness of Fear and Emptiness.

Eat with a Consciousness of Love and Spaciousness.

R$_x$ ∿∿∿∿∿ Daily

What is the difference between illness and wellness?

The first begins with 'I' and the second begins with 'We'.

Swami Satchidananda

Feeling connected to others helps you feel connected to yourself, and is a large part of the reason so many people have success losing weight when committed to another individual, a buddy, group or organization. Group session sharing and caring is an important part of Therapeutic Hatha Yoga.

Eat Consciously!

Consciousness Is Primary.

Diet Is Secondary.

"Let food be thy medicine and medicine be thy food."

Hippocrates

Take A Walk Around The Block.

Practice the Basic Core Practice For Health And Well-Being.

Practice The Triple Lock.

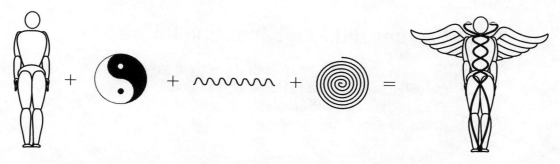

Digestion

The Digestion Pose

Inhale into the front of the body. Draw the breath down into the abdominal cavity. Relax and breathe into the organs of digestion.

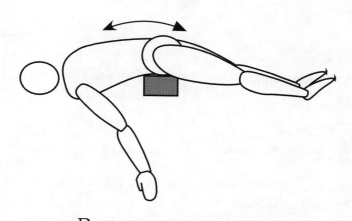

R~x~ 〰〰〰〰〰 Daily

Hold the pose for several minutes. Breathe into the sensations. Inhale and expand the front of the body. Be conscious, if the low back starts to feel too tight, hug the knee in to the chest for a moment, exhale the navel toward the spine or lower the height of the block. Taking the arms overhead will add more space in your abdominal cavity for even better digestion.

Deep Sacrum and Large Intestine Release Pose

Inhale and lengthen the front of the body from the collar bones to the pubic bone stretching out all of your organs of digestion. Feel the pelvis tilt down into the block as you inhale.

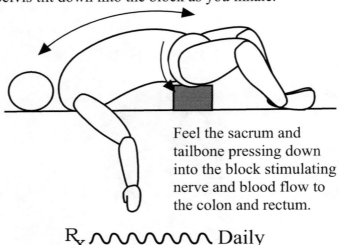

Feel the sacrum and tailbone pressing down into the block stimulating nerve and blood flow to the colon and rectum.

R$_x$ ∿∿∿∿∿∿ Daily

The Liver Cleanse

Inhale / *Nourish*

Open the front of the body and stretch out..

Feel the rib cage expand with the right hand over the liver.

Exhale / *Cleanse*

Contract and squeeze the right side of the torso down onto the liver under the right hand.

Cross the midline with the left arm.

Lift hips and shoulders so the upper back, beneath the liver, presses down on the floor.

Inhale for the count of six and exhale for the count of nine.

380

Inhale and be soft like a flower petal in the moonlight.

Exhale and be hard like a diamond sparkling in the sunlight.

R_x ∿∿∿∿ Daily

Increased circulation is the goal. Expand the area and then contract and squeeze the muscles around the liver. Inhale and nourish the liver. Exhale and cleanse the liver.

Change Sides, Raising the Left Leg and Right Arm and Continue to Nourish And Cleanse the Pancreas, Spleen, Gall Bladder, Stomach and Liver.

Burp

Practice cobra pose and gently press down with the hands and lift the chest opening the esophagus and upper abdomen.

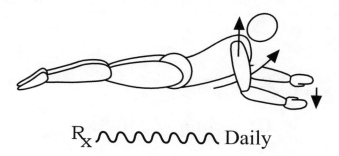

R_x ∿∿∿∿ Daily

Burp, Twist and Digest

Sit with your legs to the side and one arm behind your back. Inhale and open the chest and the upper abdomen. Raise the arm up and stretch out the esophagus. Release any gas in the stomach. Then spiral your heart and head to the front. It is amazing how often one can easily burp in these positions. Hold the pose and breathe. Each inhalation lightly lifts and unwinds you. Each exhalation deepens the twist. You could lower one elbow or both to the floor for a slightly different twist. Hold the pose for seven conscious breaths.

R~~~~~~~ Daily

Lying Twist Variations

R~~~~~~~ Daily

All the Lying Twist Postures in the Section on SciaticaStimulate the Organs of Digestion

Breathing Meditation

for

Food as Fuel and Complete Digestion

Inhale – Air, Fire and Fuel

Exhale – Combustion, Smoke and Ash

R~~~~~~~ Daily

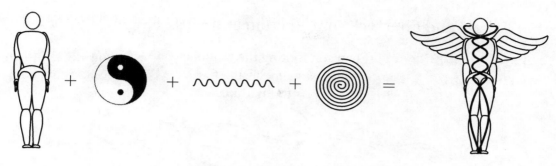

Hemorrhoids

Hemorrhoids are enlarged veins located in the lower part of the rectum and the anus. The veins become swollen due to increased pressure within them. Increased pressure can come from constipation, sitting too long or profuse diarrhea, and during pregnancy. Internal hemorrhoids are located in the inside lining of the rectum and cannot be felt. External hemorrhoids are located underneath the skin that surrounds the anus.

Hemorrhoids are more likely as you get older because the tissues that support the veins in your rectum and anus can weaken and stretch with aging.

Crocodile Variation to Strengthen the Pelvic Floor and Rectum
Begin by Lying Down

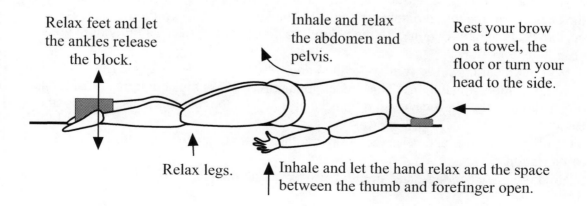

Relax feet and let the ankles release the block.

Inhale and relax the abdomen and pelvis.

Rest your brow on a towel, the floor or turn your head to the side.

Relax legs.

Inhale and let the hand relax and the space between the thumb and forefinger open.

Exhale and Contract Your Rectum and Little Finger Tightly

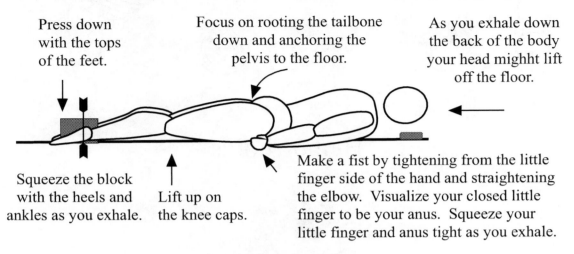

Press down with the tops of the feet.

Focus on rooting the tailbone down and anchoring the pelvis to the floor.

As you exhale down the back of the body your head mighht lift off the floor.

Squeeze the block with the heels and ankles as you exhale.

Lift up on the knee caps.

Make a fist by tightening from the little finger side of the hand and straightening the elbow. Visualize your closed little finger to be your anus. Squeeze your little finger and anus tight as you exhale.

Take Seven Empowered Exhalations

Tone Your Pelvic Floor Muscles
The Great Seal - The Triple Lock – Maha Mudra

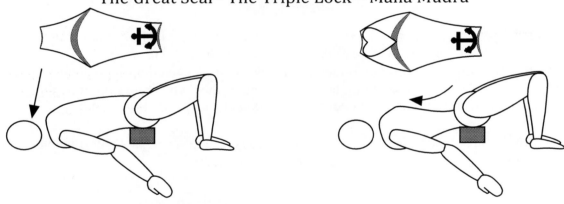

1. Inhale deeply through your nose. Then exhale quickly and forcibly through your nose, or pursed lips.
2. Hold the breath out. Contract the throat and press the chin firmly down and in towards the chest. Seal the throat diaphragm, closing the larynx and the epiglottis. This is the neck lock, Jalandara Bandha. In the beginning it might be easier to simply hold your nose with your fingers.
3. Without inhaling, relax your abdominal area while you lift and expand the heart cavity creating a "mock inhalation." This "mock inhalation " sucks the abdominal muscles and organs up into the chest cavity and reduces pressure on the rectum. This is Uddiyana Bandha.
4.Contract your anus and perineum, drawing the tailbone towards the pubic bone. This is Mula Bandha.
5. Hold the three bandhas, and strengthen your pelvic floor.

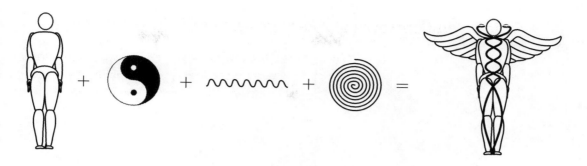

Inguinal Hernia

Each of us has unique issues and history and yoga has a unique and important gift for us. We are all wounded healers and our wellness stories are the fuel that ignites healing and well-being in others. Dealing with a hernia has been one of my wellness stories.

Why Me?

I believe that my hernia was in part the result from physical and structural imbalances from the aggressive yoga practices I have had. My doctor said that traditionally farmers and other hard laborers were prone to hernias. He also told me that people could have a genetic predisposition to hernias. It is interesting to note that my grandfather and I both had an inguinal hernia operation when we were 50 years old. However, there might be additional shadow and or hidden contributing factors to an inguinal hernia. The hernia protrudes from the exact same spot where the vas, which carries sperm from the testicle through the abdominal wall and to the urethra. I generally felt my hernia more after sex. Just as my left foot is bigger than my right, the vas canal on my right is wider than my left. This canal is supposed to shrink after puberty, sealing the testicle in the scrotum. However, my right testicle got pushed back up the canal at various times in my life. This helped create a passageway for the small intestines to drop into once the abdominal wall was ripped where the vas enters the abdominal cavity.

Light on Yoga by B.K. S Iyengar was my first yoga book. I wanted to be a supreme seeker. I wanted to do the most advanced postures possible. I especially wanted to do Natarajasana.

Natarajasana / Royal Dancer Pose

Through years of practice, I noticed that my psoas and my hip flexors on the left side were tighter than on my right. I was much more open on the right side of my body for postures such as Natarajasana and Eka Pada Raja Kapotasana / Pigeon Pose.

Pigeon

Over the years, I unevenly stretched my right groin and destabilized it in a slightly unconscious manner, in an effort to achieve these postures. However, it was neither of these postures that directly created my inguinal hernia. It was an aggressive standing side bend to the left, Nitambasana for Richard Hittleman or Arda Chandrasana for Bikram,

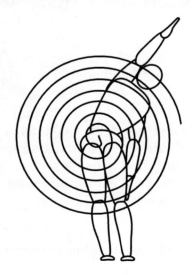

Side Bend

In forcing the pose and not maintaining a connection between my navel and spine the moment it happened. I knew something had been pulled or torn. I thought it was my psoas or hip flexor. I rested a bit, though I did not alter my yoga practice. I thought it would get better and kept practicing challenging postures. This tear ruptured and developed into an inguinal hernia. The dynamics of the hernia spiraled out into even larger issues that have taught me so much about my body and my spirit, about my heart and my mind. My inguinal hernia has been one of my greatest teachers.

My inguinal hernia typically popped out when I ate too much, when I was angry or when I coughed abdominally. Basically, my hernia popped out when my internal abdominal downward pressure was too much. It looked like a ping-pong ball under my skin. The easiest way to reverse my inguinal hernia was uddiyana bandha. I must say that it is extremely dangerous when the intestines pop out like this. **If the intestines do not make it back into the abdominal cavity immediately the blood flow will be strangled, which potentially can be fatal.** If the intestines pop out and they are not returned immediately call 911. Practicing uddiyana bandha should be viewed as a preventative measure for an inguinal hernia or as a practice for recovering from surgery, but not a substitute for surgery. I had hoped to heal my hernia without surgery. I now believe once the hernia is popping out regularly it is virtually impossible to reverse it and keep a normal lifestyle. Now, after surgery, I practice with greater awareness to keep pressure off of the area. It is important to consciously witness your edge, and not force them.

There are always shadow psychological factors to consider with any physiological condition. Louise Hay attributes hernias to ruptured relationships, strains, burdens and incorrect creative expression.

In my case, anger and unresolved emotional tension created internal pressure that irritated my hernia. Was I leading my life with my second chakra too much, not pulling the energy of my second chakra and sexual activity up into love and wisdom?

Balancing and integrating the chakras,
the psycho-physical vortexes, related to your ill,
is an important part of any healing.

I adopted this affirmation for my second chakra hernia condition.

I am a spiritual being.
I am moderate in my appetites.
I am in perfect harmony and balance.
I am filled with unconditional love.
I use my energy in Divine service.

Uddiyana Bandha

The most beneficial way I found to release pressure on the inguinal area was uddiyana bandha. The best way to practice deep healing uddiyana bandha was to practice in a supported bridge pose. This is because there is a slight inversion of the torso, as the hips are raised, allowing gravity to assist in taking pressure off of the lower abdomen. Exhale everything out. Try exhaling through pursed lips in a controlled slow manner though traditionally exhalation would be done with an ujjiyi breath. At the bottom of the exhalation, close your mouth and throat and then lift and suck the diaphragm high up into the thorax, so that the abdominal organs are pulled back and up into the chest cavity.

This movement relieves the downward pressure on the hernia. This is only a temporary solution, not a substitution for corrective surgery.

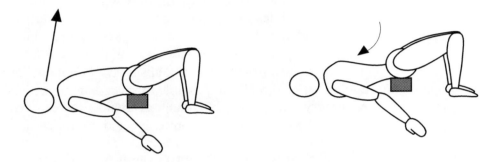

Excellent Recuperating-From-Surgery Postures

R$_x$ ∿∿∿∿∿ Daily

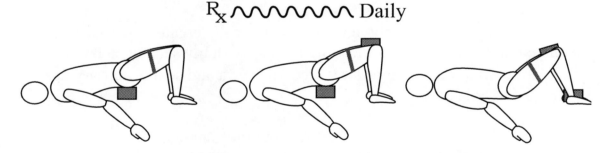

Take 5, 10 or 15 minutes in any one of these postures after surgery.

Relieve Lower Abdominal Pressure

For me, the first really helpful postures to relieve abdominal pressure were Upavista Konasana and Kurmasana. They are recommended yoga postures for hernias in the rear of Iyengar's book *Light on Yoga*. These postures include headstand and headstand cycle, shoulder stand and its cycle, Ubhaya Padangustahasana, Urdhva Mukha Paschimottanasana I & II, Krounchasana, Akarana Dhanurasana, Supta Padangusthasana, Upavista Konasana, Baddha-Konasana, Samakonasana, and Yoganidrasana.

Postures for Hernias from *Light On Yoga.*

Upavistha Konasana
Upavistha=seated kona=angle

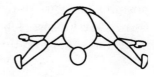

Kourmasana
Kurmasana

Sarvangasana
Sarva=all, whole, entire, complete; anga=limb

Ubhaya Padangusthasana
Ubhaya=both padangustha=big toe

Supta Padangusthasana

Hanumanasana
Hanuman=the mythic monkey god and
devoted servant of Rama

Urdhva Mukha Paschimottanasana I & II
Upward Facing Forward Fold

Krounchasana
Heron Pose

Samakonasana
Sama=Same, kon=angle

Yoganidrasana
Nidra=sleep

The Lying Bound Angle Pose
(Supta Bandha Konasana)

Rx ∿∿∿∿∿∿ Daily

389

Prevention of Hernias

Stabilizing the lower abdomen and preventing a hernia while practicing challenging postures is about rooting down through the sacrum, specifically on the side where the hip flexors are loosest. This produces a stable ground floor in the muladara chakra, which holds the small intestines in place. A hernia is like a ruptured dam.

All of the second chakra can flow out through an inguinal hernia including small intestines, sexuality, emotions and passion. Raising the pelvis in a bridge pose helps reverse this down and out flow of energy. Practicing uddiyana bandha while in a supported bridge posture is very powerful technique and is a for sure way to pull that ping-pong ball of small intestines back into the body, but it will not mend it.

Safest   Caution   Dangerous

Postures, which open the front of the second chakra, like standing back arch, variations of Kneeling Lunges, Camel/Ustrasana and even Warrior I must be done with the sacrum well rooted. Rooting the sacrum and establishing a firm foundation will support the internal organs and create less downward and outward pressure in the area of the hernia. Stretching the hip flexor area without adequate sacral support will begin to both pinch the back and overstretch the groin area. Leaning and dropping back without any structural root support in the sacrum and buttocks is risky for everyone.

These postures could tear the abdominal wall without adequate root support.

Dynamic Tension in the Breath

Another way to keep the pressure off of the inguinal area is to initiate the inhalation in the upper chest and back, rolling the shoulders back and down, then filling the side ribs and finally barely inhaling to the abdomen. Initiate the inhalation in the chest and hold the abdomen lightly in. To keep pressure off of the lower abdomen during exhalation squeeze more of the breath out and up with the intercostals. A slight engaging of mulabandha will further strengthen your exhalation and lift the subtle energy of the body up through the torso. Keep the collarbones lifted as you exhale. Feel as if there were buckets of water on your shoulders, and as you inhale the buckets tip backwards and the water runs down your back towards the floor like a waterfall. Beginning the inhalation in the lower abdomen while sitting creates pressure on the inguinal area.

Be Aware of your Lower Abdomen when Bending Forward

Pulling the lower abdominal wall in before completely bending forward is an excellent way for keeping excessive pressure off of the lower inguinal area. Teachers often say exhale and bend forward. However, if the abdomen does not lift up and in during exhalation the belly will get in the way of completely hinging and bending forward. It seems much better to have completed or nearly completed exhalation before going all the way down.

Clothing, posture and breath all have an effect the inguinal area. To keep extra pressure off of the inguinal area of the lower abdomen wear suspenders and avoid heavy belts around my waist, which push the energy down the front of the abdomen. Thong underwear can put too much friction and pressure; though support the rooting of the sacrum. Tight shorts can help keep awareness in the hernia area.

Furthermore, I noticed that I hold on with my right quadriceps much more than my left ones. My right quadriceps is always tighter than my left. This, combined with the looser psoas on the right side, makes for unevenness in the right groin area. I have started stretching my right quadriceps more to take any strain off of the right psoas and even the stretch in front of the right side in general. Asymmetrical variations of Bekasana are good for relaxing and lengthening the right quadriceps.

Wisdom Is Being Conscious

Of When You Need Help to Co-create Your Life

I never was able to close the gap in my abdominal wall and had to have nylon mesh sewn in to repair my inguinal hernia.

A friend of mine did not have the money for surgery and he, like me, had been trying to keep functioning with his hernia. Unfortunately, he had to call an ambulance for help, as he was curled on the floor in pain. His intestines got stuck and strangulated. A section of his small intestines had to be surgically removed, in addition to repairing the inguinal hernia. It was dangerous for me to postpone surgery. Do not be in denial about your health. Be wise and get help when you need it.

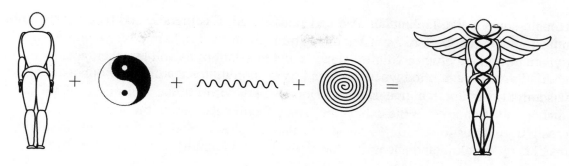

Hope

Empower Your Inhalations!

Exhale for the Count of 6.
Inhale for the Count of 9, Pause for the Count of 4 or more.

R$_x$ 〰〰〰 Daily

Hopelessness is like feeling deflated and exasperated. It is literally and figuratively being uninspired, in that both our spirit and our in-breath are not in harmony. Maintain a dynamic tension between your inhalations and exhalations as you lengthen your inhalations. Hope is lifted when the breath is anchored. It is the union of opposites and wisdom of paradox that give us hope. Hope is in the heart of the inhalation. Hope's anchor and strength is in the exhalation. Hope facilitate access to the source of infinite creative solutions to our life's issues. It is also the power to take action on those subtle insights by exhaling and anchoring those visions and intentions out your third eye.

The best way to inhale hope into our bodies, heart and or mind is to practice the infinite breathing loop, focusing on inhaling from the heart to your third ear at the inion, the small button shaped bump on the occipital ridge of the back of your head and resonate with the infinite spirit.

All of life on earth is constantly changing, expanding and evolving. For humanity it is about going beyond our five physical senses to include a sixth sense of the unfolding space of life between, around and in us. The sixth sense is a sense that deals with telepathy and empathy. Our sixth sense is like a third eye, a cosmic antenna, and a third ear that tunes into and resonates with the subtle vibrations of creativity, love and wisdom that always surround us.

Be grateful for your capacity to love and be loved.

Be grateful for the ability to experience and create

creativity, love and wisdom.

You are part the ever expanding cosmic consciousness. Have hope.

Rx  Daily

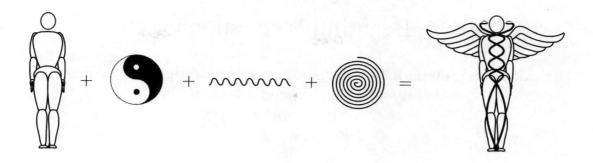

Beauty

The Beauty Rest Posture

Yoga is really a path of elimination rather than acquisition. In the yoga tradition, you already are a beautiful and divine being. Yoga helps remove the stress, thoughts, emotions and imbalances that prevent your natural beauty from shining through. Let go of any tension in your brow. Let the pose melt away any insecurities, worries or fears. Take an inhalation all the way down to the pubic bone and let the tailbone lift slightly. Exhale and let go of any tension in your brow. Inhale and soften your forehead. Exhale sunlight, and inhale moonlight--and let your beauty shine.

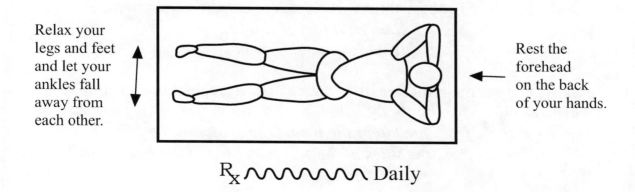

Relax your legs and feet and let your ankles fall away from each other.

Rest the forehead on the back of your hands.

R$_X$ ∿∿∿∿∿ Daily

The Be Beautiful Meditation Practice

Beauty carries with it an association of splendor, light and brilliance.
Beauty is about shining the light within.
Exhale sunlight.
Inhale moonlight.

Being beautiful is about being delightful, luscious and joyous.
Exhale and sparkle like diamond.
Inhale and glow like a flower.

Beauty has to do with attractiveness and being good-looking.
Our word for God is related to the old-German word for good.
Therefore, good-looking is literally related to looking like God.
Exhale – I am what thou art.
Inhale –Thou art what I am.

Beauty has to do with loveliness,
which is another way of expressing being loveable.
There is an openness and sweetness in being beautiful.
Beauty opens our hearts.
Inhale and liberate love in your heart.
Exhale and manifest love in your heart.

Beauty is about grace and elegance.
To be beautiful is to be graceful, limber, lithe and flowing.
Exhale into a pause, which flows into an inhalation, which flows into
pause, which flows into another exhalation.

Beauty is about being magnetic, seductive, alluring and appealing.
We can only be these things when we are centered and grounded.
Exhale and feel grounded.
Inhale and feel lifted.

Finally, there is magnificence to beauty a majesty, splendor and eminence
that shines only when our body, mind, breath and spirit are truly integrated.
Exhale from the top of the head to the soles of the feet.
Inhale from the soles of the feet to the top of the head.

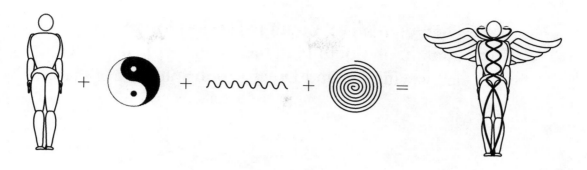

Aging

Yoga Is Not Just About Adding Years to Your Life,
It Is About Adding Life to Your Years.

R$_X$ 〰〰〰 Daily

One of the main purposes of hatha yoga is to keep the body healthy and prolong your life so there is sufficient time to complete the difficult job of 'living liberated' *(jivan mukti)* and so you can enjoy the liberated state as long as possible.

Don't Let Age Be Your Cage!

If we could stop trying to get to know someone by asking them their chronological age and instead ask them about who they really are, we would have more than a number to talk about.

Therapeutic Hatha Yoga, non-dual-metaphysical-quantum yoga, is a practice to transform and help us transcend life-long patterns and conditioning that limits our growth in creativity, love and wisdom throughout our lives.

"He who is not busy being born is busy being dying."

Bob Dylan

The Fountain of Youth Is Not in Florida.
The Fountain of Youth Is in the Cerebrospinal Fluid Flowing Up and Down Your Spine.

Historically, the 'fountain of youth' has been a mythical spring that restores youth to anyone who drinks from it or bathes in its waters. In the yoga tradition, the fountain of youth has been compared to the flexibility of the spine. A young man has been defined as a man with a flexible spine, which can undulate and twist, while an old man has been described as a man with a stiff spine.

The Purpose of Life is to Grow in Wisdom and Compassion.

Other ways of describing the purpose of your life might include your family, career, neighborhood, parks, oceans and the environment. The purpose of your life is to be free to share the gifts of creativity, love and wisdom you were borne with. The purpose of life is to follow your bliss. A sense of purpose in our lives gives us extraordinary energy to heal. The only real terminal illness is being human. Being human is being part of the evolution of life on earth and the expansion of consciousness in the universe.

Death Is Not a Defeat.

*Your feelings and thoughts will live
In the hearts and minds of those you have touched and known.*

You are an eternal soul in a temporal body.

The Magic Bullet that Kills Death and

Prevents Aging In the Hatha Yoga Tradition

The Triple Lock or the Great Seal
(See Super Yoga Healing Powers)

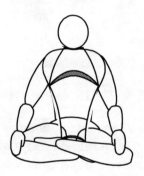

Awaken Your Timeless Infinite Self

*The Great Seal is literally described as the lion that kills the elephant death and
the cure for old age.
It is not so much a cure to prevent you from dying, though it helps heal you,
rather it allows you to experience your eternal, infinite Self.
All suffering, including the suffering of old age, is cause by the illusion of separation
from our eternal, timeless, cosmic, divine and beautiful Self.*

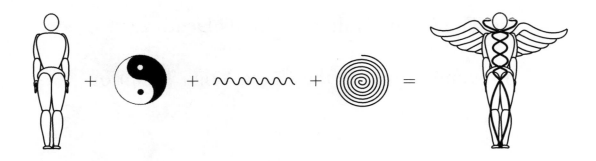

Healing the World

We Have a Crisis of Consciousness

*"We cannot solve our problems with the same thinking we used when we created them...
The unleashed power of the atom has changed everything save our modes of thinking and
we thus drift toward unparalleled catastrophe."*

Albert Einstein

*Change Your Consciousness.
Change Your Mode of Thinking about Self and World.*

Racism, sexism, and the destruction of the natural world are ultimately issues of how we perceive and conceive of ourselves, others and the planet.

Historically, modern morality has been fundamentally about how people treat other people, and primarily about how men treated men, with little reference to include treatment of animals, nature, women and people of other cultures.

Modern morality is founded on the empirical science and philosophy of the Age of Reason and exemplified in the writings of men like Descartes, Newton and Bacon. Modern morality like modern science, separates men from each other, nature, animals and the web of life, and values only that which can be objectively measured.

Modern morality is a materialistic, mechanistic, reductionist and individualistic mode of thinking. As a result, modern morality is fundamentally an individualist materialist morality, where making money is always a good thing to do, and morally justifiable as long as it is legal. At the same time, the invisible world of nature, feelings, thoughts and human relationships are sacrificed, and the profit motive reigns supreme. Modern morality is a sort of "money-theism," where money and things are worshipped.

Consciousness Is Primary and Matter Is Secondary.

Relationships Are Primary and The Exchange Secondary.

Modern morality has separated individual morality from larger questions of social and environmental responsibility. This mode of thinking promotes the idea that nature, animals and even people are resources to be used, as property to be owned, or as adversaries to be conquered in the quest for material and monetary gain.

This mode of thinking and morality creates a culture of fear, and is used to justify war, poverty and the destruction of natural world. It is as if the body of humanity is currently suffering from an autoimmune-like self-destructive disease, in which people, the individual cells of the body of humanity, attack one another from a limited and narrow sense of self. Modern morality has been more focused on fearing life rather than loving life, and thus has been comfortable declaring war on everything from cancer, to drugs, to other peoples and countries in a fruitless effort to be well.

Don't Succumb to a Culture of Fear!

There are no solid separate individual human beings just as there are no solid separate pieces of matter. Quantum physics contradicts the concept of separate, solid particles of matter occupying empty space. No one is separate. No one is worthless. We are all borne with gifts of creativity, love and wisdom to share. We are conscious fields of energy, resonating with each other and co-creating all of life. Therapeutic Hatha Yoga is based on a love of life and a holistic mode of thinking.

We are separate unique individuals, yet we are inseparable from each other and the web of life

It is time for a quantum paradigm shift in our perception of ourselves in relationship to others, nature and life. Let us respect personal rites and rituals for healing and living, and respect social rights for the common good of all. We are all woven into the web of life and the body of humanity.

The Prescription to Heal the World:
Be A Conscious Co-creator of Yourself and the World.
Take Personal and Social Responsibility
For the Health and Well-Being
Of Yourself, Others and the Planet.

Exhale and Be Conscious of Your Personal Responsibilities.
Inhale and Be Conscious of Your Social Responsibilities.

R$_X$ ∿∿∿∿∿ Daily

Your personal thoughts, feelings, breath and lifestyle profoundly affect those around you, and vice versa. We are co-creating our health and well-being with those around us and ultimately, with all life on earth. All life is interrelated and interconnected.

Ultimately, healing THYself and healing the world are two sides of the same coin. Healing the world is about realizing that you are physically and spiritually interconnected to the health and well-being of the world, and that every human being is important to humanity's survival. In a fundamental way, this is self-liberation and self-realization. Yoga teaches us to be conscious that that there is an absolute unity of being.

Be well!

Namaste!

THY Sources

Light on Yoga- B.K.S. Iyengar
Integral Hatha Yoga - Swami Satchidananda
The Complete Illustrated Book Of Yoga - Swami Vishnudevananda
How To Know God: The Yoga Aphorisms of Patanjali - Christopher Isherwood
Yoga For A New Age - Bob Smith
Yoga For Body, Breath and Mind - A. G. Mohan
Yoga: The Spirit and Practice of Moving into Stillness - Erich Schiffmann
Buddhist Yoga - Rev. Kanjitsu Iijima
Power Yoga - Beryl Bender Birch
Yoga For Wellness - Gary Kraftsow
The Heart of Yoga - Desikachar
Introduction to Yoga - Richard Hittleman
The Sivananda Companion to Yoga - The Sivananda Yoga Center
Hatha Yoga Pradipika - Commentary by Swami Vishnudevanda
The Yoga Tradition - Georg Feuerstein
The Breathing Book - Donna Farhi
The Yoga of Breath - Richard Rosen
Hatha Yoga - Theos Bernard
Yoga Self-Taught - Andre Van Lysebeth
Yoga as Therapy Volume One and Two - Doug Keller
Anatomy of Hatha Yoga - David Coulter
Esoteric Anatomy - Bruce Burger
Anatomy of the Spirit - Caroline Myss
Anatomy Trains - Thomas Myers
Bioenergetics - Alexander Lowen
The Spectrum - Dean Ornish
Biology of Belief -Bruce Lipton
You Can Heal Your Life - Louise Hay
Acu-Yoga - Michael Reed Gach
Wheels of Life - Anodea Judith
Chakras: Energy Centers of Transformation - Harish Johari
Kundalini Yoga - Swami Sivananda
The Tantra Way - Ajit Mookerjee & Madhu Khanna
Body, Mind and Sport - John Douillard
The Runner's Yoga Book - Jean Couch
ExTension - Sam Dworkis
Yoga for Dummies - Feuerstein and Payne
Yoga Zone Introduction to Yoga - Alan Finger
Hridayasutra - Mark Whitwell
The Yoga of Heart - Mark Whitwell
Yoga Therapy - A. G. Mohan
Healing Mantras - Thomas Ashley-Farnand
American Yoga Association Beginner's Manual - Alice Christensen

TherapeuticHathaYoga.com

TherapeuticHathaYoga.com
is a 21st century, Post-Modern-New Millenial website
To support individuals and research to consciously
integrate body, mind, breath and spirit to heal.

It is a sacred site for sharing and caring relationships.

Share The Gift Of Yoga

The most powerful drug in the world is the placebo, the belief that something good will result from an empty pill. Countless of different issues are improved by the power of belief. Interestingly, a placebo works best when the participant feels personally connected to and cared for by the person dispensing the placebo.

Nothing seems to be more psychologically uplifting to our health and well-being than the sense that we feel cared for. When we feel separated, lonely, alienated and unloved our immune and metabolic systems do not function optimally. We heal better when we feel connected to others.

If you would like to help someone consciously participate in their own healing, gift them a copy of this book. Yoga is a priceless gift for everyone. Gift it.

Check out my You Tube videos

A Yoga Pill For Every Ill

Printed in the United States
By Bookmasters